Lives of the Saints Complete:

January - December

Michael J. Ruszala

Wyatt North Publishing

LIVES OF THE SAINTS
VOLUME I (JANUARY – MARCH)

Michael J. Ruszala

2

Foreword

The world needs saints to show it the way to true humanity. The Church needs saints to show it how to live out its calling. The witness of the lives of the saints is a powerful testimony to the reality of God's plan and the possibility for truly following it in one's life. So often, we do not see this witness. We see hypocrisy and mediocrity among Christians. That is why we must look to the saints — the ones who really followed the words of Christ and let them be carried out fully in their lives. The saints also give us a reason to hope. Saints were not born; they were made through a life of cooperation with God's grace despite many difficulties, weaknesses, and temptations.

This book, written from a Catholic perspective, provides an overview to the lives of the saints celebrated from January to March on the Roman calendar. It is the first in a series, which will cover the whole Church year. It makes for inspirational spiritual reading any time of the year, providing an introduction to the patron saints for many walks of life. Included are the Blessed Virgin Mary and St. Joseph, Apostles like St. Peter and St. Paul, early martyrs like St. Perpetua and St. Felicity, early evangelizers like St. Patrick, medieval giants such as St. Thomas Aquinas, American saints such as St. Elizabeth Ann Seton and St. John Neumann, and many others.

Introduction

Truly encountering a living saint can be a life-changing experience. Such an encounter can open up worlds of possibility. The words and actions of a saint can elucidate the meaning of life. They can take Christianity from a flat concept to a dynamic wonder and a work of love. Indeed, the life of one saint can speak more eloquently than many volumes of theology.

Saints are not merely the two-dimensional figures in stain glassed windows. When Mother Teresa was canonized in September of 2016, the artist for her official painting strove to depict the way she made a person feel when she was talking with them. She was smiling in the painting, mouth slightly agape, with eyes focused on a person out of view.

Saints are what we need. St. Francis is said to have admonished, "Sanctify yourself and you will sanctify society." Philosopher Peter Kreeft writes, "The deepest reason why the Church is weak and the world is dying is that there are not enough saints. No, that's not quite honest. The reason is that WE are not saints."

Saints set sanctity as their goal. St. Therese of the Child Jesus wrote of her aim to become a great saint, "This aspiration may very well appear rash, seeing how imperfect I was, and am, even now, after so many years of religious life; yet I still feel the same daring confidence that one day I shall become a great Saint. I am not trusting in my own merits, for I have none; but I trust in Him Who is Virtue and Holiness itself. It is He alone Who, pleased with my feeble efforts, will raise me to Himself...." (*Story of a Soul*).

'Saint' means 'holy.' The New Testament uses the term even for the faithful, those who are alive and are striving to become holy. While all those in Heaven are surely saints, over time the Church has come to recognize some saints officially as true models of heroic virtue for all of the faithful. The first saints to be recognized as such after their death were the early martyrs. Early Christians would gather their relics and set up altars over their tombs in the catacombs. They were living sacrifices, holy to God. Now they were surely with him in Heaven.

The gospel is for all peoples. Thus the holy men and women who let the gospel have full victory in their lives are diverse. There are saints of all ages, races, vocations, and walks of life. St. Therese of the Child Jesus wondered at the differences among saints and also among those who aren't quite saints.

She thought of it in terms of a garden. God needs not just roses but all sorts of flowers. Her desire for her own sanctity was simply to be his 'Little Flower.'

While some saints were always good people for the most part, others were once great sinners. In fact, all but one — the Blessed Virgin Mary — were sinners. They all had personal weaknesses and were well aware of their own sinfulness. Peter Kreeft writes, "Go back to Socrates: 'Know thyself.' For Socrates, there are only two kinds of people: the wise, who know they are fools; and fools, who think they are wise. Similarly, for Christ and all the prophets, there are only two kinds of people: saints, who know they are sinners; and sinners, who think they are saints."

The Church came to call upon the saints in Heaven to pray for those on earth. This is called intercession. According to the *Catechism of the Catholic Church*, "Being more closely united to Christ, those who dwell in heaven fix the whole Church more firmly in holiness.... They do not cease to intercede with the Father for us, as they proffer the merits which they acquired on earth through the one mediator between God and men, Christ Jesus.... So by their fraternal concern is our weakness greatly helped" (no. 956). The Church has also proclaimed certain saints as patron saints, encouraging the faithful in certain walks of life to look to their example and ask for their intercession. For example, there are patron saints of students, of athletes, of police officers, of politicians, etc.

Today, the process of canonization — of the Church officially recognizing a saint posthumously — is a rigorous process of discernment. First the local bishop opens a commission to study the person's life. Upon examination, the person may be given the title 'Servant of God.' The bishop may elevate the cause to the Vatican's scrutiny, which can bestow the title of 'Venerable.' The examiners will be looking closely at writings and testimony for evidence of heroic virtue. They will look for examples of all the virtues of the Christian life lived consistently beyond the norm and despite great challenges. Upon the approval of a first miracle which non-Catholic doctors cannot explain, the person may be beatified and given the title of 'Blessed' by the pope. The final step, after the second approved miracle, is canonization, by which the pope proposes the holy person to all the faithful, who may ask for their intercession. Only then are they given the title of 'Saint.'

The Church celebrates the saints throughout the year. Most commonly, saints are remembered on the anniversary of their death, because this is really their birth to eternal life. Special liturgical commemorations are divided into solemnities, feasts, and memorials, which can be either obligatory or optional. Solemnities, which are celebrations of the highest order, are reserved to commemorate events or persons of salvation history in the Bible and in Sacred Tradition. The observance of Christmas, Mary Mother of God, and Epiphany (the visit of the wise men) are examples of solemnities. While some solemnities, such as Epiphany, are always on a Sunday (in the current calendar), solemnities take precedence even if they fall on a Sunday. Feasts commemorate the Apostles, certain Apostolic men, and certain mysteries of Our Lord and Our Lady. Like solemnities, feasts always have a Second Reading, as with a Sunday Mass. Also, they always have a Gloria even if they fall during Advent or Lent when the Gloria is not permitted. Memorials are the general observances of the saints throughout the year. Some popular saints, such as St. Francis of Assisi, are honored throughout the whole Church with an obligatory memorial. Others have optional memorials. Some days have many saints with optional memorials. Also, some churches, dioceses, or regions may elevate their patron saint's commemoration. For example, the memorial of St. Kateri Tekaktwitha is obligatory in the United States, but not throughout the world.

This book — the first of a series — follows the Roman calendar in the commemoration of the saints. These commemorations help us to remember these saints and strive to become like them. As St. Clement, Bishop of Rome, said, "Follow the saints, because those who follow them will become saints."

Mary, Holy Mother of God
Solemnity, Jan. 1

The solemnity of Mary, Holy Mother of God, is celebrated on the first day of the year. It is also the octave of Christmas — that is, eight days after Christmas and a continuation of that celebration. Mary's motherhood is inseparably connected with the Son of God's becoming human at his conception in her womb and then with his birth. Celebrating the Blessed Virgin Mary on the octave of Christmas was an ancient tradition, but from 1568 to 1960, January 1 was known as the Feast of the Circumcision of Our Lord Jesus Christ. The rite of circumcision is how boys were first initiated into the Jewish community. It was also when Jesus officially received the name announced previously by the angel — the holy name which means 'God saves.' This was a joyous occasion for a mother. In this case, since the son, though fully human, was God, the mother was 'Mother of God.' Such was the decision of the bishops of the Council of Ephesus in AD 431.

Catholic theologians have long seen hints of Mary's role in salvation history in the Old Testament. After Adam and Eve disobeyed God by eating the forbidden fruit, God said to the serpent (the Devil), "I will put enmities between thee and the woman, and thy seed and her seed: she shall crush thy head, and thou shalt lie in wait for her heel" (Gen. 3:15 [Douay-Rheims Bible]). Also, Isaiah prophesied, "Behold a virgin shall conceive, and bear a son, and his name shall be called Emmanuel" (Is. 7:14 [DRB]).

Mary's beginnings were humble, as was her whole life. She lived in the very small Galilean village of Nazareth, which was home to only about 200 people, whose small dwellings were mostly hewn out of the rock of the earth. Today, the Church of the Annunciation in Nazareth preserves part of what is thought to be the home of Mary. According to the Catholic dogma of the Immaculate Conception, Mary was uniquely conceived without Original Sin. This is why the angel was able to proclaim to her even before Christ's coming, "Hail, full of grace, the Lord is with thee: blessed art thou among women" (Lk. 1:28 [DRB]). Mary also lacked the sinful tendencies that come with fallen human nature. She was free to follow to the will of God perfectly and was made worthy to bear the Son of God for nine months in her womb.

According to tradition, Mary's parents were Joachim and Anne, and they had specially chosen to present their daughter to the Lord at the Temple. Mary is said to have made a vow of virginity at a young age. In her early teens, Mary was betrothed to Joseph, a descendent of David often presumed to be a number of years older than her. Tradition has it that the two committed to practice celibacy throughout their marriage.

The Angel Gabriel came to Mary to announce to her the miraculous birth of her son Jesus. In the Old Testament, there are numerous stories in which a child destined for greatness, whose conception is unlikely, comes about through divine intervention. With Mary, the Son of God is born of a virgin — the most humanly unlikely of all. Unlike some of the others, Mary believed the angel's word immediately. Her question was only how it could happen, given her virginity. The answer the angel gave was by the power of the Holy Spirit. St. Maximillian Kolbe called the Blessed Virgin Mary the "spouse of the Holy Spirit," with whom she cooperated intimately her whole life. Mary was also present in the Upper Room on Pentecost when the Holy Spirit descended on the Apostles, ushering in the age of the Church.

Mary had a choice with regard to becoming the mother of Jesus. Despite the many social risks involved, she answered in faith, "Behold, I am the handmaid of the Lord. May it be done to me according to your word" (Lk. 1:38). Her pregnancy could have been easily misunderstood. She could have been accused of adultery because of her betrothal and stoned. But

God took care of her. According to the Gospel of Matthew, the angel then spoke to Joseph in a dream saying, "Joseph, son of David, do not be afraid to take Mary your wife into your home. For it is through the holy Spirit that this child has been conceived in her" (Mt. 1:20). Joseph humbly embraced his role as guardian and protector of his Immaculate wife and his divine son, generated not through him but by the power of God.

Still young and pregnant, Mary journeyed all the way south to the foothills of Judea to share the joy of her cousin Elizabeth, whom the angel announced was to have a son in her old age. Elizabeth greeted Mary saying, "Most blessed are you among women, and blessed is the fruit of your womb. And how does this happen to me, that the mother of my Lord should come to me?" (Lk. 1:42–43). At the presence of the baby Jesus in Mary's womb, John the Baptist leapt in the womb of his mother Elizabeth. This was reminiscent of how King David danced before the Ark of the Lord, using words similar to those spoken by Elizabeth. The Church Fathers saw Mary as the new Ark of the Covenant, bearing within herself that which is holy.

According to the Gospel of Luke, after each of the mysterious events of Jesus' childhood, "his mother kept all these things in her heart" (Lk. 2:19). According to tradition, Mary's stories may have been a source for the nativity stories in the Gospels. Tribulations were never far from Mary, whose Immaculate heart ached with the sorrows to befall her son. The angel warned Joseph in a dream that the family must flee to Egypt to escape Herod's murderous intentions for the infant Jesus. Only after the death of Herod the Great was the Holy Family to return, this time back to Nazareth.

The Gospel of Luke tells us, "The child grew and became strong, filled with wisdom; and the favor of God was upon him" (Lk. 2:40). Mary was again troubled when Jesus, at the age of twelve, stayed behind three days in the Temple to discuss the Torah, while his parents did not know where he was. Upon finding him and hearing his words, "Why were you looking for me? Did you not know that I must be in my Father's house?" (Lk. 2:29), Mary saw greater significance in the event as confirming who he was and what he was to do. Mary's commitment to Jesus continued her whole life. In John's Gospel, Mary initiates Jesus' public ministry by telling the servers at the wedding at Cana, "Do whatever he tells you" (Jn. 2:5). This led to Jesus' first miracle of turning water into wine, bringing him into public scrutiny. Jesus later told his disciples, "whoever does the will of God is my brother and sister and mother" (Mk. 3:33). Pope St. John Paul II noted that this was a great compliment of Mary — she supremely followed the will of God in all things. Fulfilling in part the prophecy of Simeon that "thy own soul a sword shall pierce" (Lk. 1:35 [DRB]), Mary was one of the few followers present to the last at her son's crucifixion. It was from the cross that Jesus gave Mary to John the Apostle as his own mother — an act symbolic of giving Mary as the spiritual mother of all the faithful.

Mary is said to have spent her final days in Ephesus, in modern-day Turkey, in the home of John the Apostle. According to Sacred Tradition, Mary was assumed into Heaven body and soul at the end of her earthly life. The dogma of the Assumption of the Blessed Virgin Mary into Heaven was at last infallibly proclaimed by Pope Pius XII in 1950. The one preserved from sin would likewise be preserved by her son from bodily corruption, and united body and soul to reign with him in Heaven. Certainly the Blessed Mother, honored so much by God, has been likewise greatly honored through the ages. Regarded as the mother of all the faithful, the Blessed

Virgin has been invoked by more names and with more devotions throughout the ages than can be enumerated.

Mary's *Magnificat*

My soul proclaims the greatness of the Lord;

my spirit rejoices in God my savior.

For he has looked upon his handmaid's lowliness;

behold, from now on will all ages call me

blessed.

The Mighty One has done great things for me,

and holy is his name.

His mercy is from age to age

to those who fear him.

He has shown might with his arm,

dispersed the arrogant of mind and heart.

He has thrown down the rulers from their thrones

but lifted up the lowly.

The hungry he has filled with good things;

the rich he has sent away empty.

He has helped Israel his servant,

remembering his mercy,

according to his promise to our fathers,

to Abraham and to his descendants forever (Lk.

1:47–55).

Sts. Basil the Great and Gregory Nazianzen
Bishops and Doctors of the Church
St. Basil (ca. 329 – 379) and
St. Gregory (325 – 389)
Memorial, Jan. 2

Church Fathers St. Basil the Great and St. Gregory Nazianzen were friends and collaborators, upholding orthodox and true faith in a time when many bishops, priests, and laity denied Christ's full divinity. Together with St. Basil's brother St. Gregory of Nyssa, they are known as the Cappadocian Fathers (Cappadocia being an ancient region in what is now Turkey). St. Basil, perhaps the first non-martyr popularly recognized as a saint, also developed the first true monastic rule. Known as the Rule of St. Basil, it paved the way for monks and nuns to live together in community rather than only as hermits. It influenced the later Rule of St. Benedict which is foundational for many religious orders in the West. The Rule of St. Basil remains to this day the standard rule for religious in the East.

It is not uncommon to find that saints come in clusters. Christian holiness is especially fostered in the context of community of others likewise striving for holiness. Saints inspire and support each other and call each other on when they are straying from the narrow path. St. Basil was one of ten children from a devout family. His mother's father had been a martyr. His sister St. Macrina the Younger was a nun and his brothers Peter of Sebaste and St. Gregory of Nyssa were bishops. His father, St. Basil the Elder, was a noted catechist and man of virtue. St. Basil's grandparents had suffered as refugees because of religious persecution (newadvent.org).

St. Basil the Great, also known as St. Basil of Caesarea, became a great scholar at a young age. Studying at Caesarea, Constantinople, and then Athens, he became friends at Athens with another great mind — the future St. Gregory Nazianzen. St. Gregory Nazianzen later wrote that the two shared a common goal — a life in the pursuit of true wisdom. But though St. Basil was a noble youth, he was prone to worldliness and self-sufficiency because of his academic success. His sister, St. Macrina, corrected him, and he had a change of heart, desiring to pursue God alone. St. Basil withdrew to learn the path of perfection from the hermits, traveling to Egypt, Palestine, Syria, and Mesopotamia.

Religious life began in the Church with the hermits, but the latest trend in religious life at the time involved hermits coming together to live near each other and in community — namely, coenobitic monasticism. St. Basil himself founded a monastic community in Pontus, which is now in northern Turkey just south of the Black Sea. St. Basil wrote his rule for monastic life grounded in Scripture and based on his experiences of hermits and monasticism throughout the

Christian world. Religious community without a common stated purpose and shared discipline is prone to become fractured or misguided. St. Basil's rule provided the necessary foundation for religious communities to begin to flourish and to lead the way to spiritual perfection in all charity. As distinguished from later rules, one notable feature distinguishing Basil's rule is his emphasis on wisdom and prudence to be exercised differently in various situations and circumstances.

After Basil's days at Pontus, he and St. Gregory came for several years at Tiberina in Cappadocia to live a monastic life together. Both St. Basil and St. Gregory Nazianzen felt unworthy to become priests but were persuaded to accept ordination. St. Basil was a great administrator and was a forceful supporter of orthodoxy, making his positions clearly known. He became the assistant to Eusebius, archbishop of Caesarea, but was more effective in leadership than him. He withdrew to Pontus to ease the tension but was called back when the threat from the heretics became critical. Basil became the archbishop of Caesarea and metropolitan of Cappadocia.

The challenge of the day was Arianism — a heresy that denied Jesus' full divinity, insisting instead that he is a creature and came to be in time. St. Basil, a man of strong will and forceful and clear argumentation, would not allow Arianism to continue in his domain, even boldly standing up to the Arian emperor Valens. Gregory Nazianzen, likewise a great orator, preached strongly against this heresy and in favor of belief in Christ as fully God and fully man. Unlike Basil, administration was not a primary strength for Gregory. Having served as coadjutor bishop under his father, the bishop of Nazianzen (before the rule of celibacy), Gregory was made archbishop of Constantinople. The task there was to restore that important church to orthodoxy. Key to this was hosting the First Council of Constantinople in 381, which affirmed, clarified, and strengthened the teachings of the Council of Nicea on Christ's divinity. Gregory Nazianzen resigned only six months into his tenure as archbishop, citing poor health. He retired to Nazianzen to live as a monk.

When Basil died in 379, Gregory was unable to attend his funeral on account of his failing health, so he composed a series of poems in honor of his friend. Gregory died in 389. Both St. Basil the Great and St. Gregory Nazianzen are regarded as doctors of the Church. In the East, Gregory is given the title "the Theologian." St. Basil, listed among the saints invoked in many Eastern liturgies, persists in his influence above all in his monastic rule.

Both St. Basil and St. Gregory believed that embarking on the work of theology required living a holy life. Only someone in tune with the Spirit of God could correctly speak of the divine mysteries. St. Gregory writes, "Now when I eagerly go upon to the Mount — or, to use a truer expression, when I both eagerly long and at the same time am anxiously fearful (the one through my hope and the other through my weakness) to enter within the cloud and hold converse with God, for so God commands — then, if any be an Aaron, let him go up with me, and let him stand near, being ready, if it must be so, to remain outside the Cloud...But if any belong to the multitude who are unworthy of this height of contemplation, if they are altogether impure let them not approach at all, for it would be dangerous for them. But if they are at least temporarily purified, let them remain below and listen to the Voice alone and to the trumpet, the bare words of piety, and let them see the mountain smoking and lightning, at once a terror and a marvel to those who cannot go up" (Second Theological Oration, no. 2).

St. Basil the Great and St. Gregory Nazianzen, pray for us!

St. Elizabeth Ann Seton
Religious (1774 – 1821)
Memorial, Jan. 4

St. Elizabeth Ann Seton is the first American-born saint canonized in the Catholic Church. She was born Elizabeth Ann Bayley in 1774 in New York City to an upper class and influential Protestant family. Her father was a high-ranking doctor and medical officer, and her mother was the daughter of an Anglican priest. Growing up, Elizabeth loved to read and was well versed in the Bible. She drew strength from her faith and from the pages of Scripture in the midst of tragedy, hardship, and misunderstanding. Elizabeth came to know loss early in life, understanding the temporary nature of human life. When Elizabeth was only three years old, her mother died. Young Elizabeth also experienced the loss of her younger sister. Her father remarried, but the marriage ended after a number of years and Elizabeth was disowned by her stepmother. Elizabeth grew up in a large family. Her father had four children from his first marriage and five children from his second. Elizabeth enjoyed poetry and playing the piano. She was very charitable, and often made rounds to visit the poor and provide for their needs.

In 1794, at the age of nineteen, Elizabeth married William Magee Seton, aged twenty-five, who was from a noble Scotch family. The two first settled on Wall Street in New York and were parishioners of the famous Trinity Church on Lower

Manhattan. They had five children and also took in William's younger siblings after their father's death. Elizabeth suffered greatly in enduring the loss of two of her daughters in childhood. When William's father died, he inherited his father's trading business. Later, however, the business was greatly harmed after several ships were lost at sea and other ships were detained because of a British blockade of shipping to America.

To add to this hardship, William developed tuberculosis and became dangerously ill. His doctor recommended a warmer climate to aid in a possible recovery. Because of this, William, Elizabeth, and their eldest daughter traveled to Italy, where William had friends connected to his trading company. William died in Italy in 1803, but Elizabeth was touched by the welcoming, generous, and devout spirit of the Italian Catholics she came to know. Her friends in Italy introduced her to the Catholic faith and taught her about Christ's Real Presence in the Eucharist, which she longed to receive. Having suffered the loss of her mother and rejection from her stepmother, Elizabeth came to look to the Blessed Virgin Mary as her new mother.

Upon returning to New York, Elizabeth was received into the Catholic Church by Fr. Matthew O'Brien in 1805 and a year later was confirmed by Bishop John Carroll of Baltimore, the first Catholic bishop in the United States. Elizabeth's in-laws were quite dismayed at her conversion to Catholicism and came to greatly misunderstand her. As was common for upper class widows in need of a livelihood, Elizabeth started a school. Sustaining enrollment, however, became a challenge, given the climate of anti-Catholic prejudice at the time. Most families pulled their children out of her school after learning of her conversion to the Catholic faith. Elizabeth was troubled, but came in contact with a Salesian priest from Emmetsburg, Maryland, who encouraged her to start a Catholic school there. She accepted his invitation in 1809 and founded St. Joseph's Academy and Free School, which was open to Catholic girls. It was the first Catholic school in America, laying the foundation for many others. After her children entered adulthood, Elizabeth answered the call to a religious vocation. Under the guidance of Bishop Carroll, she founded the Sisters of Charity of St. Joseph, based on St. Vincent's rule for the Daughters of Charity.

Mother Seton left behind several volumes of letters which show her spiritual development. Once she wrote, "We must pray without ceasing, in every occurrence and employment of our lives — that prayer which is rather a habit of lifting up the heart to God as in a constant communication with Him." Ever resigned to the will of God in all things, Mother Seton, was known for her tenderness, devotion, and culture. She died at the age of forty-six in 1821. Her Sisters of Charity went on to found a number of orphanages and Catholic schools throughout the United States. Canonized in 1975, St. Elizabeth Ann Seton is patroness of Catholic schools. A female saint and educator who lived out both the vocations of marriage and religious life, St. Elizabeth Ann Seton is also looked to by those suffering troubles with in-laws, the loss of children, and the loss of parents.

St. Elizabeth Ann Seton, pray for us!

St. John Neumann
Bishop (1811 – 1860)
Memorial, Jan 5

St. John Neumann, frontier parish priest and Bishop of Philadelphia, was an early pioneer of the Catholic Church in America. John Nepomucene Neumann was born in Bohemia in 1811 in what is today the Czech Republic and was then part of the Austrian Empire.

There was much faith in his homeland at that time, which was flooding over with vocations to the priesthood. John, too, discerned a strong calling to become a priest, but his bishop halted all ordinations since they could not make accommodations for any more priests at the time. Though John had the prerequisite education and theology, he could not gain entrance anywhere else in Europe either. He heard, however, about the desperate need for priests in America, where German Catholic immigrants were losing their faith because no one was ministering to them.

John set sail for New York City in 1836, where he was promptly ordained by the Bishop of New York, John Dubois. Bishop Dubois assigned Fr. Neumann a large territory in western New York state as his parish. He had to build the churches for his parish, since there were none. The German immigrants there appreciated having a priest who ministered to them and spoke their language. Fr. Neumann, actually, was gifted in a number of languages and was ready to learn more as needed. Because of this, he was able to build not only churches but trusting relationships with Catholic immigrants of various backgrounds, whether German, Irish, or Italian. Language was very important for his ministry.

Though a man of short stature, Fr. Neumann was willing to go anywhere or do anything for his flock. He would climb mountains and travel for miles on horseback to reach parishioners in need. Feeling the need for spiritual community, Fr. Neumann joined the Redemptorist order in 1842 in Ohio, where he likewise built more churches and later became the order's provincial superior in America. Then in 1848, Fr. Neumann went to Baltimore to became a naturalized American citizen.

Attracting the attention of Rome for his leadership in large frontier regions, Fr. Neumann was appointed Bishop of Philadelphia in 1852. The head of a poor diocese, Bishop Neumann was known for his frugality. He wore only one pair of shoes and lived and traveled very simply. He did much as bishop to build the infrastructure of the diocese, increasing the number of Catholic schools from two to 200 and building about one new church each month in his diocese.

Bishop Neumann traveled to Rome for Pope Pius IX's solemn definition of the Immaculate Conception in 1854. Finally, worn out by his labors, Bishop Neumann collapsed on a street in Philadelphia and died on January 5, 1860, at the age of only forty-eight. St. John Neumann was canonized in 1977 as the first male American saint and is regarded as a patron saint of Catholic Education.

St. John Neumann, pray for us!

St. André Bessette
Religious (1845 – 1937)
Optional Memorial, Jan. 6

St. André Bessette, also known as Brother André, is the first Canadian-born male saint. Canonized in 2010 by Pope Benedict XVI, St. André is remembered for his humility and unswerving devotion to St. Joseph despite all obstacles. Pilgrims continue to seek St. André's healing intercession at the Oratory of St. Joseph in Montreal, which he built. Countless crutches from those healed by Brother André line the walls of the vestibule of the Oratory to this day, a testament to God's healing power through Brother André and especially his patron St. Joseph.

Alfred Bessette, the future St. André Bessette, was the eighth of twelve children, born in 1845 to devout parents in the outskirts of Montreal. He was very frail and sickly from infancy, never growing even to reach five feet tall in adulthood. Alfred's father, a lumberjack, died in an accident on the job when Alfred was only nine. Alfred loved his mother very much, and she did her best to care for her children and bring them up in the faith. But then she too became ill and passed away when André was only twelve. The younger children, then orphaned, were taken in by their uncle and aunt. His uncle was also a woodworker and Alfred had to do a lot of work with his hands growing up. Thus, it was natural for

Alfred to grow in devotion to St. Joseph the Worker, under whose patronage he remained his whole life.

Alfred remembered his First Communion as a particularly special moment in his early life. As he grew older, he did his best to support himself through hard work, though he was uneducated and illiterate since he had to work most of the time. Being quite weak and ill, he had a hard time holding a job for long, whether as a farmhand, shoemaker, baker, or blacksmith. He even spent some time as a factory worker in Vermont in the United States. Alfred did, however, grow to become a very prayerful young man. At the age of twenty-five, he sought entrance to the Congregation of the Holy Cross with a glowing recommendation from his pastor and close mentor André Provinçal, who wrote, "I am sending you a saint." The Congregation of the Holy Cross, an order of teaching priests, nonetheless denied him entrance because of his frailty and lack of education. Alfred, however, returned determined with a recommendation from the archbishop, and the Holy Cross Fathers reluctantly allowed him entrance.

Alfred took the religious name André after his pastor André Provinçal, who had helped him so much on his journey to religious life. Brother André took his final vows in the

Congregation of the Holy Cross at the age of twenty-eight, but he was never to become a priest or a schoolteacher. He later remarked, "When I joined this community, the superiors showed me the door, and I remained 40 years" (www.franciscanmedia.org). He was given the job of porter at one of their secondary schools, Notre Dame College in Montreal, and was given other lower-level tasks. But André grew faithful in his duties and in his devotion to St. Joseph. This enabled him to show God's love powerfully to the many people who came through those doors over the years. He provided them with wise counsel and efficacious prayers for healing, with a touch of holy oil. So many people were cured that word of him spread, but he always told the people, "I do not cure. St. Joseph cures."

After many years, Brother André came to have a strong sense in prayer that St. Joseph wished to be honored with a statue enshrined atop Mount Royal, the hill from which Montreal derives its name. There people could come to pray to St. Joseph and become aware of his powerful intercession. A shrine to St. Joseph would also relieve the immense burden placed on the school by the thousands of pilgrims who came for prayers for healing. All this attention did not win Brother André the good graces of his superiors or of the school's administrators because of all the problems that came with the influx of visitors who were often desperate and ill. The superiors even saw them as possibly superstitious. Brother André was so very popular, though, that the Congregation had to provide him with four secretaries to process the 80,000 letters sent to him annually.

After some time, negotiations, and prayers from Brother André and his friends, the Congregation was a last able to purchase a plot of land on Mount Royal. Starting with just $200 and a few boards, Brother André built a chapel himself around a statue of St. Joseph. Pilgrims flocked to the site and countless people were cured of various diseases. Construction on the larger Oratory of St. Joseph took place as donations trickled in. Brother André was not concerned with the slow progress of the construction. St. Joseph would provide what he wanted for himself.

The aged Brother André asked one last time to be taken to the Oratory, which still did not yet have a roof. He did not live to see the Oratory's completion, but was pleased to see that the statue of St. Joseph was indeed enshrined atop Mount Royal. Brother André died on January 6, 1937, at the age of ninety-two. A million people came to pay him their respects upon his passing. He was buried at the Oratory, which was finally completed in 1967, some two decades after his death and fifty years after the start of construction.

The completed Oratory of St. Joseph is a massive and ornate domed structure protruding from the skyline of Montreal, reminding all of the intercession of St. Joseph. It has been designated a minor basilica, a national shrine, and a National Historic Site of Canada, receiving some two million visitors each year.

Prayer to St. André for Healing

Saint André,
I come to you in prayer for healing.
(state your intention)
You were no stranger to illness.
Plagued by stomach problems,
you knew suffering on a daily basis,
but you never lost faith in God.
Thousands of people have sought your healing touch
as I do today.

Pray that I might be restored to health
in body, soul and mind.
With St. Joseph as my loving Protector,
strengthen my faith and give me peace
that I might accept God's will for me
no matter what the outcome.
Amen (www.holycrosscongregation.org).

St. Antony (of Egypt)
Abbot (251 – 356)
Memorial, Jan. 17

The hermit St. Antony was an early desert father and an inspiration for many later saints in living an ascetic life of self-denial. Antony battled demons, denied himself all pleasures, strove for virtue, and cultivated a strong interior life. Though not the first hermit, his example, as recorded by the great theologian and bishop St. Athanasius of Alexandria (d. 373), helped spearhead in the Church the newly developing vocation we call religious and consecrated life. He is given the title 'St. Antony the Great.'

Antony was born into a Christian home in upper Egypt and spent most of his time at home. After his parents died, he was entrusted with the care of his younger sister and was provided their sizable farmland as his inheritance. As a young man, Antony felt a strong calling to give up everything to follow Christ. He went to church, and just then the gospel was read in which Jesus told the rich young man that to be perfect, he must give all he had to the poor and follow him. So Antony went and gave much of his land to his neighbors and sold everything else, except what he needed for his sister. Then he entrusted his sister to the care of consecrated virgins — early nuns. She later became one herself and eventually became an abbess (as the role would later be called).

Young Antony went in search of ways to learn Christian perfection. He set out for the next village, away from his friends and relatives, where there was a pious man who lived in the wilderness in its outskirts. Learning wisdom from this man, Antony spent his time in manual labor, in prayer, and in reading Scripture. He also sought out other people who were exemplary in virtue so as to learn from them as well. Antony then went on to the tombs to do battle with the demons, and then, like Christ during his temptation, into the desert, where Antony spent the rest of his life. He spent the next twenty years on a mountain in an abandoned Roman fort across the Nile, refusing to see anyone except a man who would occasionally bring him bread.

Demons came in many visible forms to battle Antony and offer him many temptations, and with God's help, Antony proved victorious through these temptations. St. Athanasius wrote of Antony's first confrontation with a manifested demon, "One would suggest foul thoughts and the other counter them with prayers: the one fire him with lust, the other, as one who seemed to blush, fortify his body with faith, prayers, and fasting. And the devil, unhappy wight, one night even took upon him the shape of a woman and imitated all her acts simply to beguile Antony. But he, his mind filled with Christ and the nobility inspired by Him, and considering the spirituality of the soul, quenched the coal of the other's deceit" (no. 6). The demons' manifestations to Antony on other occasions were even more dramatic. St. Athanasius writes, "And the place was on a sudden filled with the forms of lions, bears, leopards, bulls, serpents, asps, scorpions, and wolves, and each of them was moving according to his nature. The lion was roaring, wishing to attack, the bull seeming to toss with its horns, the serpent writhing but unable to approach, and the wolf as it rushed on was restrained; altogether the noises of the apparitions, with their angry ragings, were dreadful" (no. 9).

Antony prayed and meditated constantly, and also worked, weaving baskets and growing a garden in the desert. He slept on a mat or the bare ground and ate very little — only meager cakes and dates — sometimes going days without even this much. In his old age, he added some oil for his cakes. Throughout his long life, Antony only reentered civilization on a few occasions. Once, for example, was to support Christian martyrs during a persecution and another time to testify to the full divinity of Christ during the Arian crisis.

Antony was very wise and gave prudent counsel to those who came to him. He also worked many healings and miracles. Others were attracted to Antony's way of life and desired to become hermits, so he established communities for them in the desert. These were precursors of monks and monasteries. While Antony exhorted them and may have written a kind of rule for their way of life, he spent most of his time in seclusion as a hermit, with only loose ties to the other hermits.

Once in exhorting his followers, he did so in this way: "Wherefore, children, let us not faint nor deem that the time is long, or that we are doing something great, for the sufferings of this present time are not worthy to be compared with the glory which shall be revealed to us. Nor let us think, as we look at the world, that we have renounced anything of much consequence, for the whole earth is very small compared with all the heaven. Wherefore if it even chanced that we were lords of all the earth and gave it all up, it would be nought worthy of comparison with the kingdom of heaven ... Why not rather get those things which we can take away with us — to wit, prudence, justice, temperance, courage, understanding, love, kindness to the poor, faith in Christ, freedom from wrath, hospitality? If we possess these, we shall find them of themselves preparing for us a welcome there in the land of the meek-hearted" (no. 17).

St. Antony of Egypt, pray for us!

St. Sebastian
Martyr (d. 288)
Optional Memorial, Jan. 20

St. Sebastian, the patron saint of athletes and soldiers, is held in high regard for his rigorous zeal and endurance to the last. According to legendary accounts, St. Sebastian was a devout Christian from his youth, but joined the army in Rome as a cover while providing support to the martyrs and confessors (those imprisoned on account of their confession of faith). Because of his character and bravery, he was appointed by both the emperors Diocletian and Maximian as a captain of the Praetorian Guard — an elite group of veterans from Italy charged with special assignments such as the protection of the emperor (*Butler's Lives of the Saints*).

When two deacons, twin brothers Marcus and Marcellian, who were in prison facing death, were becoming shaken in their resolve, St. Sebastian went to them and passionately exhorted them to stand strong. They were encouraged by his words. St. Sebastian's prayers for healing were very effective. Their father Tranquillinus had been trying to persuade them to renounce Christ to save themselves, but St. Sebastian healed his gout and converted him to Christianity. The governor of Rome, Chromatius, heard of it and sought St. Sebastian for prayers because he had the same condition. St. Sebastian healed him as well, and he became a Christian. The governor freed his Christian prisoners, resigned from his position, and retired into obscurity in the countryside. St. Sebastian also healed a woman named Zoe who had lost the ability to speak, and she converted to Christianity. A number of others also came into the faith because of St. Sebastian's witness.

Later a persecution broke out and many of those converted or ministered to by St. Sebastian were martyred along with other Christians. The twin deacons Marcus and Marcellian, their father Tranquillinus, and the mute woman Zoe who was healed were all among those martyred. St. Sebastian was also exposed as a Christian and brought before the emperor Diocletian himself. The enraged emperor ordered him tied to a tree and used as target practice for the archers of Mauritania. St. Sebastian was shot through so many times that an account says he resembled a porcupine. He was left for dead, but Irene, the widow of the martyr St. Castulus, recovered his body. To her amazement, she found that he was still alive and nursed him back to health.

After his recovery, St. Sebastian refused to flee Rome, but instead exposed himself to a second martyrdom. He stood along the emperor's route and vocally denounced him for his brutality against the Christians. Diocletian was speechless to see the one he had put to death standing there denouncing him. But he regained his composure and ordered St. Sebastian clubbed to death. This time St. Sebastian entered into eternal life. The soldiers cast his body into the sewer, where the Christians would be unlikely to find it. But St. Sebastian appeared to a woman named Lucina and told her where to recover his body, which was venerated by Christians throughout the centuries.

St. Sebastian's prayers were especially sought in times of plague because of his effective prayers for healing and resilience to bodily harm.

St. Sebastian, pray for us!

St. Agnes

Virgin and Martyr, ca. 291 – 304

Optional Memorial, Jan. 21

St. Agnes was a young martyr who died at Rome, venerated as a heroic model of purity. There are various legendary accounts of her martyrdom. What is known for sure is that the bones of a young female martyr lie under the main altar at the Church of *Sant'Agnese fuori le mura* in Rome. The skull, meanwhile, is venerated at a side chapel in the church. St. Agnes' name means 'pure' in Greek. In Latin, it resembles *agnus*, or lamb. St. Agnes has the honor of being venerated in the canon of the Mass. On her feast day, two sheep are brought to be blessed by the pope. Then on Holy Thursday, they are shorn and the wool made into palliums, which are white collar-like vestments indicating the rank of archbishop. The pope will then present these palliums to the the new archbishops of the world over the coming year.

According to legendary accounts, St. Agnes was very beautiful and was from a Christian family that was both devout and wealthy. She consecrated her virginity to God, but was sought after by numerous noble youths of Rome. She rejected them, saying that she already had a heavenly husband. After many attempts to win her over, her suitors became enraged because of her faithfulness to her vow to God. One of them turned her into the authorities as a Christian. So St. Agnes, who was only about thirteen years old, was arrested and brought before a magistrate, who ordered her to renounce her God and offer sacrifices to the emperor. She refused. She was offered many promises and threatened with fire, iron hooks, and racks for torture, but none of this had any effect on her despite her young age. St. Agnes was placed in chains, but she was undeterred by this, too, and rejoiced in her sufferings. She continued to insist that she would preserve her purity for Christ, her spouse.

Since it was not allowed for virgins to be put to death, the magistrate announced that any man who wished was free to assault her. According to one account, St. Agnes was dragged naked through the streets, but God heard her prayers for purity and made her hair grow as a covering. Men who looked lustfully or attempted to assault her were immediately blinded by a flash from Heaven. By another account, men were so moved by her prayerful resolve that that they did not dare touch her — except for one, who was blinded until his companions brought him to St. Agnes, who healed him through her prayers.

St. Agnes, still unmoved from her resolve to maintain her purity for Christ, was led to execution. By one account, she went to her place of execution as happy as a bride who goes to her husband. Bystanders were moved to tears and tried in vain to persuade her simply to renounce Christ and save her life. She then bent her neck and was beheaded with a single blow. By another account, she was tied at the stake to be burned, but either the flames would not touch her or the fire would not light. For that reason, St. Agnes was either beheaded or stabbed in the throat. Her blood spilled into the streets and was mopped up by devout Christians. Several days later, a Christian girl — the daughter of St. Agnes' wet nurse — was found praying at the place where St. Agnes was buried. She was discovered and lamented St. Agnes' death to the pagan crowd. The girl was stoned on the spot, likewise martyred for her Christian faith.

St. Agnes is the patron saint of young girls, rape survivors, chastity, and the Children of Mary.

St. Agnes, pray for us!

St. Francis de Sales

Bishop and Doctor of the Church

(1567 – 1622)

Memorial, Jan. 24

St. Francis de Sales, Bishop of Geneva, is a doctor of the Church, remembered for his charitable and clear Catholic teachings during the period of the Counter-Reformation (or "Catholic Reformation") and continuing to wield influence to the present day.

Francis was born in 1567 to a noble Catholic family in Château de Sales in the Duchy of Savoy on the eastern edge of France. He was given the name Francis since there was a painting of St. Francis of Assisi in the room in which he was born. Francis was devout from a young age, even taking the tonsure as a child as a sign of commitment to Holy Orders. His father, however, had other plans for his eldest son, who was an excellent student and grew to be an attractive young man.

Francis' father sent him to the University of Paris, providing the best education available for his son, whom he intended to become a lawyer and government official. Francis excelled in law and theology and even had to learn dance and fencing. Even during his sporting endeavors, however, God reminded him of his vocation. Several times he dropped his weapons while on horseback, and each time, they fell on the ground in the shape of a cross. He later earned his doctorate in both civil and ecclesiastical law at the University of Padua and then returned to Savoy. There, his father made his plans for him known, though Francis confided with his mother about his discerning a vocation to the priesthood. Francis' father arranged for him to marry and expected him to accept the seat on the senate of Savoy which he was offered. The Bishop of Geneva, Claud de Granier, understanding the situation, appealed to the pope to offer Francis a prestigious church position as an alternative. Francis accepted the position, to his father's chagrin, and was soon ordained a priest.

The Duke of Savoy requested that the Bishop of Geneva send priests to build up the faith in the region of Chablais (today split between France and Switzerland), which had recently become converted to Calvanism. The assignment was a very dangerous one in this time of religious belligerence following the Reformation. There would be constant risk of assassination or mob lynching. Fr. Francis volunteered. When his father found out, his father went to the bishop, who was a friend of his, to demand that Fr. Francis not go. The bishop went to Fr. Francis with the concern. But Fr. Francis insisted on going on the mission, quoting the gospel and saying, "Would you make me unworthy of the Kingdom of God? Having put my hand to the plough, would you have me look back?" (*Butler's Lives of the Saints*).

Fr. Francis, together with companions, spent several years in the region, risking great dangers and escaping death on multiple occasions. Fr. Francis, loved in Catholic regions for his sermons, tried to preach in Chablais, but could not continue to do this safely. So he wrote tracts explaining the Catholic faith and had them hand-copied and placed under the doors of the populace. These tracts were later compiled into the *Catholic Controversies*, or *Meditations on the Church*, in which he argued that Christ had given the sole authority for the interpretation of Scripture and Sacred Tradition to the Catholic Church.

Francis had experienced temptations in his youth to despair of God's salvation, as some of the Calvinists did on account of their doctrine of predestination. Thus Fr. Francis was particularly empathetic to the concerns of those who had left the Catholic faith whether because of matters of belief or lifestyle. He was always gentle and meek, but also clear and firm. Little by little through his words and loving example, he converted the majority of the populace of Chablais back to the Catholic faith so that Bishop de Granier was even warmly welcomed to come to the city to celebrate the sacrament of Confirmation. In an age where violence was the norm, St.

Francis de Sales later wrote, "I have always said that whoever preaches with love is preaching effectively against the heretics, even though he does not say a single controversial word against them" (*Butler's Lives of the Saints*).

Bishop de Granier was impressed with Fr. Francis and recommended him to the pope to become the coadjutor bishop to someday succeed him in office. Fr. Francis went to Rome to be questioned and was chosen for the post. Upon Bishop de Granier's death in 1602, he became Bishop of Geneva. Bishop de Sales was particularly concerned with catechizing his people by organizing the teaching of the faith throughout the diocese and also by his own teaching. His writings, which were clear, simple, but profound, were distributed widely in his day and in the following centuries. He wrote *A Treatise on the Love of God* and *An Introduction to the Devout Life*, his most famous classic, which came out of his work as a spiritual director. He wrote it especially for his cousin, a lay woman, who came to him for spiritual direction. The book is very practical and wise and was ahead of its time in promoting the universal call to holiness. St. Jeanne de Chantal, a pious widow dedicated to prayer and works of charity, also came to him for spiritual direction and found much comfort in his counsel. He guided her in founding an order for women religious known as the Sisters of the Visitation. Centuries after his death, several other religious orders for both men and women were founded under his patronage and in the tradition of his spirituality.

While en route to meet with the King of France, Bishop de Sales fell ill. He died at Lyons in 1622, uttering the name of Jesus as his last words. In 1661, Francis de Sales had the privilege of being the first to be solemnly beatified at the Vatican. He was canonized in 1665. Then in 1877, St. Francis de Sales was given the rare honor of being proclaimed doctor of the Church. This title was given him by Pope Pius IX, who lifted up St. Francis de Sales' example of clear and charitable teaching against the errors of the day.

St. Francis de Sales is the patron saint of Catholic writers, the Catholic press, journalists, and adult education. Always looking for ways to more effectively teach the faith, St. Francis de Sales even developed a sign language to teach a deaf man. Thus he is also the patron saint of the deaf.

St. Francis de Sales, pray for us!

The Conversion of St. Paul the Apostle
Feast, January 25

St. Paul the Apostle was born ca. AD 5 in Tarsus in modern-day Turkey. Born to Jewish parents of the tribe of Benjamin, he was circumcised on the eighth day and given the Jewish name Saul (Phil. 3:5–6). Saul's father was a Roman citizen, and he passed the privilege of citizenship on to his son. At a young age, Saul had the good fortune to be educated in the Temple in Jerusalem in the Torah, the Law of God, and he joined company with the Pharisees. In fact, he studied under the famous rabbi Gamaliel. Saul was a very zealous practitioner and enforcer of the Law of God — so much so that he became a fierce persecutor of Jesus' followers, perceiving their cult to be a perversion of that Law and a danger to it. According to the Acts of the Apostles, the witnesses to the stoning of the martyr St. Stephen laid their cloaks at Saul's feet, who watched in approval.

Saul, in fact, took the initiative in persecuting the followers of Jesus and hunting them out on behalf of the chief priests. He went so far as to drag them from their own homes in Jerusalem. Saul then traveled with a band of men to Damascus, in modern-day Syria, to find followers of Jesus among the Jews there and bring them back to Jerusalem as prisoners. It was while traveling that Jesus came to him in a voice and with a great light saying to him, "Saul, Saul, why are you persecuting me?" Saul asked, "Who are you, sir?" And the Lord replied, "I am Jesus, whom you are persecuting. Now get up and go into the city and you will be told what you must do" (Acts 9:4–6). Saul, blinded by the light, was shaken to his core. We read, "For three days he was unable to see, and he neither ate nor drank" (Acts 9:9).

The Lord instructed the disciple Ananias in Damascus on where to find Saul. The Lord reassured Ananias despite his fear of Saul, "Go, for this man is a chosen instrument of mine to carry my name before Gentiles, kings, and Israelites, and I will show him what he will have to suffer for my name" (Acts 9:16). So Ananias went to Saul and prayed, laying hands on him for healing. We read, "Immediately things like scales fell from his eyes and he regained his sight. He got up and was baptized, and when he had eaten, he recovered his strength" (Acts 9:18–19). Saul experienced a death to self before he would rise again with Christ in baptism. As he writes in the Letter to the Romans, "We were indeed buried with him through baptism into death, so that, just as Christ was raised from the dead by the glory of the Father, we too might live in newness of life" (Rom. 6:4).

Saul joined with the community of disciples at Damascus and preached about Jesus in the very synagogues where he originally intended to find the Christians and capture them. When he was informed about a plot against his life, he escaped the city, lowered by the disciples down over the city walls in a basket. After returning to Tarsus, he then spent three years in the desert in prayer and reflection (Gal. 1:17). After this, he went to Jerusalem and presented himself to Peter, the leader of the Apostles. He also preached about Jesus publicly while in Jerusalem.

The Church in Apostolic times came to the realization that the gospel was not only for Jews but also for Gentiles, and that Gentile believers did not have to convert to Judaism to enter into the New Covenant. Saul, who then went by his Roman name Paul, became the 'Apostle to the Gentiles.' Paul went on three missionary journeys together with companions throughout Asia Minor and Greece, visiting churches already established and founding others. Paul is recognized as the chief vehicle for bringing Christianity to Europe and the Gentile word. He strove to be "all things to all" (1 Cor. 9:22), and he suffered much. He writes, "Three times I was beaten with rods, once I was stoned, three times I was shipwrecked…" (2 Cor. 11:25).

Paul had great solicitude for the churches and kept in contact with them through letters, or epistles, which were read before the whole worship assembly. He also wrote several letters to those he had formed in ministry. Thirteen epistles attributed to St. Paul were included in the canon of the New Testament and cherished for their authentic inspired teaching. His epistles provide some of the first pieces of Christian theology, reflecting on the meaning of Christ's coming.

St. Paul's writings are the first to speak of the "Lord Jesus Christ," thereby ascribing to him, in Koine Greek, the titles of King and Messiah. He also taught vigorously on salvation by faith in Jesus in the New Covenant and not the Law of Moses. He writes in his Letter to the Romans, "But now the righteousness of God has been manifested apart from law, although the law and the prophets bear witness to it, the righteousness of God through faith in Jesus Christ for all who believe" (Rom. 3:21–22 [RSV]). St. Paul, perhaps because of his experience of Christ on the road to Damascus, was among the first to recognize the unity of Christ and his Church as one Body. He writes in his First Letter to the Corinthians, "As a body is one though it has many parts, and all the parts of the body, though many, are one body, so also Christ. For in one

Spirit we were all baptized into one body, whether Jews or Greeks, slaves or free persons, and we were all given to drink of one Spirit" (1 Cor. 12:12–13).

Paul was threatened by a mob in Jerusalem and taken in by Roman authorities for protection and questioning. As a Roman citizen, Paul appealed to have his case heard by Caesar himself. Thus he was sent to Rome by ship. Though shipwrecked in the wintertime, he arrived at his destination. During his captivity, he continued to communicate with the churches by letter, writing the 'Captivity Epistles.' In Rome, the erratic and brutal Emperor Nero famously used the Christians as scapegoats for the Great Fire in Rome. Around this time, ca. 67, Paul was beheaded in Rome.

St. Paul writes in his Second Letter to Timothy, "I am already being poured out like a libation, and the time of my departure is at hand. I have competed well; I have finished the race; I have kept the faith. From now on the crown of righteousness awaits me, which the Lord, the just judge, will award to me on that day, and not only to me, but to all who have longed for his appearance" (2 Tim. 4:6–8).

St. Paul is recognized as the patron saint of missions, theologians, and Gentile Christians.

St. Paul on Imitating Christ

> Have among yourselves the same attitude that is also yours in Christ Jesus,

> Who, though he was in the form of God,
> did not regard equality with God something to be grasped.

> Rather, he emptied himself,
> taking the form of a slave,
> coming in human likeness;
> and found human in appearance,

> he humbled himself,
> becoming obedient to death, even death on a cross.

> Because of this, God greatly exalted him
> and bestowed on him the name
> that is above every name,

that at the name of Jesus

every knee should bend,

of those in heaven and on earth and under the earth,

and every tongue confess that

Jesus Christ is Lord,

to the glory of God the Father (Phil. 2:5–11).

Sts. Timothy and Titus
Bishops (First Century)
Memorial, Jan. 26

Sts. Timothy and Titus were early bishops of the Church and close associates of St. Paul the Apostle. Mentioned numerous times in Paul's epistles in the New Testament, his First and Second Letters to Timothy and Letter to Titus are addressed to them, respectively. These letters are called his "Pastoral Epistles." They provide sound advice for Christian leaders and give us a glimpse of the structure of the early Church. Both Timothy and Titus were from Asia Minor and served throughout their lives in various churches as bishops on temporary assignment, dealing with specific challenges within those communities. Paul, "all things to all" (1 Cor. 9:22), had Timothy, who was part Jewish, circumcised so he could better witness to the Jews, while he had Titus, a Gentile, remain uncircumcised to show that circumcision was not required in the New Covenant.

Timothy's father was a Gentile. His mother, however, was Jewish, and she taught him the Scriptures growing up. At the time of Paul's writing (probably in the mid-60s AD), Timothy was young, somewhat shy, and prone to illness. He had, however, earned Paul's highest trust and admiration in the faith. Paul exhorted Timothy in a fatherly way, "Let no one have contempt for your youth, but set an example for those who believe, in speech, conduct, love, faith, and purity" (1 Tim.

4:12). Timothy was ordained a presbyter (priest) by the laying on of hands from Paul himself (2 Tim. 1:6). Later, because of a word of "prophetic utterance," he was ordained a bishop (1 Tim. 4:14). Tradition regards him as the first bishop of Ephesus, where Timothy was stationed when Paul wrote to him. (The Apostle John arrived in Ephesus some time after Timothy.) Paul lists Timothy, as his close collaborator and companion, as a cosigner of several of his epistles, and also notes him as having been sent to other churches besides Ephesus. In 2 Timothy, Paul, anticipating his own impending martyrdom, expresses his desire for Timothy to come to Rome to see him one last time. It is believed that Timothy did visit and remain with Paul in his last days.

St. Paul charged Timothy as a bishop to stand firm in right teaching: "proclaim the word; be persistent whether it is convenient or inconvenient; convince, reprimand, encourage through all patience and teaching" (2 Tim. 4:2). He also admonished him to piety: "Train yourself for devotion, for, while physical training is of limited value, devotion is valuable in every respect, since it holds a promise of life both for the present and for the future. This saying is trustworthy and deserves full acceptance. For this we toil and struggle, because we have set our hope on the living God, who is the savior of all, especially of those who believe" (1 Tim. 4:9). Paul exhorted Timothy to be strong in the Lord and to rely on the graces of his ordination: "I remind you to stir into flame the gift of God that you have through the imposition of my hands. For God did not give us a spirit of cowardice but rather of power and love and self-control. So do not be ashamed of your testimony to our Lord, nor of me, a prisoner for his sake; but bear your share of hardship for the gospel with the strength that comes from God" (2 Tim. 1:6–8). Tradition holds that Timothy died a martyr's death, beaten and stoned by pagans ca. AD 97.

Titus, a Gentile Christian, was a secretary to Paul and a bishop given various assignments. At the writing of Paul's epistle to him, Titus was serving on the island of Crete — a place known for its pagan immorality. His task was to build the church throughout the island, appointing upright bishops who would be models of right action. According to tradition, Titus continued his ministry in Crete until his death in natural old age.

Paul wrote to Titus, "the grace of God has appeared, saving all and training us to reject godless ways and worldly desires and to live temperately, justly, and devoutly in this age, as we await the blessed hope, the appearance of the glory of the great God and of our savior Jesus Christ, who gave himself for us to deliver us from all lawlessness and to cleanse for himself a people as his own, eager to do what is good. Say these things. Exhort and correct with all authority. Let no one look down on you" (Ti. 1:11–15).

Pope Pius IX, in the mid-nineteenth century, was first to give Titus a place on the Roman calendar — February 6. Whereas Timothy was celebrated on January 24, the new calendar of Pope Paul VI includes both recipients of Paul's Pastoral Epistles on January 26, the day after the Feast of the Conversion of St. Paul.

Saints Timothy and Titus, pray for us!

St. Thomas Aquinas
Priest and Doctor of the Church
(ca. 1225 – 1274)
Memorial, Jan. 28

Ever humbly illuminated by divine Truth, St. Thomas Aquinas is one of the greatest models for Catholic students, scholars, and theologians. His writings have also become foundational in the study of theology and philosophy.

St. Thomas was born at the castle of Rocca Secca in the small Italian town of Aquino. Descended from the Lombards, his father was a knight by the name of Landulf, and his mother was named Theodora. St. Thomas grew to become tall and have a large build, but he was always afraid of lightning. This is because as a child, he experienced the death of his younger sister, struck by lighting while sleeping in the same room (*Butler's Lives of the Saints*).

St. Thomas' parents sent him, at the age of thirteen, as an oblate to the nearby prestigious Benedictine abbey of Monte Cassino, where they hoped he would one day become abbot. When he was about fifteen, the Benedictines sent him for further studies in Naples, where he remained for five years. There he became acquainted with the Order of Preachers (the Dominicans), a mendicant order recently founded by St. Dominic. Attracted by their teaching and learning, St. Thomas expressed interest in joining the order, which he did after the three years of discernment that they had given him. He and the Dominican friars were convinced that joining the Order of Preachers was God's will for him, and he took the habit at the age of nineteen.

St. Thomas' parents were very displeased with his decision and his mother made an unsuccessful trip to Naples to persuade him against joining, but the friars whisked him away to the convent of Santa Sabina. Then his parents sent his older brothers, who were soldiers, to pursue him. They found him on the side of the road, captured him, and brought him home by force. Later, they locked him in the castle of Monte San Giovanni, just outside Aquino. He would remain there for two years, unshaken in his resolve to follow God's will. St. Thomas made good use of his time in captivity, memorizing large sections of Scripture and studying the Sentences of Peter Lombard, the chief theological work of the time. His sister Marotta, his only visitor, would come to try to dissuade him from joining the mendicant order, which lacked the prestige of the Benedictines at the time. When all else failed, his brothers brought in a prostitute to stay with him and seduce him. He preserved his chastity, chasing her out with a red-hot fire brand. St. Thomas later converted his sister Marotta, who became a nun and abbess.

Seeing that the imprisonment was of no use, his family set him free in 1245, and he returned to the Order of Preachers in Naples. There, he studied under St. Albert the Great, who frequently lectured on the texts of the Greek philosopher Aristotle. St. Thomas' peers gave him the nickname "The Dumb Ox" because of his large build and silent disposition. But St. Albert was quite impressed with St. Thomas' learning and said, "We call Brother Thomas 'the dumb ox'; but I tell you that he will make his lowing heard to the uttermost parts of the earth" (quoted in *Butler's Lives of the Saints*).

St. Albert the Great and Cardinal Hugh of Saint-Cher sent St. Thomas to teach at the University of Paris. There he wrote his *Commentary on the Sentences of Peter Lombard*. He also wrote his *Summa Contra Gentiles*, which was an apologetic work in dialogue with Islamic thought, explaining and defending the teachings of Christianity. Later, he spent five years writing what would become one of the greatest theological works of all time — the *Summa Theologica*, which literally means 'Theological Summary.' Many *summas* were written by theologians during this time, called the Scholastic period. They were systematic works in question-and-answer format. St. Thomas would begin each article by first explaining the objections of his opponents, which were often said to be better arguments than they made for themselves.

Because he was a member of the Order of Preachers, one of St. Thomas' assignments was to be a preacher for the papal court, following the travels of the pope around Italy. He was also a visitor at the court of St. Louis, the king of France. The University of Paris held him in such respect that they asked him to settle a dispute among the professors regarding the theology of the Eucharist. St. Thomas' fervor in prayer was even greater than his scholarship, and this event became the occasion for one of St. Thomas' mystical experiences. The Lord spoke to him from the crucifix while he was praying and said out loud, "Thou has written well of the sacrament of my Body." St. Thomas was then seen by the friars levitating above the ground in ecstasy. Later in his life the Lord spoke to him saying, "Thou hast written well of me, Thomas; what reward wouldst thou have?" His answer was, "Nothing but thyself, Lord." After another mystical experience, St. Thomas stopped work on his *Summa Theologica*, which he never finished, saying, "The end of my labours is come. All that I have written appears to be as so much straw after the things that have been revealed to me." In addition to his many theological and philosophical works, St. Thomas wrote numerous hymns and religious poems (including *Tantum Ergo*) as well as catechetical teachings on the Lord's Prayer and Apostles' Creed. St. Thomas died in 1274, en route to the Council of Lyons to which he had been summoned by Pope Gregory X.

St. Thomas Aquinas has been held as a model theologian because of his humility before God and others, his confidence in the unity of faith and reason, his respect for and understanding of the Church Fathers, and his willingness to kindly dialogue with those with whom he disagreed. Pope Leo XIII writes, "Among the Scholastic Doctors, the chief and master of all towers Thomas Aquinas, who, as Cajetan observes, because 'he most venerated the ancient doctors of the Church, in a certain way seems to have inherited the intellect of all'" (*Aeterni Patris*, no. 17). Pope St. John Paul II writes of St. Thomas' thought, "Faith therefore has no fear of reason, but seeks it out and has trust in it.... This is why the Church has been justified in consistently proposing Saint Thomas as a master of thought and a model of the right way to do theology" (*Fides et Ratio*, no. 43).

St. Thomas Aquinas was canonized in 1323. His *Summa Theologica* was placed on the altar next to the Bible at the opening of the Council of Trent in 1545, symbolic of its guidance for the Council's proceedings. He was proclaimed doctor of the Church by Pope St. Pius V in 1567. In 1880, Pope Leo XIII, who had established St. Thomas' philosophy as the foundation for studies in seminaries, declared the 'Angelic Doctor' as the patron saint of all Catholic schools, seminaries, and universities.

Adoro Te Devote (excerpt), Eucharistic Hymn written by St. Thomas Aquinas

> Devoutly I adore You, hidden Deity,
> Under these appearances concealed.
> To You my heart surrenders self
> For seeing You, all else must yield.
>
> Sight and touch and taste here fail;
> Hearing only can be believed.
> I trust what God's own Son has said.
> Truth from truth is best received (trans. Robert Anderson and Johann Moser).

St. John Bosco
Priest (1815 – 1888)
Memorial, Jan. 31

St. John Bosco, also known as Don Bosco, was an Italian priest dedicated to the welfare and faith development of abandoned boys. He was also the founder of the Salesian order, a popular religious writer, and a builder of churches and religious institutions.

John Bosco was born in the Piedmont region of northern Italy. When he was only two, his father died, leaving his mother to care for him and his two older brothers. John's mother, the Venerable Margherita Bosco, instilled devotion and charity into her son. Though the family was very poor, Margherita still provided for the less fortunate who came to her. As a child, John helped his family tend sheep and grow crops.

At the age of nine, John's vocation was laid before him in the first of several dreams. Young John dreamt that he was surrounded by a large gang of foul-mouthed boys, whom he tried to correct first by words and then by blows. It was no use. Then a majestic Man and Lady appeared before him. The Man told him that he must win them over by kindness and gentleness. The Lady told him, "Be strong, humble and robust. When the time comes, you will understand everything" (catholic.org).

Not long after, John's interest became piqued by traveling circus performers that came to his area. He thought he could attract the attention of other youths if he learned to first entertain them. So John learned acrobatics and magic tricks and was lauded by his peers for his skills.

Inspired by his dreams, John felt called to become a priest, though he lacked the prerequisite education. So, despite being harassed by his older brother to give up on this and remain like the rest of his family, he left home at the age of twelve to work as a farm laborer to raise money for his education. Two years later, a priest, the future St. Joseph Cafasso, helped fund John's education. John entered seminary in 1835 and was ordained a priest in 1841.

Don Bosco (priests in Italy were addressed with the generally honorific title of 'Don') soon began work among troubled youth in Turin. He considered becoming a foreign missionary, but Don Cafasso persuaded him that his talents did not lie there, but in serving the youth. That was God's will for him. Don Bosco attracted the boys with his magic tricks and then befriended them and taught them about God. He would also go to the places they worked to strike up conversations with them. He took a genuine interest in the boys, and many, abandoned by their parents during the Industrial Revolution, were drawn to him.

At first, Don Bosco rented a property for the large number of abandoned boys that he found. The landlady, however, was bothered by the noise the boys made and by the flowers they ruined in her garden. So she told Don Bosco that either the boys must go or he must give up the property. Don Bosco brought the boys to his mother Margherita, who became known to the boys as Mamma Margherita. She helped house and care for the boys on the family farm property.

Wherever Don Bosco went with the boys, people saw trouble brewing since abandoned boys were associated with crime in the public consciousness. Sometimes pastors considered Don Bosco to be stealing their boys. Sometimes the anticlerical local government also opposed him as subverting the youth by teaching them the Catholic faith. Several times, Don Bosco was interrogated by the authorities and several attempts were even made on his life by anti-Catholic schemers. A large, mysterious gray dog he called Grigio would come to his defense throughout his life when he most needed it. The appearances of the dog happened over thirty years in different places, so Don Bosco believed that Grigio was miraculous protection from his guardian angel (Fr. Paul O'Sullivan, *All About the Angels*).

Don Bosco knew that the boys would need to learn a trade if they were to become upright citizens. He sent them out for apprenticeships and also tried to instill in them a formation of the heart. He soon realized that for the younger boys, the conditions at work were not suitable for them. Conditions were harsh and his efforts at fostering godly men were being undermined by the bad influences they encountered there. So Don Bosco brought in opportunities for learning trades within the community he had established for the boys and taught them other subjects as well. For older boys, he advocated worker's rights in a time when they were not yet common, insisting that their managers give them off on Sunday and give them reasonable hours and working conditions.

Don Bosco later raised funds and set up a new institution for housing and training the hundreds of boys that came to be under his care. Remembering the dream he had as a youth, Don Bosco avoided the harsh punitive methods common for discipline in the day and always treated the boys with kindness. He wanted not only to love them but let them know that they were loved.

Other priests came to assist Don Bosco from time to time, but they did not usually stay for long. So Don Bosco sought to form a religious order particularly dedicated to working with the youth. He called it the Society of St. Francis de Sales, or the Salesians. The government at the time was very anticlerical, opposing and constricting most religious orders as part of the rich establishment. But an important official looked favorably on Don Bosco's new type of religious order. Many of the vocations to this new order came from the boys themselves as they grew older. They understood the need, shared Don Bosco's passion, and were dedicated to the cause of lifting up the youth.

The Salesians began in 1859 with 22 members. They grew to include priests, seminarians, brothers, and laity, and opened houses for the youth throughout Italy and then Europe and the Americas. After founding a house for girls with Mary Mazarello in 1871, Don Bosco then helped found the Daughters of Mary Help of Christians for women religious working with the youth.

Don Bosco was known for his practical spiritual advice. He was a mentor to the young St. Dominic Savio, who associated with his organization for boys. Don Bosco also published a number of popular religious books to provide wholesome and spiritually up-building materials to his readership. Refusing to retire or rest, St. John Bosco died on January 31, 1888. He was canonized in 1934 and is the patron saint of Christian apprentices, editors, publishers, schoolchildren, young people, magicians, and juvenile delinquents. Today, there are over 15,000 Salesians serving all around the world.

St. John Bosco's Advice
Listen: there are two things the devil is deadly afraid of: fervent Communions and frequent visits to the Blessed Sacrament ...

Do you want many graces? Visit Him often. Do you want Him to grant you only a few? Visit Him but seldom. Do you want the devil to attack you? Rarely visit the Blessed Sacrament. Do you want the devil to flee from you? Visit Jesus often. Do you want to overcome the devil? Take refuge at Jesus' Feet. Do you want to be overcome by the devil? Give up visiting Jesus.

Visiting Jesus in the Blessed Sacrament is essential, my dear boys, if you want to overcome the devil. Therefore make frequent visits to Jesus. If you do that, the devil will never prevail against you (truechristianity.info).

St. John Bosco, pray for us!

St. Blaise

Bishop and Martyr (d. ca. 316)

Optional Memorial, Feb. 3

St. Blaise, a fourth-century martyr, was the bishop of Sebastea in Armenia. He is known for his intercession for ailments of the throat, and his memorial is often an occasion for special blessings of the throat. St. Blaise is also one of the "Fourteen Holy Helpers," or *Nothhelfer*, traditionally sought in German devotion during times of need.

The earliest mention of St. Blaise comes from the "Acts of St. Eustratius" (or St. Eustace), a martyr who is also venerated among the Nothhelfer. That early document tells us that St. Blaise was bishop of Sebastea and that he was the faithful executor of St. Eustratius' will after his martyrdom (*Butler's Lives of the Saints*).

Legends about St. Blaise were written several centuries later. They tell us he was a nobleman who was made bishop of Sebastea while still young, but that he later became a hermit after persecutions broke out. According to legend, wild beasts, the only inhabitants near his mountain-cave dwelling, would come to him for a blessing. People found St. Blaise, though, and came to ask him for prayers for healing.

Agricolaus, the Roman governor of Cappadocia and Lesser Armenia, ordered that St. Blaise be found and arrested for being a Christian. Hunters, sent out to capture animals for the amphitheater games, found St. Blaise, surrounded by various beasts that came to him. They arrested him and led him to his trial and death. On the way, a very poor woman came to him for help. A wolf had carried off her pig. St. Blaise summoned the wolf, who then brought back the pig to the poor woman, and sustained her livelihood. Also, a woman brought her son, who was choking on a fishbone, and the saint cured him.

The judge Licinius ordered St. Blaise scourged and then thrown in a dark and foul dungeon to starve. But the poor woman whose pig he had restored remembered him and brought him food and two candles. St. Blaise is said to have been thrown into a lake to drown, but he emerged on shore. Licinius then had St. Blaise tortured by having him hung by the hands and his skin torn open with iron wool combs. According to legend, seven women were found piously collecting his blood, and were then tortured and beheaded before St. Blaise. At last, St. Blaise was beheaded along with two youths brought in with him and condemned for being Christian.

The blessing of the throats on St. Blaise's memorial is administered with two blessed candles bound together with a red ribbon to form a St. Andrew's cross. The candles are extended to the person's throat along with this prayer: "Through the intercession of Saint Blaise, bishop and martyr, may God deliver you from every disease of the throat and from every other illness." The candles recall those brought to St. Blaise by the poor woman while he was in the dungeon. St. Blaise is often portrayed wearing a bishop's miter and accompanied by several of his symbols, whether the crossed candles, a wool comb, or surrounded by wild animals. He is venerated by the Eastern Orthodox on February 11, but on the Roman calendar on February 3.

St. Blaise, pray for us!

St. Agatha
Virgin and Martyr (ca. 231 – ca. 251)
Memorial, Feb. 5

St. Agatha was a third-century Sicilian martyr and model of purity, and is one of the several early saints venerated in the canon of the Mass. She is the patron saint of those suffering from breast cancer. Both the Sicilian towns of Catania and Palermo claim to be her birthplace. Various accounts of her martyrdom are legendary and differ from each other, but emphasize St. Agatha's heroic chastity.

Reputed to have been beautiful and of noble birth, St. Agatha made a vow of chastity at a young age, resolving never to marry. Nonetheless, she was approached by numerous men, including the powerful Quintian, a Roman prefect and a pagan. Enraged by her refusal of his advances, Quintian had St. Agatha arrested for being a Christian and had her given over to the madam of a brothel. Though St. Agatha was assaulted for weeks at the brothel, she proved unshaken in her resolve for chastity. At last, the madam of the brothel sent her back, and Quintian had her beaten and thrown in prison. Still resolved to follow Christ, St. Agatha was subjected to torture on the rack, but she endured cheerfully. The judge was enraged and ordered her breasts to be cut off. Sent back to prison, where she was denied both food and medical attention, she was left to die.

However, St. Peter appeared to her in a bright light and miraculously healed her wounds and comforted her. Seeing that she would not die easily nor be shaken in her resolve, Quintin had St. Agatha rolled naked over burning coals mixed with sharp potsherds. At last, St. Agatha's body had had enough. She prayed, "Lord, my Creator, thou hast always protected me from the cradle; thou hast taken me from the love of the world and given me patience to suffer. Receive now my soul" (*quoted in Butler's Lives of the Saints*). Having been taken back to the prison, St. Agatha died of her injuries.

St. Agatha's name appears several centuries later in sacramentary books containing the prayers for the Mass, and her cult of veneration was confirmed by Pope St. Gregory the Great. She is often portrayed carrying a dish with two severed breasts. Her feast day is celebrated in Sicily with a blessing of loaves of bread, owing to the paintings in which she is depicted carrying her breasts on a platter. Traditionally, Sicilians have prayed to St. Agatha for protection against eruptions of Mt. Etna, since the volcano was stilled from an eruption the year after her death. She is buried in Catania in Sicily, and her feast day is February 5. St. Agatha is a model of chastity, willing to sacrifice her body and even her life to please God.

St. Paul Miki and Companions
Martyrs (d. 1597)
Memorial, Feb. 6

Twenty six Catholic martyrs crucified together in Nagasaki, Japan, in 1597 were canonized together in 1862 by Pope Pius IX. They are remembered throughout the universal Church by a memorial in the Roman calendar under the name of St. Paul Miki and Companions.

The number of Christians in Japan the generation after St. Francis Xavier's arrival in 1549 grew to 200,000, bringing concern to the emperors of Japan. According to *Butler's Lives of the Saints*, one emperor, Cambacundono, forbade Christian missionaries in Japan. A few years later, another emperor, Tagosama, decided to take violent action against them after meeting the captain of a Spanish ship. The captain reportedly boasted to the emperor that the Europeans would conquer Japan through the many missionaries stationed there. So the emperor ordered a group of Catholic missionaries to be arrested to make an example of them.

Six Franciscan missionaries and three Jesuit missionaries were arrested, along with a number of Japanese lay associates and even several boys. Some of the missionaries were of European ancestry while others were from Asia. Many of the associates were lay Franciscans who served as catechists, translators, and workers. The teenage boys, two of whom were sons of lay associates, served at the altar. St. Paul Miki himself was born to a noble family in Japan, the son of a high-ranking soldier. Educated by Jesuits, he joined the order and was in formation for the priesthood. He was a great preacher and converted many to the faith.

The martyrs were mutilated, having one ear partly cut off, which was actually a commuted sentence from further mutilation. Then, their faces bloodied, they were marched several hundred miles from Kyoto down to Nagasaki, passing through many towns as an example to any other Christian missionaries. They sang the Te Deum hymn as they went.

At Nagasaki, after having been allowed to make their last Confession to two local Jesuits, the 26 martyrs were lifted onto crosses to which they were bound. To the surprise of the officials, they considered it an honor to die in the same way as their Lord. St. Paul Miki even preached to the crowds from his cross. He was heard to say, "Like my Master, I shall die upon the cross. Like him, a lance will pierce my heart so that my blood and my love can flow out upon the land and sanctify it to his name" (ignatianspirituality.com). Then they were impaled to death all at once, as was the Japanese custom for execution. Before they died, St. Paul Miki and the other martyrs were heard to forgive their persecutors. Christians came to the place of their martyrdom and collected relics, and the site became a place of pilgrimage for Christians in Japan, though Catholicism was forced underground by 1630.

The names of the martyrs, compiled and compared from various sources, are as follows:

Jesuit missionaries:

St. Paul Miki, scholastic (seminarian) and preacher, from Japan

St. John Goto (or John Soan de Goto), lay brother and catechist, from Japan

St. James (or Diego) **Kisai**, lay brother and temporal coadjutor of the Jesuits, from Japan

Franciscan missionaries:

St. Peter Baptist (or Pedro Bautista), friar and superior, from Spain

St. Martin de Aguirre (or Martin of the Ascension), friar, from Spain

St. Francis Blanco, friar, from Spain

St. Francis of St. Michael, lay brother, from Spain

St. Philip de las Casas (or Philip of Jesus), in formation for the priesthood, from Mexico City

St. Gonsalo (or Gundisalvus) **Garcia**, lay brother, from India

Japanese Lay Associates

St. Cosmas Takeya of Owaro, catechist

St. Francis of Nagasaki (or Francis of Miyako), catechist, cared for the sick

St. Gabriel de Duisco

St. Gaius Francis (or Kichi Franciscus or Francis Kichi), soldier, arrested while devoutly watching the passion of the other Christians

St. Joachim Sakakibara (or Saccachibara), cook for the Franciscans

St. John Kisaka, silk weaver

St. Leo Karasuma (or Karasumaru), of Korea, catechist, former Buddhist monk, brother of St. Paul Ibaraki, uncle of St. Louis Ibaraki

St. Matthias of Miyako, offered himself up as a Christian

St. Michael Kozaki (or Kosaki), carpenter, cared for the sick, father of St. Louis Kozaki

St. Paul Ibaraki, catechist, interpreter, father of St. Louis Ibaraki, brother of St. Leo Karasuma

St. Paul Suzuki, cared for the sick

St. Peter Sukejiroo, arrested while coming to help the prisoners

St. Thomas Kosaki

St. Thomas Xico

St. Ventura (or Bonaventure) **of Miyako,** renounced the Catholic faith to become a Buddhist monk but returned to the Catholic faith through the ministry of the Franciscans

Altar Servers:

St. Louis Ibaraki, age twelve

St. Antony Deynan (or Danian), age thirteen

St. Thomas Kozaki (or Kosaki), age fifteen, son of St. Michael Kozaki, nephew of St. Leo Karasuma

St. Paul Miki and companions, pray for us!

St. Josephine Bakhita

Virgin (ca. 1869 – 1947)

Optional Memorial, Feb. 8

Warmly remembered as the "Black Mother," the kind-hearted St. Josephine Bakhita, a former slave in Africa, aspired to the religious life and sanctity in the Catholic Church. Canonized in the Jubilee Year of 2000 by Pope St. John Paul II, she is recognized as the patron saint of the Sudan.

The future St. Josephine Bakhita was born outside Darfur in Sudan around 1869. At the age of seven, she was kidnapped by slave traders and reduced to a life of captivity, hard work, and abuse. Her new masters gave her the name Bakhita, which means 'fortunate one' in Arabic. She was bought and sold repeatedly in the marketplace and was harshly mistreated by many of her masters. She was branded, sometimes beaten daily, and cut with knives with salt poured into her wounds. After many years, Bakhita was purchased by a Genoese man, Callisto Legnani, the Italian consul to Sudan. He at first treated her more humanely, so she begged him to take her back with him when he returned to Italy, and he did. Legnani later gave her to a friend of his, Augusto Michieli, who gave her charge of young Mimmina Michieli (www.franciscanmedia.org).

Bakhita took good care of Mimmina. One of her duties was to take Mimmina to catechism classes with the Canossian sisters. Bakhita had experienced God in her life, but did not know him, so the sisters answered many of her questions. Bakhita later said, "Seeing the sun, the moon and the stars, I said to myself: Who could be the Master of these beautiful things? And I felt a great desire to see him, to know Him and to pay Him homage" (www.vatican.va). Bakhita too desired to receive the sacraments, which she did around the age of twenty-one. She took Josephine as her baptismal name. Josephine Bakhita grew very much in love with God, the "Master" of all, as she often called him.

Josephine Bakhita further felt a vocation to the religious life, however the Micheili family was planning on returning to Sudan. Josephine Bakhita refused to go, and the sisters helped her, filing a complaint on her behalf with the Italian authorities. The matter went to court and was decided in her favor, on the basis of Italian law at the time. Josephine Bakhita was declared to be a free woman, and could make her own decisions.

Josephine Bakhita entered the Institute of St. Magdalene of Canossa, or the Canossian Sisters, in 1893, taking her final vows in 1896. Performing tasks such as cooking, cleaning, and greeting visitors, Sister Josephine Bakhita became known and loved among the people. In times when there was a spread of disease, Bakhita was there to nurse the people to health. Though she also faced racial prejudice, Sister Josephine Bakhita was remembered for her wise sayings, warm smile, enthusiasm, tender service, and her gentle and expressive eyes. Rather than consider the trauma of her earlier life, she focused on the wonders that God had done for her. She once said, "The Lord has loved me so much: we must love everyone...we must be compassionate!" She served among the Italian people as a Canossian sister for fifty years, until her passing in 1947. Towards the end of her life, Sister Josephine Bakhita suffered illness and hardship. In her final moments, she saw the Blessed Virgin Mary. Her last words were, "Our Lady! Our Lady!"

St. Josephine Bakhita, pray for us!

Our Lady of Lourdes
Apparitions of the Blessed Virgin Mary
(1858)
Memorial, Feb. 11

The apparitions of Our Lady of Lourdes in 1858 to young St. Bernadette Soubirous were approved by the Catholic Church after much examination. They are not proposed to be held in faith by all believers since that is reserved only for Scripture and Sacred Tradition. Still, these apparitions are held in such high regard that the Blessed Virgin Mary is honored on the Roman calendar with the optional memorial of Our Lady of Lourdes. There were eighteen apparitions of Our Lady of Lourdes, all occurring in the year 1858 before ceasing. The message of Our Lady of Lourdes was similar in theme to that of other Marian apparitions of this time to the present — a call to prayer and penance.

Lourdes is a small town in southwestern France in the foothills of the Pyrenees Mountains. On Thursday, February 11, 1858, a thirteen-year-old peasant girl named Bernadette Soubirous had an encounter with a mysterious Lady. Bernadette went along with her sister and a friend collecting wood for the fireplace that evening. While the others waded across the chilly waters of the River Gave, Bernadette tarried behind because of her asthma. Suddenly she noticed a rose bush in the grotto at Massabielle blowing as if in a strong wind. A cloud appeared, and then a young, beautiful Lady appeared. The Lady did not speak. Bernadette grabbed her

Rosary and began praying. The Lady, who carried a pearl Rosary, fingered the beads as Bernadette prayed, but only joined in at the Glory Be. When the Rosary was finished, the Lady disappeared ("Our Lady of Lourdes," www.catholicnewsagency.com).

The other girls made fun of Bernadette for dallying behind, and when she told them about the Lady, they had further sport. They told their parents about the event, and they were not pleased. But on Sunday, Bernadette, winning the support of a prominent woman in town, returned to the grotto and the Lady appeared again. The next time, the Beautiful Lady spoke, only asking Bernadette to come every day for fifteen days. Over that time, the Lady asked Bernadette to do a number of unusual things. She asked her to always come with a blessed candle, to kiss the ground in penance, to repeat to the crowd, "penance, penance, penance," and to wash in the spring, even though there was no visible spring in the place.

Bernadette dug slightly in the ground and rubbed the dirt over her face so that people thought she was mad. But water soon emerged from where she had dug, and there is a voluminous spring that flows to this very day. Not long after, a severely disabled boy was cured in its waters. The Lady also asked Bernadette to tell the parish priest that she wished that a chapel be built at the place and to let processions come.

Some of the townspeople of Lourdes were concerned about all the commotion that these events were causing and the large crowds that trampled through the farmland. Some accused Bernadette of lying or of mental illness. Town authorities tried to prevent Bernadette from continuing to visit the Lady, whom she called *Aquero*, "that one." Seen with her face transfigured when she looked upon the Lady, the authorities also ordered for her to be examined by doctors. The doctors found nothing wrong with her.

Bernadette's parish priest was not interested in the request of the mysterious Lady, but he insisted that she ask *Aquero* her name. The Lady would not tell Bernadette her name right away, but at a later apparition, she told her in a voice filled with emotion, "I am the Immaculate Conception." Bernadette, an illiterate peasant girl, did not understand the meaning of these words. All the way to the priest's house, Bernadette kept repeating the phrase she remembered from the Lady without knowing what it meant. When she gave the words to the priest, he was deeply moved and began to believe. Only a few years earlier, in 1854, Pope Pius IX had solemnly proclaimed the dogma of the Immaculate Conception of the Blessed Virgin Mary — that from the first moment of her conception, the Virgin Mary was free from Original Sin.

At the age of twenty-two, Bernadette joined the Sisters of Charity at Nevers in central France. Given the name Sister Marie-Bernarde, she tended to the sick and embroidered altar vestments. Sister Marie-Bernarde lived to know that the chapel the Lady asked for was being built, but she never saw it. The Lady had told her she could not promise her happiness in this life but in the next. Sister Marie-Bernarde contracted tuberculosis of the bone and died at the age of thirty-five on April 16, 1879. Her body was exhumed some thirty years later, in 1909, and found remarkably intact and without any stench. Buried once more, the body was exhumed again in 1919 and found mysteriously incorrupt. Then preserved in wax, the body of St. Bernadette is kept open for viewing and veneration at the convent at Nevers to this day.

Bernadette's visions of Our Lady were approved by her local bishop and then in 1870 by Pope Pius IX himself — the same pope who had proclaimed the dogma of the Immaculate Conception several decades before. Today, the grotto is preserved, and over it towers a magnificent basilica — the

Sanctuary of Our Lady of Lourdes — known for its beautiful candlelight Marian processions. Lourdes is one of the most popular Catholic destinations, attracting several million pilgrims each year. Many, including hundreds of thousands of people with serious or terminal conditions, go each year into the waters of the baths from the spring seeking healing. There are countless stories of healing, dozens of which have even been carefully examined and approved by the Catholic Church.

Our Lady of Lourdes, pray for us!

St. Bernadette Soubirous, pray for us!

Sts. Cyril and Methodius

St. Cyril, Monk (ca. 826 / 827 – 869) and

St. Methodius, Bishop (815 – 885)

Memorial, Feb. 14

Sts. Cyril and Methodius, brothers by birth and by spirit, are remembered as the apostles of the Slavic peoples. Born in Thessalonica to noble parents, the two had to overcome many obstacles — particularly political ones involving tensions between East and West — to bring the gospel into the lives and culture of the Slavic peoples. Concerned with bringing the Bible and the liturgy to the Slavs in their own language but in written form, the brothers are credited with inventing the alphabet that became the Cyrillic alphabet of today, used in Russia and several other Eastern European countries.

Cyril and Methodius are both names taken by the brothers at religious profession (*Butler's Lives of the Saints*). Cyril's birth name was Constantine and Methodius' was Michael. Their father was a high official in the imperial government. The future St. Cyril was at first a philosopher, studying under the most eminent Eastern scholars at Constantinople. During that time he was also ordained as a deacon. The future St. Methodius was governor of a Slavic colony of the Eastern Empire. Methodius, however, decided to become a monk and was elected abbot. Cyril, having gained a reputation for his erudition, withdrew to live a life of prayer and asceticism on the Bosphorus. Known as "the Philosopher," he was found and brought back to serve as a teacher and scholar at Constantinople.

Emperor Michael III sent Cyril to evangelize the Khazars on the far side of the Black Sea, and he made a great many converts. Then the prince Rastislav of Moravia (now in the Czech Republic), interested in tempering the Western influence of German missionaries, petitioned Constantinople for missionaries to teach the Slavic people in the own language. Photius, Archbishop of Constantinople and former teacher to Cyril, recommended Cyril and Methodius since they knew the Slavonic language. At the time, many in the Western Church insisted only on the use of Latin for both the Bible and the liturgy, even in Eastern lands. Cyril and Methodius were readily welcomed since the people were glad that they made use of their own language for sacred matters. Nonetheless, controversy swirled among influential Western churchmen, and the German bishop would not ordain any priests for them.

So Cyril and Methodius, having found the relics of Pope St. Clement I in a church in Crimea, went to Rome to present the relics to Pope St. Nicholas I and win his favor. The Holy Father is said to have summoned them to an audience. The pope died before they arrived, but his successor Adrian II likewise was favorable to the brothers. They impressed him very much with their efforts at bringing the faith to the Slavs in their own language. Pope Adrian also greatly appreciated receiving the relics of such an early and revered Bishop of Rome. Pope Adrian announced that he would consecrate the brothers as bishops and the Slavic converts who accompanied them as priests. Then as bishops, the brothers would be able to ordain priests as desired.

But it happened to be the time of Cyril's passing. He was a priest but not as yet a monk. He was consecrated as a monk at this time, and only then took the name by which we know him — Cyril. We do not know if there was actually an opportunity for the pope to consecrate Cyril a bishop before his death. His brother Methodius was, however, consecrated a bishop by Pope Adrian himself, who insisted that Cyril be buried with honor at Rome. Then Methodius and his priests returned to the land of the Slavs. He later became archbishop of Sirmium, a restored ancient see. Support from the Bishop of Rome and high rank, however, did not prevent other churchmen from trying to stall the progress of the Slavic liturgies and Bibles.

Svlatopluk, a prince, usurped his uncle Rastisalv's power and took a hostile stance towards Methodius, who had rebuked him for his sinful ways. Methodius was imprisoned for two years, falsely charged with intruding on another bishop's territory. Pope John VIII had Methodius freed, but he was at first suspicious when Methodius was again denounced for heresy. But upon summoning Methodius and hearing directly from him about the matter, he exonerated him and praised his work. Still obstructed in his efforts at home, Methodius spent much of his latter days translating the Scriptures into the Slavic languages, making use of the alphabet that his brother Cyril in particular had pioneered. When he died, he was greatly mourned by the people. But then his chief opponent, Wiching, who used to go so far as to forge papal documents against Methodius, became bishop and suppressed the Slavonic liturgy and translations of the Bible, even exiling Methodius' supporters. A later pope also forbade the Slavonic liturgy and Bibles, which previous popes had approved. But Methodius' supporters kept them alive, and they became of great influence in the future Eastern Orthodox and Eastern Catholic churches.

Today, Sts. Cyril and Methodius are celebrated in both Catholicism and Eastern Orthodoxy. Utilizing the highest ordinary use of papal teaching authority, Pope St. John Paul II wrote an encyclical *Slavorum Apostoli* in 1985 to recall the lessons of Sts. Cyril and Methodius. He sets up their example of unity between East and West and their presentation of the unchanging gospel in new cultural ways — what he calls "inculturation" (no. 21). John Paul II, the only Polish pope, regarded the apostles of the Slavs as his own spiritual fathers. The Eastern Orthodox, moreover, venerate them with the title of "Equal to the Apostles."

There are a number of days on which the two have been commemorated both throughout history and by the various Eastern churches. Pope Leo XIII likewise dedicated an encyclical to Sts. Cyril and Methodius in 1880. There he raised their observance, previously only celebrated in certain local Catholic churches, to the calendar for the universal Catholic Church. The date chosen was February 14, the date of St. Cyril's death. Sts. Cyril and Methodius are venerated as the patron saints of ecumenism and co-patrons of Europe, together with St. Benedict of Nursia.

Sts. Cyril and Methodius, pray for us!

The Chair of the Apostle Peter
St. Peter, Apostle (ca. 1 BC – ca. AD 64 / 68)
Feast, Feb. 22

The feast of the Chair of the Apostle Peter celebrates St. Peter's papal authority. As when Jesus sat down to preach his Sermon on the Mount in Matthew's Gospel, a teacher sat down in ancient Jewish culture to demonstrate his authority. Thus the chair of Peter refers both to the actual chair purported to be St. Peter's and to his office in general. In fact, the term 'Holy See' is derived from the Latin and French usage for the 'Holy Seat' and remains the term used to indicate the pontifical office and the authority stemming from it. There used to be two separate feasts of the Chair — January 18 for the Chair at Rome, St. Peter's final city, and February 22 for the Chair at Antioch, St. Peter's prior city where he presided over the church before setting out for Rome. In 1960, Pope John XXIII combined the two feasts into the Feast of the Chair of the Apostle Peter on February 22.

Already by the year AD 250, there is mention of a physical chair associated with St. Peter at Rome and with his official duties of baptizing and presiding over worship. By the middle of the first millennium, there appear references in the sacramentary books for Mass for feasts of the Chair of the Apostle Peter. In the seventeenth century, the artist Bernini designed a glorious construction around the purported actual chair of St. Peter in the apse of St. Peter's Basilica. It features the Holy Spirit in stained glass descending from above the chair and encircled by gilded angels.

Peter is often seen as a relatable figure in the Bible. He was a candidly-spoken Galilean fisherman, not particularly well educated, and yet well-off enough that his father could hire several helping hands for his fishing business. From the start, Peter had a big heart and an open mind, but early in his formation as a disciple of Jesus, he was often impetuous, naturally slow to understand, and sometimes cowardly. But after the Pentecost event, it was Peter who boldly led the charge to evangelize at Jerusalem, leading to the baptism of some 3,000 persons.

The New Testament shows that Peter had a special role among the Apostles and in the early Church. Peter is always first in all the lists of the Apostles in the Gospels. The Beloved Apostle (traditionally John) is said in John's Gospel to have waited before entering the empty tomb of Christ after the Resurrection, deferring to Peter and allowing him to be the first to enter. After Paul's conversion, it was to Peter that he went to present himself for ministry.

When Jesus asked the disciples who he was, Simon (later called Peter) stepped forward in faith, saying, "You are the Messiah, the Son of the living God" (Mt. 16:16). Jesus replied, "Blessed are you, Simon son of Jonah. For flesh and blood has not revealed this to you, but my heavenly Father. And so I say to you, you are Peter, and upon this rock I will build my church, and the gates of the netherworld shall not prevail against it. I will give you the keys to the kingdom of heaven. Whatever you bind on earth shall be bound in heaven; and whatever you loose on earth shall be loosed in heaven" (Mt. 16:17–19).

Jesus gave the name Peter to Simon. Often in Scripture, with a new mission comes a new name. The name Peter means "Rock," and must have been unique since it is not found as a name prior to this in all of antiquity. Jesus named Peter as the rock of the Church which he would build. The word for 'church' is the same used in the Greek Bible for the assembly of Israel. Thus, Peter's role is a very important one in salvation history.

The reference to binding and loosing has precedent in the Old Testament where the prophet in Isaiah 58 speaks in the same terms to the prime minister. There too, keys are the symbol of the prime minister's authority. Jesus, the king, is apparently naming Peter as his prime minister. Jesus further declares that Peter, the first of the Apostles to acknowledge him as "the Messiah, the son of the living God," was given special help from God to make this statement of faith. Though fallible in his nature, Peter was infallible in this matter of faith. Thus the Catholic Church, from early on, began to speak of the successors of Peter, the popes, as infallible on matters of faith and morals, though the dogma of papal infallibility was not solemnly defined until the nineteenth century.

Peter famously denied Jesus three times during his passion, but unlike Judas, he came to the risen Christ with heartfelt repentance. Jesus gave him his penance, asking Peter three times if he loved him. Each time, after eliciting an affirmative response in faith, Jesus asked him to feed his flock. Peter was to be a chief shepherd of souls. Jesus also prophesied, "Amen, amen, I say to you, when you were younger, you used to dress yourself and go where you wanted; but when you grow old, you will stretch out your hands, and someone else will dress you and lead you where you do not want to go" (Jn. 21:18).

According to tradition, Peter went to Rome as the leader of the church there since it was the capital of the Roman Empire.

When Nero's persecution broke out, he began to flee the city when he met Jesus, who appeared to him. Peter asked Jesus, *Quo Vadis, Domine?* "Where are you going, Lord?" And Jesus replied, "I am returning to Rome to be crucified." So Peter returned to Rome to accept his martyrdom. He was captured and condemned to crucifixion, but he insisted on being crucified upside down since he did not feel worthy to die in the same manner as his Lord. There was an Egyptian obelisk which had been repositioned by the ancient Romans near the place Peter was crucified. That same obelisk is preserved to this day in St. Peter's Square. In the 1940s, archaeologists finally found the bones of Peter in an ossuary (bone box) deep under St. Peter's Basilica, which was traditionally said to be built on the place of his burial. Along with it was an inscription with Christian symbols written in Latin with the words, "Peter is here."

St. Peter, pray for us!

St. Polycarp
Bishop and Martyr (69 – 155)
Memorial, Feb. 23

St. Polycarp, who in his youth was taught at the feet of John the Apostle, was a saintly bishop of Smyrna in Asia Minor. Martyred at the venerable age of eighty-six, his story was recorded by the early church in a document called "The Death of Polycarp." Polycarp leaves us an epistle to the Philippians, in which he exhorts the church there to submit to their presbyters and deacons and to remember the sound advice given them years ago by St. Paul. Polycarp was also the recipient of a surviving epistle from his friend and colleague St. Ignatius of Antioch, who was traveling to Rome to meet with his own martyrdom.

Angered by the Christians, pagans at Smyrna cried out against Bishop Polycarp, so the Roman authorities sought Polycarp's arrest. They charged him with promoting 'atheism' — that is denying the Roman gods. Other Christians warned Polycarp to flee, providing him harbor in various houses outside Smyrna. Polycarp's whereabouts, however, were given up by one of his servants who had been arrested and tortured for the information. The bishop of Smyrna, meanwhile, had a dream in which he was surrounded by flames. When the soldiers arrived, Polycarp accepted his fate. He offered his captors a meal and in return they allowed him two hours of fervent prayer. Though moved by his devotion, the soldiers brought him to the magistrates, who ordered him to hail Caesar as Lord and offer sacrifice to him. Polycarp refused. Though at first respectful to his age, they became enraged at his constancy. They began to mistreat the old man, shoving him out of a carriage. Though his leg was dislocated, he boldly continued on foot.

Polycarp was brought into the amphitheater where he was met by a vicious pagan crowd. There he heard a voice from Heaven saying, "Be strong, and show yourself a man, O Polycarp!" ("The Death of Polycarp"). His persecutors gave him another chance, urging him to curse Christ. Polycarp replied, "Eighty and six years have I served Him, and He never did me any injury: how then can I blaspheme my King and my Saviour?" Following several more threats and immoral commands, Polycarp refused to give in, and was condemned to die at the stake. He said, "You threaten me with fire which burns for an hour, and after a little is extinguished, but are ignorant of the fire of the coming judgment and of eternal punishment, reserved for the ungodly. But why do you tarry? Bring forth what you will." The soldiers then went to nail him to the stake, but he persuaded them only to tie him, since he was resolved to remain in place.

Polycarp prayed a great and moving prayer as the pyre was built, and God worked powerful miracles at his martyrdom. When the fire was lit, the flames rose up, but billowed around Polycarp without touching him. The Christians who recorded it thought it resembled bread baking in an oven — an image reminiscent of the Eucharist. They also noted a sweet aroma like frankincense — symbolic of a fitting sacrifice offered to God. Seeing that Polycarp would not die by fire, the soldiers stabbed him with a dagger. Out of the wound, a dove flew out as his spirit departed and so much blood — like that which came from Christ's side — that it extinguished the fire.

The magistrates refused to give Polycarp's body to the Christians but instead had it burned. Afterward, the Christians collected the bones, considering them "more precious than the most exquisite jewels, and more purified than gold." They then kept them aside in an honorable place "to celebrate the anniversary of his martyrdom." After Polycarp's martyrdom, the magistrates paused their persecution of Christians in Smyrna.

St. Polycarp, known throughout his life for his holiness, was remembered throughout the centuries as one of the great martyrs of the early church. His heroic fortitude and perseverance remains a model for all in their struggle against denying Christ by word and deed.

St. Polycarp, pray for us!

St. Katharine Drexel
Virgin (1858 – 1955)
Optional Memorial, Mar. 3

St. Katharine Drexel is the second American-born individual to be made a saint. An heiress to a massive fortune, she ultimately gave it away, and in the process gave herself completely as well. Founding the Sisters of the Blessed Sacrament, she used her wealth to build boarding schools and missions for marginalized communities of Native Americans and African Americans throughout the United States.

Katharine, or Kate, was born in Philadelphia in 1858. Her father, Francis Anthony Drexel, was a wealthy financier and a devout Catholic. Her mother, Hannah Langstroth Drexel, died several weeks after giving birth to Katharine due to complications from childbirth. Francis married Emma Bouvier in 1860 who accepted Katharine and Katherine's older sister Elizabeth as her own children. Emma, who also gave birth to a daughter named Louise, was also a devout Catholic and introduced the girls to charitable work. Years later, Emma became seriously ill and died in 1883. While caring for Emma during her illness, Katharine became awakened to a possible calling to the religious life. Then when her father passed away in 1886, he bequeathed ten percent to charity but the rest — some $14 million — to his three daughters. The estate continued to grow, providing further income to the sisters and thus making Katharine very wealthy. But Katharine remembered what her father had taught her — that they were merely stewards of the great wealth with which God had blessed them.

Discerning the religious life, Katharine submitted to spiritual direction under her pastor, Fr. James O'Conner, who later became bishop of Omaha in Nebraska. He thought it best for her to remain a layperson and do good with her inheritance. Moved by the plight of the Native Americans who she learned had suffered much injustice, Katharine became deeply involved with and provided support to missions serving them. But more missionaries were needed, so she went for an audience with Pope Leo XIII in Rome and asked him to send missionaries to serve the Native Americans. The Holy Father gave his answer: "Why not my child, yourself become a missionary?" (www.stkatharinedrexel.org). Katharine was troubled and felt sick when she left the audience, but consulting with then-Bishop O'Connor, she resolved to enter the religious life to become a missionary. Katharine would receive formation from the Sisters of Mercy in Pittsburgh, but would found her own order so as to be able to distribute her wealth through her charitable endeavors. The heiress' unusual move even made newspaper headlines in Philadelphia when she entered the convent in 1889.

The Drexel sisters, who were also keenly interested in Katharine's charitable work, went out with Bishop O'Connor to visit Native American communities in the northern and northwestern
United States, where they met with the famous Chief Red Cloud. After her formation, then-Mother Katharine traveled to Native American communities in the southwestern United States with thirteen religious sisters for her new order — the Sisters of the Blessed Sacrament. First, Mother Katharine reopened a school for Native Americans in New Mexico. Then she opened another school for the Navaho and then one for African Americans on the James River in Virginia. She reached out to African American communities both in rural areas and the inner city.

Mother Katharine ultimately spent her fortune building schools and missions for the marginalized all over the country — a total of 145 missions, fifty schools for African Americans, and twelve schools for Native Americans. The school Mother Katharine founded in 1915 for African Americans in New Orleans later became Xavier University, the only predominantly African-American Catholic university in the country. The sisters had to brave many difficulties, both because of the challenges of the frontier and racial prejudice. All the while, Mother Katharine inspired many women to join the Sisters of the Blessed Sacrament to serve in the boarding schools and missions. Mother Katharine was bedridden for the last two decades of her life. During that time, she experienced much spiritual growth before her passing in 1955 at the age of ninety-six.

St. Katharine Drexel was beatified in 1988 and canonized in 2000, both by Pope St. John Paul II. She is the patron saint of philanthropy and racial justice.

St. Katharine Drexel, pray for us!

Sts. Perpetua and Felicity
Martyrs (d. 203)
Memorial, Mar. 7

Saints Perpetua and Felicity, both married women and catechumens recently baptized, were martyred together at Carthage in North Africa on March 7 in the year 203. Their story is recorded in "The Passion of Saints Perpetua and Felicity," much of which is purportedly taken from the dairy of St. Perpetua herself, and was read in church in North Africa alongside the Scriptures.

St. Perpetua was a well-educated, married Carthusian lady who had a young child. Her mother was a Christian, and Perpetua became a catechumen. She was martyred at the age of twenty-two. St. Felicity was a slave girl who, after her death, rose with Perpetua to become one of the most universally venerated saints in the liturgy.

Upon hearing of her resolve to become Christian, Perpetua's pagan father, who loved her dearly, became enraged because of the dangers to which she was exposing herself under Roman law. Perpetua took a vessel and asked her father if it could be called anything other than what it was. He replied that it could not. Perpetua said that neither could she be called by any other name than that of Christian.

Perpetua and Felicty were found out and arrested along with other catechumens and their teacher. They were confined under horrible conditions. Perpetua recalled the extreme heat, the terrible smell, and the pitch darkness. During this time, Perpetua cared for and breastfed her infant, until it was taken away from her and given to her family.

Perpetua's brother suggested that she should ask God to show her what was to happen to her, so Perpetua prayed and had a dream. She dreamt that she was ascending a golden ladder to the heavens. On the sides of the ladder were all sorts of sharp weapons to entrap anyone who would falter, and at the base of the ladder was a dragon to devour anyone who would fall. Perpetua made her way up the ladder into Heaven, where she was warmly greeted by the Shepherd, who fed her with a cake which she received with folded hands. This was likely an image of the Eucharist. Another time while praying, Perpetua received an image of one of her brothers, who had died in childhood from a hideous cancer on his face. She saw him in a place of suffering — likely what would later be called Purgatory — and prayed earnestly for him. Later, when she was confined to the stocks, she saw another image of her brother, healed and happy because of his sister's suffering and prayers. Perpetua had another dream in which she was led into the arena by a deacon who had been martyred and who promised to be with her. In the arena, she met the Devil who was dressed as a gladiator. She was victorious over him and won the prize. From this, Perpetua knew that martyrdom awaited, but also the crown and victory over Satan.

When the Christians were brought to trial, they confessed to their belief in Christ and refused to offer sacrifices to the emperor. Perpetua's father tried hard to persuade his daughter to renounce Christ to save her life, but the magistrates ordered him to be beaten, and condemned the Christians to be devoured by wild beasts. Perpetua's concern was firstly for her infant, but God gave her the grace to let go and trust that her mother and brother would care for the child.

Felicity was pregnant at the time, and pregnant women were not allowed to be exhibited in the games. Felicity was distraught at the thought that she would not go to the wild beasts with the Christians but later with criminals. The Christians prayed, and Felicity began to go into labor. She cried out in pain, and one of the pagans chided her that this was nothing compared to the pain of being devoured by wild beasts. Felicity responded that God would give her the grace to endure at the right time. She gave birth, and her child was cared for by a woman in the Christian community.

When the day came for the games, the group of Christians were led into the amphitheater. Some of the Christian men warned the jeering and bloodthirsty crowd of God's coming judgment, and the crowd called for them to be scourged. God gave each martyr the grace to endure what they could. One, who boldly desired to fight with multiple beasts so as to win a greater crown, was given just that. Another, who wished to die at once from the jaws of a leopard, was indeed martyred quickly in that fashion. The women were attacked by a wild cow. Perpetua came to Felicity's aid when the latter was trampled on by the cow. The two gave the kiss of peace.

The crowd had enough of the savagery to these young mothers, so they were given to be slain instantly by gladiators. Perpetua did not realize how badly she had been wounded by the cow until she saw her wounds. A trembling gladiator stabbed Perpetua in the side of the chest, wounding her so that she gave out a loud cry, but not killing her. Perpetua, with her own hand, guided his sword to her neck. The editor of the ancient account of their martyrdom writes, "Possibly such a woman could not have been slain unless she herself had willed it, because she was feared by the impure spirit."

Saints Perpetua and Felicity are universally celebrated in early martyrologies and on the various traditional liturgical calendars, representing also the many early martyrs of the Church. Their stories provided inspiration to other martyrs and to generations of Christians.

Saints Perpetua and Felicity, pray for us!

St. Patrick
Bishop (ca. 384 – ca. 461)
Optional Memorial (Ireland Solemnity), Mar. 17

St. Patrick, Apostle of Ireland, was born in Roman Britannia to wealthy Christian parents in the late fourth century. Through him, by strong witness and mighty deeds, Ireland was brought from Druid nature worship to Christianity. Even in his day, people who had grown up in paganism were becoming priests, monks, and nuns. For many centuries to the present day, Ireland would become a bulwark of Christianity.

It's unclear in which year exactly St. Patrick was born, but as footprints in the sands of history, he leaves us not only legends and the sudden conversion of Ireland to Christianity, but also two letters — namely his *Confession* and his *Letter to Coroticus*. In his *Confession*, he gives testimony to his faith in Christ and the teachings of the Church, also giving an account of his life and a defense of his actions in light of detractors in the church back in Britain. St. Patrick tells us that his father was a deacon and his grandfather was a priest (in the days before celibacy was required of priests), but that he had paid little attention to God or his laws as a youth. Around the age of sixteen, Patrick was captured by Irish raiders — a misfortune he attributed to God's punishment — and was reduced to slavery in Ireland, where he tended sheep for his master.

Patrick saw his lonely time in captivity as providential. It occasioned him to grow close to the God he had learned about as a youth. He recalls praying a hundred times a day and a hundred time a night, fasting often. He writes in his *Confession*, "I used to stay out in the forests and on the mountain and I would wake up before daylight to pray in the snow, in icy coldness, in rain, and I used to feel neither ill nor any slothfulness, because, as I now see, the Spirit was burning in me at that time." God had other plans for Patrick than caring for sheep. At night, he heard a voice, "You do well to fast: soon you will depart for your home country." Later he heard, "Behold, your ship is ready." So after six years of slavery, Patrick set out some two hundred miles to where the Lord directed him. When he came to the ship, the men turned him away angrily. But while walking away, Patrick prayed — and just then, the men relented. They set sail, landing perhaps in Gaul. They wandered through uninhabited land for many days, nearly starving because they had run out of provisions. The men told Patrick to pray to his God to provide food and prove his divine power. Patrick prayed, and he recounts that in that moment, they saw and slaughtered a herd of swine and had their fill.

Patrick eventually made it home to Britain, where he was welcomed back heartily by his family. They asked him to remain there with them always, which is what Patrick intended to do. But then he had a dream in which the people of Ireland appeared to him, saying, "We beg you, holy youth, that you shall come and shall walk again among us." Patrick obeyed the dream, and submitted to formation and studies for the priesthood, perhaps in Gaul. Providentially, Patrick was indeed ordained a priest and a bishop and was sent to Ireland.

Patrick does not tell us what he did first in Ireland, but according to legend, he went right back to his old master, paid him for his freedom, and proved to him the power of the Lord God. There are many legendary accounts of Patrick's miraculous deeds among the Druids, accounting for the dramatic fact of the country's conversion to Christianity. These legends include his driving the snakes out of Ireland and walking unharmed through fire. They also include a story that Patrick lit a forbidden fire on the hill of Tara on the evening of Holy Saturday, which was also the Druid Feast of Darkness. The Druids were unable to put out the fire, whose light they feared would spread throughout all Ireland. Patrick was summoned the next day to appear before the king, which occasioned a battle of mighty deeds between the gods of the

Druids and Patrick's God. Patrick's God proved more powerful, thus securing toleration for Patrick's evangelistic activities throughout the land.

Though prepared daily for death, robbery, or enslavement for the sake of the gospel, Patrick was spared. He was recaptured once, but was set free after just two months. He writes, "I fear nothing, because of the promises of Heaven; for I have cast myself into the hands of Almighty God, who reigns everywhere." According to later stories, St. Patrick used the three leaves of the shamrock to explain the Trinity — one God in three persons. Like the Druids, St. Patrick was awed by the presence of the divine in nature, but he rightly attributed it to God as his creation and as a reflection of his power and goodness.

In his *Confession*, we see that despite Patrick's saintly heroism, leaders of the church in Britain were unfavorable to him and treated him with suspicion. He even had to remind them of how evangelizing nations is part of Christ's command in the gospel. Apparently his detractors saw his ministry among the pagans as reckless and his success as motived by worldly gain. Patrick lived to an old age, spending his days committed to the evangelization of Ireland. He rejoiced at baptizing multitudes, ordaining men to the priesthood, and consecrating men and women in virginity to the Lord. Though there may have been some pockets of Christianity already on the Emerald Isle at Patrick's arrival, he was the primary instrument for laying the foundations for the church in Ireland and of bringing about the nation's conversion to Christ. St. Patrick is a patron saint of Ireland and a symbol of the Irish people. Though St. Patrick is remembered on the Church's general calendar with an optional memorial, in Ireland, March 17 is both a solemnity and a holy day of obligation.

St. Patrick's Breastplate

> Christ with me,
> Christ before me,
> Christ behind me,
> Christ in me,
> Christ beneath me,
> Christ above me,
> Christ on my right,
> Christ on my left,
> Christ when I lie down,

Christ when I sit down,

Christ when I arise,

Christ in the heart of every man who thinks of me,

Christ in the mouth of everyone who speaks of me,

Christ in every eye that sees me,

Christ in every ear that hears me.

St. Joseph

Spouse of the Blessed Virgin Mary

Solemnity, Mar. 19

Scripture does not give us many details about St. Joseph, but it does give information of the most important kind: "he was a righteous man" (Mt. 1:19). Rather than be concerned for biological progeny of his own, Joseph, spouse of the Blessed Virgin Mary, became the foster father of God's own Son. As far as the world was concerned, however, Jesus would be called "the son of Joseph."

According to the Gospel of Luke, Joseph belonged to the "house of David" (Lk. 1:27), and Matthew's Gospel traces Jesus' lineage from Abraham through David down to Joseph (Mt. 1). Luke's Gospel tells us that Joseph lived in Nazareth in Galilee, but that his hometown was Bethlehem, the city of David (Lk. 2:4). Jesus was born in Bethlehem, not Nazareth, because Joseph was required to register in his hometown on account of the census of Caesar Augustus. This served to fulfill the prophesy that a great ruler would rise up from Bethlehem, like David once had risen from that city (Micah 5:2).

Despite belonging to the ancient royal line, Joseph was neither socially prominent nor wealthy. We know from the Gospel of Matthew that Joseph was a carpenter. There we find that people at Nazareth said of Jesus, "Is he not the carpenter's son?" (Mt. 13: 55). The Greek *tekton* indicates a craftsman who works with wood, or possibly with stone. Joseph's trade is the reason he is called upon as the patron saint of workers. In Mark's Gospel, the townspeople say of Jesus, "Is he not the carpenter...?" (Mk. 4:3). As was the custom, Joseph would have handed on his trade to his son.

Though hardworking, Joseph was poor. When he went to the Temple to offer sacrifice at Jesus' presentation, he could only afford a sacrifice of two turtle doves, as prescribed for the poor (Lk. 2:24). Nazareth was a very small village, although some speculate that Joseph may also have found work in the burgeoning city of Sepphoris, a few miles off. There is no mention in the Bible of Joseph's activities during Jesus' adult ministry. Thus it is traditionally believed that he had already died. St. Joseph is recognized as the patron saint of a happy death since he likely passed in the loving presence of Jesus and Mary.

The Bible shows us that Joseph was especially open to changing his own plans once he became aware of God's will. Thus the name 'Joseph,' which means "God will give increase," seems fitting for him. The Bible also implies that Joseph was humble and ready to serve, protect, and guide. Matthew's Gospel shows us that he received three dreams from an angel.

Joseph was immediately obedient to each dream, which lead to God's will being carried out and prophesy being fulfilled in salvation history.

The first change of plans for Joseph took place when he found that Mary, his betrothed, was pregnant, though the two had been apart. Betrothal was a binding commitment prior to living together, thus Joseph "decided to divorce her quietly" (Mt. 1:19). A straightforward reading of Luke's Gospel would have it that Joseph was troubled, thinking that his betrothed had committed adultery. Being merciful, Joseph resolved to spare Mary the fate of being stoned to death for adultery. There is a tradition, however, which holds that the humble Joseph, knowing Mary's flawless and pure character, already perceived that the child was miraculously conceived and that he was unworthy of the role of caring for so great a child. Either way, the matter would be resolved by Joseph's first dream, in which an angel showed him the divine plan for the child, whose name was to be 'Jesus' and who was conceived through the Holy Spirit.

We then read, "When Joseph awoke, he did as the angel of the Lord had commanded him and took his wife into his home" (Mt. 1:24). Joseph was prepared to forgo the usual cultural norms for naming a son, and named him simply as the angel said. Matthew's Gospel also tells us of Joseph and Mary, "He had no relations with her until she bore a son," which serves to show that Jesus was not conceived through Joseph. According to Catholic tradition and dogma, Mary was ever-virgin, thus the couple remained celibate throughout their marriage. This is further why St. Joseph is seen as a model of chastity.

Joseph and Mary, who was pregnant with the baby Jesus, traveled together for the enrollment at Bethlehem, where providence would have it that Jesus would be born. It must have pained Joseph that he could not find room for Mary to give birth anywhere in the city except in a stable. Shepherds, told by an angel of Jesus' birth, "went in haste and found Mary and Joseph, and the infant lying in the manger" (Lk. 2:16). Since "all … were amazed" by their account (Lk. 2:18), Joseph too must have wondered at their stories of their visions of the heavenly hosts above. Joseph saw to it that the proper religious customs were adhered to with Jesus, having him circumcised and named on the eighth day and then presented in the Temple as the firstborn of Mary. At the presentation in the Temple, Joseph would have listened in wonder as the prophet Simeon foretold the sorrows the child and his mother would suffer.

According to Matthew's Gospel, after the magi visited the infant Jesus, Joseph received a second dream in which the angel warned him that King Herod sought to kill the child. The angel said to him, "Rise, take the child and his mother, flee to Egypt, and stay there until I tell you" (Mt. 2:13). Ready to protect the infant Jesus, Joseph obeyed the angel at once. Like Joseph the patriarch, St. Joseph's dream led him into Egypt, and again his dream served to fulfill a prophecy: "Out of Egypt I called my son" (Mt. 2:15). Meanwhile in Bethlehem, Herod's soldiers slew all male children two years and younger. After hearing of Herod's death, Joseph received a third dream telling him not to remain in Judea, but to go to Nazareth, because of Herod's son then ruling in Judea. This too was to fulfill a prophesy about Jesus: "He shall be called a Nazorean" (Mt. 2:23).

The last time we hear of Joseph's activities in the Bible is when Jesus, then aged 12, was lost on pilgrimage to Jerusalem. We are told that his parents both spent three days searching for the young Jesus. They found him in the Temple, discussing God's Law with the teachers. Jesus said to his parents, "Why were you looking for me? Did you not know that I must be in my Father's house?" (Lk. 2:49). This incident of being lost for three days and then found foreshadowed his death and Resurrection. It also highlighted his unique connection to his heavenly Father. Luke's Gospel then tells us of Jesus, "He went down with them and came to Nazareth, and was obedient to them" (Lk. 2:51). Thus Jesus submitted to Joseph as a father on earth, who we can surely assume raised him in a most virtuous manner. Luke's Gospel tells us, "Jesus advanced [in] wisdom and age and favor before God and man" (Lk. 2:52).

Often portrayed with a white lily representing chastity and with tools of carpentry, St. Joseph is a model of many virtues and is a saint with numerous patronages. Among these are families, fathers, workers, carpenters, travelers, immigrants, a happy death, and many localities throughout the world. As guardian of Jesus, the founder of the Church, and the spouse of Mary, Mother of the Church, St. Joseph is celebrated as the patron of the Universal Church.

St. Joseph, pray for us!

Epilogue

Therefore, since we are surrounded by so great a cloud of witnesses, let us rid ourselves of every burden and sin that clings to us and persevere in running the race that lies before us while keeping our eyes fixed on Jesus, the leader and perfecter of faith.
— Heb. 12:1–2

LIVES OF THE SAINTS
VOLUME II (APRIL - JULY)

Michael J. Ruszala

Introduction

If we want to see the greatest and best of what Christianity is capable of, we must look to the saints. Bishop Fulton Sheen challenges us to judge the Church "not by those who barely live by its spirit, but by the example of those who live closest to it." God's plan for everyone, in fact, is sainthood. To quote St. Irenaeus of Lyons: "The glory of God is the human person fully alive." Saints are the people who truly become the best version of themselves. They find this personal best not through the humanistic process of "self-actualization," but through losing themselves in the pursuit of God. Jesus taught, "Whoever seeks to preserve his life will lose it, but whoever loses it will save it" (Luke 17:33).

Saints spark a desire for sanctity in others. Many of the saints themselves renewed their thirst for God through reading and rereading the lives of other saints that went before them. These stories purified their minds, inspired them to strive further, and showed them the path that they must take.

St. Paul wrote to the Philippians, "It is not that I have already taken hold of it or have already attained perfect maturity, but I continue my pursuit in hope that I may possess it, since I have indeed been taken possession of by Christ [Jesus]. Brothers, I for my part do not consider myself to have taken possession. Just one thing: forgetting what lies behind but straining forward to what lies ahead, I continue my pursuit toward the goal, the prize of God's upward calling, in Christ Jesus" (Philippians 3:12–14).

In imitating the saints who went before them, the saints who followed were responding to God's gift of grace. Taking notes from the past saints, they were able to better understand themselves and God's action in their lives and in the lives of those around them. Then, having allowed God to gain victory in their own lives, they were able to attract other people and move their world toward God by their strikingly holy example. Their authenticity and genuine love became strong enough to turn the tide from evil to good. Some faced seemingly insurmountable evils and even gave up their lives as martyrs for the faith. But by the power granted by God through their death, many others came to be drawn to the light.

This book is the second in a series of four volumes on the lives of the saints. In this volume, saints are selected from the Roman Calendar from April to July. The Church has specified various types of observances of these holy persons. Solemnities are of the highest order and celebrate core mysteries pertaining to Jesus, Mary, or a saint of highest significance. Feasts are second in order and celebrate secondary events in the lives of Jesus and Mary or mark the celebration of an apostle. Memorials are general observances for saints important to the universal Church or to a particular community. Optional memorials are provided, finally, because there are more saints than there are days on the calendar! Many popular saints are celebrated through optional memorials. Particular churches also have certain local variations in order to emphasize God's work in a specific region.

The Church's calendar provides us with a healthy balance of saints from every walk of life. There are sure to be many saints' stories that readers from various backgrounds will find inspirational or relatable to their own lives.

St. John Baptist de la Salle
Priest, 1651–1719
Memorial, April 7

St. John Baptist de la Salle was born to a noble family in Rheims, France, in 1651. He was devout from a young age, receiving the tonsure at age eleven as a sign of commitment to the priesthood. Due to his noble birth, intelligence, connections, and good looks, it seemed that John Baptist was destined for high ranks within the Church. At the young age of sixteen, John Baptist was named canon of Rheims Cathedral.

Canon John Baptist earned his master of arts at the College des Bons Enfants in Paris, but he was forced to take a temporary leave from his studies at the esteemed Seminary of Saint-Sulpice, also in Paris, at the age of twenty-one, after both of his parents died within the course of about a year of each other. As the firstborn son, Canon John Baptist inherited the family fortune when his parents passed away, but he also assumed the responsibility for the education and welfare of his younger siblings. Later returning to his studies, he was eventually ordained a priest at the age of twenty-six and earned a doctorate in theology at the age of twenty-eight.

As one of his fellow canons lay on his deathbed, he entrusted Fr. John Baptist with the care of a new congregation of sisters that the canon had helped establish. This congregation, known as the Sisters of the Child Jesus, ran an orphanage and a school for girls in Rheims. Serving the sisters was not something that Fr. John Baptist wanted to do at the time, but through his commitment to his friend's final wishes, he came to find his further call. A man named Adrian Nyel came to the sisters for help in founding a school in Rheims for poor boys, and Fr. John Baptist resolved to help him raise the funds. A wealthy woman in town came forward with the money, but only on the condition that Fr. John Baptist would be a part of the school. This was not something he wanted to do, but he agreed to help. Two schools, in fact, came about in Rheims for poor boys because of these efforts.

Many people at the time were opposed to the idea of providing an intellectual education for the poor, and good teachers for them were hard to come by. The teachers for the schools at Rheims were themselves very poorly educated and lacked the proper manners in which Fr. John Baptist had been cultured. He at first invited them to have dinner each night at his home, with the intention of forming them in table manners. Some members of his own family were aghast at their lack of culture and his willingness to personally host them. And despite his efforts, the teachers did not make fast enough progress, so he had them come to live with him at his house to be trained under his own discipline. When he eventually lost his house due to a lawsuit, he rented a house for himself and the teachers. Some of the teachers were unhappy with the discipline he provided and they left, but others soon came to join the group. This was the beginning of the Institute of the Brothers of the Christian Schools. Later on, parish priests sent boys to him to train as teachers for their hometowns. This was the beginning of the first of the teacher colleges.

As things progressed, Fr. John Baptist noticed a divide come up between himself and the teachers, namely in his own financial security and their lack of financial security. To rectify this situation, he gave up his position as canon of Rheims Cathedral, along with the income it provided. Fr. John Baptist also resolved to give away all of his wealth, but the question arose as to whether he should give it to the poor or fund his own growing institution. A priest from Paris named Fr. Barre convinced him that he ought to give it away entirely, since "if you endow it, it will founder" (*Butler's Lives*). Thus, Fr. John Baptist gave his entire fortune to those suffering from famine in the region of Champagne, and he entrusted his own endeavors to Providence. Fr. John Baptist was also known to practice asceticism, often forcing himself to go hungry.

Fr. John Baptist's schools were revolutionary. Students were taught in French rather than in Latin, as they were in other schools. Also, students were taught together in classes based on ability level and with parental involvement. Soon, Fr. John Baptist had founded a network of schools across France, providing solid educational opportunities for the less fortunate, with the help of properly trained instructors. He even founded a reform school for boys from wealthy families who had set out on the wrong path—another first. Although his methods and aims might seem commonplace to us today, they were controversial in his time, and he met a great deal of resistance from other educators. He also met resistance from Church authorities, having been falsely accused of undue harshness toward the brothers.

Toward the end of his life, Fr. John Baptist retired to a life indistinguishable from that of the other brothers. He died on Good Friday of 1719 in Rouen, France. St. John Baptist de la Salle was canonized in 1900 by Pope Leo XIII and proclaimed patron of all teachers in 1950 by Pope Pius XII. Today, the four thousand Brothers of the Christian Schools and their collaborators continue to educate students in some one thousand educational institutions in seventy-nine different countries around the world, including some three hundred educational centers in places where there is little to no access to education (lasalle.org). Furthermore, the Institute has produced fourteen saints, and 150 brothers have been beatified and eight declared venerable by the Church.

St. John Baptist de la Salle, pray for us!

St. Stanislaus
Bishop and Martyr, 1030–1079
Memorial, April 11

St. Stanislaus, bishop of Krakow and patron saint of Poland, was martyred for his opposition to a tyrannical and immoral king. St. Stanislaus was born in Szczepanow, outside Krakow, to noble and devout parents in 1030. He was born very late in their marriage, which had been childless until then, and his parents intended to raise him to be offered in God's service. St. Stanislaus pursued holiness from a very young age and often practiced acts of self-denial. He was first educated at the local cathedral school and then at Paris. He was offered a doctorate, but he turned it down out of humility (*Butler's Lives*).

Upon returning to Poland, St. Stanislaus was ordained a priest. When the bishop died, he was voted overwhelmingly by the laity, clergy, and king to be the bishop's successor. He accepted this position with much reluctance and served for only seven years, until his death. As bishop, St. Stanislaus took close care of his flock, visiting all the churches annually and personally dealing with issues and problems that arose. During his tenure, he was also able to restore Krakow to its former dignity as an archiepiscopal see.

Soon, however, St. Stanislaus came into tension with King Boleslaus II, also known as the Cruel, admonishing him privately for his immoral lifestyle and his many injustices against human dignity. The king at first feigned repentance, but then angrily turned on the bishop rather than change his ways. He first accused St. Stanislaus of stealing a certain piece of property, upon which he had built a church. The king brought forth witnesses who lied, claiming to be the rightful heirs and owners of the property, and he intimidated the truthful witnesses. St. Stanislaus had purchased the land from a man named Peter, who had since died. St. Stanislaus fasted and prayed for three days before going with his clerics to visit Peter's grave. He then called Peter forth from the dead, and Peter arose and testified to the king on the saint's behalf before returning to his grave.

174

Having been visited by a witness who was actually resurrected from the dead, the king let the matter pass. But when King Boleslaus kidnapped a nobleman's wife and had her bear him several children, St. Stanislaus could not remain silent. He admonished the king again and prayed and fasted for his repentance. But when the king persisted in his stubbornness and continued to ignore further warnings, St. Stanislaus had him excommunicated from the Church. This was a serious penalty for a political leader in those days, even for a godless king, because people generally regarded excommunication as a divine withdrawal of the king's right to rule.

St. Stanislaus knew to flee from the king's wrath, and he withdraw to a chapel outside the city. He even cancelled the chanting of the divine office at the cathedral. The king pursued the bishop, ordering his men to have him slain for treason. Thrice, however, the king sent men into the chapel, but each time they withdrew, claiming to have been dispelled by a heavenly light. Finally, the king himself stormed the chapel during holy Mass and slew the bishop with his own sword. He then had his men dismember the saint's body and scatter the pieces, to be devoured by wild beasts. The holy remains, however, were guarded by eagles until the bishop's clerics could gather the pieces three days later. They then had them secretly buried at the chapel where he had been killed, since the king had forbidden any mourning over the bishop's death.

When the matter became public, however, people rose up against the sacrilege of the murderous king, and Pope Gregory VII also pronounced him excommunicated. Boleslaus was forced to flee to Hungary, where he ended his days. Ten years later, St. Stanislaus's remains were buried with honor at the Wawel Cathedral in Krakow, where they were venerated. According to another traditional source, however, the bishop had actually been killed at the Wawel Cathedral itself. St. Stanislaus has been honored in the naming of many Polish churches. With the nation later suffering from many long years of foreign domination, the Polish people came to pray to St. Stanislaus to gather back together the scattered pieces of the nation.

The year of Pope St. John Paul II's first historic visit to Poland in 1979 coincided with the ninth centenary of the martyrdom of St. Stanislaus. This held great significance to St. John Paul II, both because St. Stanislaus had been his own predecessor to the See of Krakow and because of St. Stanislaus's heroic opposition to a hostile government. St. John Paul II's 1979 visit was in tension with the Communist Polish government and served as an opportunity for millions to gather together and taste freedom and dignity for the first time. Only a few years later, Communist rule in Poland came to an end in the face of popular nonviolent resistance.

St. Stanislaus, pray for us!

St. Anselm of Canterbury
Bishop and Doctor of the Church,
ca. 1033–1109
Optional Memorial, April 21

A scholar by night and an administrator by day, St. Anselm of Canterbury was noted for his accomplishments both in learning and in political will for the Church. Regarded as the father of scholasticism, it is from him that the classic definition of theology comes, as "faith seeking understanding."

Anselm was born in Aosta in northern Italy around 1033. Inspired by his devout mother, he aspired to become a monk, but he was blocked by his father, who dissuaded the monastery from accepting him. Discouraged and annoyed, Anselm gave in to a life of youthful passions and disregard for religion before being again converted to God after the loss of his mother. Having pursued studies in Burgundy, Anselm determined to leave his father, with whom he continued to have difficulties, and he set out for Normandy, where he entered the Benedictine Abbey of Bec. There he studied under the learned prior Lanfranc.

After some time as a simple monk, he succeeded Lanfranc as prior when the latter became an abbot. During his time as prior of the Abbey of Bec, Anselm wrote his *Monologion*, which was one of the first texts of scholastic theology ever penned. The new scholastic movement in theology sought to provide a more systematic and well-reasoned teaching based on that of the Church Fathers of centuries before, and it was supported by the fundamentals of Greek philosophy. Also during this time he wrote his *Proslogion*, from which came his famous ontological argument for the existence of God. Following much meditation and realization of a certain truth grasped, Anselm sought to put his proof into words. It rests on the existence of a concept in the human mind "than which nothing greater can be conceived" (*Proslogion* 2). Though St. Thomas Aquinas, who formulated his Five Ways for God's existence several generations later, rejected the argument, St. Anselm was convinced that "if a being than which a greater is inconceivable can be even conceived, it cannot be

178

nonexistent" ("In Reply to Gaunilon's Answer in Behalf of the Fool" 1, CCEL). The argument held sway, however, in the minds of many great philosophers down the ages, perhaps more as a meditation to gain insight into the reality of God.

Anselm was made abbot of Bec in 1078. Meanwhile, Lanfranc was made archbishop of Canterbury in England. After Lanfranc's passing following years of struggle with the kings over the rights of the Church, Anselm was appointed archbishop of Canterbury, though he made numerous attempts to turn down the position. Further, King William Rufus, though himself a Norman king of England, opposed the idea of having Anselm (a Norman abbot), or anyone else for that matter, assume the position, since it suited him politically to leave it unfilled. The king is said to have sworn that he would leave it unfilled as long as he lived. As it happened, however, the king became gravely ill and gave in to the pressure to allow Anselm to assume his post as archbishop of Canterbury (*Butler's Lives*).

King William Rufus, however, struggled with Anselm over the perennial issue known as lay investiture—the practice of kings, rather than the pope, appointing church offices. The king, who was an immoral man, also despised Anselm's initiatives for genuine reform in the Church, and he tried to prevent many church offices from being filled at all. When an antipope challenged the successor of Peter, the king forbade anyone in England from making allegiance to either claimant. Anselm, however, made it clear to everyone the identity of the true bishop of Rome, recognizing his own authority as coming from him (*New Advent*).

Later, the king sought to have the pope depose Anselm, but he refused. The king's envoy received a pallium (the woolen vestment of an archbishop) for Anselm from the pope, but the king then tried to sell it to Anselm for a large sum. Anselm refused to pay, so the king tried to sell it to others, but they would not buy it. The king then insisted on at least bestowing it on Anselm personally, as if archiepiscopal authority came from him. Anselm refused even this, and the king finally conceded. Anselm took it up himself from the altar at the Canterbury Cathedral in June of 1095.

The king had Anselm banished from England on two occasions. During one of his times in exile, Anselm participated in a Church council that denounced the actions of King William Rufus, but he prevented the other bishops from excommunicating him. After the king died, his brother and successor, Henry I, heartily welcomed Anselm, but he continued to struggle with him over lay investiture. Henry, too, forced Anselm into exile before allowing him to return.

While archbishop, Anselm still found time to write numerous works of theology, including *Cur Deus Homo*, "Why God Became Man," on the topic of the Incarnation. There he argued that since God is infinite, any offense against God is an infinite offense. Restitution can only be made by a Person who is infinite, but who is also fully human—namely, the God-man, Jesus Christ.

St. Anselm was declared a doctor of the Church by Pope Clement XI in 1720 with the title "Magnificent Doctor."

St. Anselm on faith seeking understanding:

> Be it mine to look up to thy light, even from afar, even from the depths. Teach me to seek thee, and reveal thyself to me, when I seek thee, for I cannot seek thee, except thou teach me, nor find thee, except thou reveal thyself. Let me seek thee in longing, let me long for thee in seeking; let me find thee in love, and love thee in finding.... For I do not seek to understand that I may

believe, but I believe in order to understand. For this also I believe,—that unless I believed, I should not understand (*Proslogion* 1, CCEL).

St. Anselm of Canterbury, pray for us!

St. Mark
Evangelist, First Century
Feast, April 25

The evangelist and missionary St. Mark was privileged to be among the first generation of Christians, collaborating closely with the Apostles. He is traditionally believed to be the "Mark" mentioned in the Acts of the Apostles, in the First Letter of Peter, and in several of Paul's letters.

In the Acts of the Apostles, we find mention of a certain John Mark, a cousin to Barnabas, who was an assistant to Paul and Barnabas as they preached the Word in synagogues on the island of Cyprus and in Asia Minor (Acts 12–13). But at Pamphylia in Asia Minor, John Mark left and returned to Jerusalem (Acts 13:13). Later on, Barnabas expressed the desire to return along with John Mark to the churches they had established, but Paul was strongly opposed to it because of Mark's departure from the missionary voyage. As a result, Barnabas went with John Mark back to Cyprus, and Paul took Silas and continued to Syria and Cilicia (Acts 15:37–41).

We can deduce, however, from Paul's letters a forgiveness and reconciliation that took place between Paul and Mark, for Mark later accompanied Paul during very difficult times. In his letter to the Colossians, written from captivity, Paul mentioned that Mark, the cousin of Barnabas, was with him and was someone whom the church at Colossae should welcome (Colossians 4:10). Likewise, in his Letter to Philemon, Paul sent greetings from Mark, saying that he was present with him during his captivity. Writing his second letter to Timothy later on from Rome, Paul asked that Mark be sent to him, because he had been very helpful to him (2 Timothy 4:11). Then in the first letter of St. Peter, we find mention of a Mark who was an associate to St. Peter at Rome. Peter, there, sends greetings from Mark, whom he calls a son (1 Peter 5:13). Some even believe that Mark was the one who penned Peter's letters for him.

It is possible that Mark was a disciple of Jesus, but according to tradition, Mark wrote his gospel for the community at Rome based on the teaching and stories of St. Peter. St. Irenaeus of Lyons wrote, around AD 180: "After their departure [namely, the martyrdom of St. Peter and St. Paul at Rome], Mark, the underline disciple and interpreter of Peter, did also hand down to us in writing what had been preached by Peter" (*Against Heresies* III.1.1, text in brackets added for clarity). St. Irenaeus also argued that for a gospel to be authentic, it must go back to the teaching authority of the Apostles.

Some modern scholars have also noted a similarity between the preaching of Peter about Jesus in the Acts of the Apostles and the narrative structure of the Gospel of Mark (*Ignatius Catholic Study Bible*). There, Peter preached to the God-fearing Roman centurion Cornelius, saying, "You know the word [that] he sent to the Israelites as he proclaimed peace through Jesus Christ, who is Lord of all, what has happened all over Judea, beginning in Galilee after the baptism that John preached, how God anointed Jesus of Nazareth with the holy Spirit and power. He went about doing good and healing all those oppressed by the devil, for God was with him" (Acts 10:36–38). Peter then concluded by teaching on Jesus' death and resurrection and the mission He gave to His followers.

John Mark was a Jew, possibly from Galilee. "Mark" is a Roman name, but "John" is a Jewish name. His gospel, though written in Greek, seems to have been written by a non-native speaker of Greek and one with a Jewish manner of expression (*Butler's Lives*). Still, he recognized many of his readers as non-Jews, finding it necessary to explain the customs of the Jews, particularly in Judea (Mark 7:3–4). This would have been helpful for his gospel's Roman Christian audience, which consisted of both Jewish and Gentile believers. His focus on Jesus' words to those who would be persecuted (Mark 13:9) may also be tailored to the situation of the church at Rome in the late 60s AD, during the persecution of Nero, when Mark likely wrote his gospel.

From its first verse, Mark's gospel proclaims "the gospel of Jesus Christ [the Son of God]" (Mark 1:1), thereby declaring faith in Jesus as God's Messiah. The gospel, in only sixteen chapters, moves briskly to persuade the reader by Jesus' words and deeds that He is the Christ, the Son of God. Mark's gospel reaches two climax points by which this conclusion is attained. The first comes with the confession of Peter, a Jew, that Jesus is the Christ, which means the Messiah (Mark 8:29). The second comes with the confession of the Roman centurion at the foot of the cross: "Truly this man was the Son of God!" (Mark 15:39).

In the gospel of Mark, Jesus began in Galilee proclaiming the Kingdom of God not only with words but also with mighty deeds, such as casting out demons, healing the sick, and demonstrating authority even over nature, sin, and the Mosaic Law. He was often seen to urge people to silence over His identity as the Messiah, or the Son of God, until the right time for its full revelation, which came when He went up at last to the holy city of Jerusalem to suffer, die, and rise again.

Before He ascended to heaven and after giving His disciples their mission, Jesus said, "These signs will accompany those who believe: in my name they will drive out demons, they will speak new languages. They will pick up serpents [with their hands], and if they drink any deadly thing, it will not harm them. They will lay hands on the sick, and they will recover" (Mark 16:17–18). Though these verses come from the "longer ending" of Mark's gospel, which may not have been written by Mark himself, it seems true to his own experience. He knew and visited Paul around the time a deadly serpent bit him without effect on his body (Acts 23:3–6). Further, according to traditional sources, St. Mark set out from Rome to evangelize

185

in Egypt and establish churches, with much success because of the many miracles that he worked there.

Mark is said to have returned to Rome before coming back to Alexandra in Egypt, where he was bishop. Angry pagans were waiting for him there, who remembered how he had destroyed their temples. They bound his feet to the back of a cart and dragged him through the streets all day. He survived and was imprisoned for the night, during which time he received two visions from the Lord. The next day, he was dragged once more through the streets, where he gave up his spirit and won the crown of martyrdom. St. Mark's Basilica in Venice, Italy, claims his body, which an ancient journal suggests may have been brought from Alexandria to Venice at some point before AD 870 (*Butler's Lives*).

St. Mark, pray for us!

St. Catherine of Siena
Virgin and Doctor of the Church, 1347–1380
Memorial, April 29

Mystic, writer, peacemaker, and charitable worker St. Catherine of Siena is one of the great women of Church history. Catherine was born in 1347 in Siena, Italy, to a wealthy cloth-dyer, James Benincasa, and Lapa, his forty-year-old wife. Lapa bore twenty-five children, although only half survived past infancy. Catherine herself had a twin sister who died as a baby. Catherine grew up in her father's large house, and as she went up and down the steps of the house, sometimes she would kneel on each step as a child to pray a Hail Mary (*Butler's Lives*). Her future was sealed when she had a vision of Christ at the age of six. This led her to consecrate her virginity to God.

Catherine's family tried to dissuade her from this path, first by distracting her with many chores to keep her from a prayer life they considered excessive. Despite this, Catherine fostered a peaceful awareness of God's presence, even within the hustle of daily life. At last, Catherine's mother and her sister Bonaventura were able to persuade her at the age of twelve to receive a makeover according to the fashions of the times. Catherine soon repented of this with great tears as vanity and an infidelity to her heavenly spouse, always considering it her greatest fault. Her vow was challenged again when her sister Bonaventura died at the age of only sixteen, leaving behind a husband. Catherine's father intended to offer Catherine's hand in marriage to Bonaventura's widower, but Catherine refused and cut her golden-brown hair short to make herself less attractive. At last, her father relented, also impressed with her fasting and care for her family. She tended to her father as Christ, her mother as Mary, and her brothers as the apostles (Catholic Online).

Catherine was freed at the age of fifteen to pursue a life of dedicated holiness through fasting, prayer, and charitable works. Catherine received the habit as a third order Dominican at the age of eighteen. Through the Dominicans, she learned to read and write. She spent three years in solitude, enjoying contemplation and mystical experiences, and speaking only to Jesus and her confessor. The devil, however, came to tempt her more strongly, assailing her with sexual thoughts and sometimes even manifesting in visible forms. Catherine remained steadfast and Jesus came to her mystically after these experiences:

> ...she said to him, "Where wast thou, my divine Spouse, while I lay in such an abandoned, frightful condition." "I was with thee," he seemed to reply. "What!" said she, "amidst the filthy abominations with which my soul was infested!" He answered: "They were displeasing and most painful to thee. This conflict therefore was thy merit, and the victory over them was owing to my presence" (*Butler's Lives*).

Catherine was directed again to charitable works, visiting the sick and imprisoned, to whom she dedicated herself wholeheartedly. She even tended to those suffering from the most repulsive illnesses with great love and care, dressing and bathing them as need be. The Lord blessed her charity with miracles to provide for the needs of the poor. But certain women she cared for spread false stories about her, and the people in Siena became suspicious of her. Catherine tried to win them over through love, and even had to account to the Dominican Order for her conduct, but she was at last cleared and won back her reputation through her love and good works. She was given Blessed Raymond of Capua as her spiritual director, and the association proved quite fruitful for both. Blessed Raymond ultimately also became Catherine's biographer and helped her with her writings.

At the age of twenty-one, while she was praying silently in her room while the city was reveling for Shrove Tuesday, Catherine experienced a mystical marriage with Christ, in

189

which He gave her a ring, visible only to her. Later, while traveling in Pisa, Catherine was also given a unique sharing in Christ's sufferings through the stigmata, the wounds of Christ manifested in her body. These wounds were likewise visible only to her, but they became visible to all after her death. At times, Catherine was also known to levitate above the ground in mystical prayer. Sometimes this even happened in public.

Catherine became a blessing among the people. It was a time of plague epidemics, and she was always there to tend to the sick, comfort the dying, and even personally help to bury the dead. She was also a solace to those with leprosy. Once she tenderly comforted and spiritually prepared a young knight who was condemned to death for making a jest against the Sienese state, receiving his head into her hands at his execution. Catherine also would exhort sinners, and they would repent. People would gather around Catherine in the town to hear her speak and because of her many miracles and healings.

As a known figure, Catherine also became a peacemaker, working to broker peace among the warring kingdoms in Italy, and she came to be sought after for that purpose. She did advocate, though, for a crusade in the Holy Land, and this brought her into communication with the pope. She favored the claims of the Papal States in Italy, but she also exhorted the pope to mercy as needed. At this time, Pope Gregory XI, like a number of popes before him, had taken up residence at Avignon in France, leaving behind the troubles of life in Rome. She incessantly urged him to return to Rome, the traditional seat of the papacy, and he did so in 1376, two years before his passing. His successor in Rome was Urban VI, who, though legitimately elected, was harsh and unbending in his style. Cardinals at Avignon rejected him and elected their own anti-pope at Avignon. Catherine continued to support Urban, but she exhorted him to clemency.

Thus, Catherine became a respected consulter in the papal court, and the popes and their cardinals would listen respectfully to her sisterly counsel. But at this time, Catherine's fasting for the Church had taken its toll on her body. Though her confessor, Raymond of Capua, ordered her to eat, she could not. Catherine eventually suffered a stroke that left her paralyzed from the waist down. Two weeks later, she breathed her last at the age of just thirty-three. She was canonized in 1461 by Pope Pius II, who stated that no one left Catherine's presence without becoming better. Together with St. Teresa of Avila, St. Catherine of Siena was declared the first woman doctor of the Church by Pope Paul VI in 1970, and she was named as a patron saint of Europe by Pope John Paul II in 1999.

Be who God meant you to be and you will set the world on fire.
—St. Catherine of Siena

St. Catherine of Siena, pray for us!

St. Athanasius
Bishop and Doctor of the Church,
ca. 296–373
Memorial, May 2

St. Athanasius, "father of orthodoxy," was instrumental in securing a decisive statement on Christ's divinity at the Council of Nicea. He later became bishop of Alexandria in Egypt, but he was exiled multiple times by the Arian heretics before being finally reestablished.

We can tell from St. Anthanasius's writings that he was very learned, had great clarity of thought and expression, and made faithful use of the teachings of the earlier fathers and the martyrs. We also know that he was the assistant to Alexander, bishop of Alexandria, who was his mentor. At a young age, St. Athanasius wrote his famous treatise "On the Incarnation." Athanasius pursued holiness, and he went out into the desert in Egypt to learn the ways of the hermit St. Antony the Great. From this encounter, Athanasius left us with the classic hagiography "The Life of Antony," which inspired many future saints in the religious and consecrated life.

While still a deacon, Athanasius went along with Bishop Alexander to the Council of Nicea in 325, providing the decisive terminology to secure its key pronouncement. When Arius, a priest in Alexandria, furthered the heresy about the Son of God, that "there was a time when he was not," a great controversy came over the newly Christianized Roman Empire. Thus, Emperor Constantine called a council of bishops to settle the matter at Nicea. For Arius and his followers, Jesus was only "the firstborn of all creation" (Colossians 1:15), but not actually God. But Jesus Himself also taught that "the Father and I are one" (John 10:30). Thus, Deacon Athanasius proposed that the creed devised by the Council of Nicea profess that the Son is, in Greek, *homoousios*, translated as "one-in-being," or consubstantial, with the Father. Athanasius's term, based on the Greek philosophical concept of *ousia*, or "being," won out and was enshrined in the Nicene Creed.

Athanasius was regarded as a hero by the faithful of Alexandria and the orthodox throughout the empire. On his deathbed, Alexander called for Athanasius to make him his successor, but Athanasius had withdrawn. Alexander said, "Athanasius, you think to escape, but you are mistaken" (*Butler's Lives*). The people and clergy also called for his succession, and Athanasius did assume the See of Alexandria after Alexander's death.

Emperor Constantine, however, was persuaded to sympathize with the Arians later in life. He called the great heretic Arius out from the exile imposed on him at the Council of Nicea, and Arius sought reentry to the church at Alexandria. Athanasius refused. The Arian bishop Eusebius of Nicomedia, likewise recently released from exile, wrote to Athanasius to have Arius brought back into the Church, but he again refused. So, Eusebius and his followers sought to find a way to have Athanasius removed from Alexandria and replaced with one of their own (*Butler's Lives*).

Eusebius accused Athanasius of "various ecclesiastical and political charges, which, though unmistakably refuted at their first hearing, were afterwards refurbished and made to do service at nearly every stage of his subsequent trials" ("Athanasius," *New Advent*). Eusebius and his party accused Athanasius to Emperor Constantine of corruption and supporting a traitor. Constantine rejected these first allegations, so then charges were brought that Athanasius was accused of murdering an elderly Arian bishop named Arenius and having his arm cut off for magical use. Athanasius was summoned to Tyre for a synod to determine his fate, but he refused to go, since it was composed mostly of his enemies. But word got to Constantine that Athanasius would not cooperate, so he grew angry and ordered him to appear (*Butler's Lives*). Athanasius's accusers even produced a severed arm to prove their case. Athanasius had Arenius sent for, and the bishop, who had withdrawn for a time, was found. Athanasius thus presented him alive and well with both arms intact. His accusers then accused Athanasius of magic in producing the appearance of Arenius. Arenius, however, converted to orthodoxy and restored friendship with Athanasius. Still, Athanasius's enemies accused him of many other things and, even though everything was disproven, they had him exiled to Triers, in present-day Germany. Constantine, however, left the See at Alexandria vacant rather than appoint a replacement to Athanasius.

At Triers, Athanasius was warmly greeted by St. Maximinus, the bishop, and by Constantine the Younger, who remembered him after his father died in 336. The empire was divided among three of the sons of Constantine the Great. So, when Constantine the Younger assumed power over the western Empire, he restored Athanasius to his See, where he was greeted by the people with a hero's welcome. Athanasius's enemies then accused him of violating the decision of a synod, and Athanasius was forced to flee. This time, the Arian heretic Gregory of Cappadocia took control of the Church in Alexandria.

Athanasius journeyed to Rome, where he was declared innocent by Pope Julius and where he also furthered the cause of the monastic life, pioneered by St. Antony and his hermits in Egypt. Then Pope Julius called a council at Sardica to give Athanasius a fair hearing, but the Arians, being outnumbered, withdrew to Philippopolis, where they again condemned Athanasius. The Council of Sardica, however, exonerated him. But Constantius, who reigned over the part of the empire where Alexandria was situated, was an Arian, and he vacillated in his stance toward Athanasius. At first, he threatened him with death should he return. Later, however, Athanasius succeeded in convincing him to restore him to his See. Athanasius was received again in triumph by the people of Alexandria and he reigned for ten years. Then the Arians rose up again and Constantius's men forced him back into exile. He was replaced by another Arian heretic, George of Cappadocia.

After Emperor Constantius died, Julian "the Apostate," a pagan, became emperor. He disdained the Christians and sought to sow division among them, so he sought to cause disruption. He had the Arian bishop of Alexandria, George of Cappadocia, imprisoned. George was later killed by a pagan mob. Meanwhile, those whom the Arians had exiled were allowed to return home. Athanasius returned to his See, but later on, Julian expelled Athanasius, perceiving him as too powerful, or perhaps too successful in his evangelization of the city. But soon after, Julian died in battle, and Jovian, an orthodox believer, became emperor. Athanasius again returned to Alexandria and won the favor of Emperor Jovian. Then Jovian died suddenly, replaced by the Arian Emperor Valens, and Athanasius again had to flee. But there was such public outcry in Alexandria in favor of Athanasius that Valens allowed him to remain there as bishop. Athanasius remained in his See of Alexandria, promoting orthodoxy and fighting heresy, until his passing in the year 373.

St. Athanasius, pray for us!

Sts. Philip and James
Apostles, First Century
Feast, May 3

The Apostles Philip and James are honored with a single feast that commemorates the dedication of their churches at Rome in the sixth century. Both saints were called by Jesus Himself to be among the Twelve, to be witnesses to the world of the mysteries of His life, death, and resurrection. James the Lesser, the traditional writer of the epistle of St. James, commemorated here, is not to be confused with James the Greater, also an Apostle, who was the brother of John.

James the Lesser is usually considered to be the same as James, the son of Alphaeus, listed as one of the Twelve Apostles. James the Lesser, who was called as such perhaps because he was younger than James the Greater, became the leader of the local church in Jerusalem. He also presided at the Council of Jerusalem, which determined the Church's new approach to Gentiles (Acts 15). He is often considered to be the James who was a cousin (literally a "brother") of Jesus mentioned in Mark's gospel, although it is not certain (Mark 6:3). We learn in 1 Corinthians that Jesus specially appeared to him after the resurrection (1 Corinthians 15:7).

James the Lesser is traditionally believed to be the writer of the epistle of St. James, although scholars are not certain of the authorship. The epistle begins with these words: "James, a slave of God and of the Lord Jesus Christ, to the twelve tribes in the dispersion, greetings" (James 1:1). In the letter, we read of the need to put faith into action: "Be doers of the word and not hearers only, deluding yourselves" (James 1:22). Also, "Indeed someone may say, 'You have faith and I have works.' Demonstrate your faith to me without works, and I will demonstrate my faith to you from my works" (James 2:18).

Philip, who came from Bethsaida in Galilee, was a disciple of John the Baptist (John 1:44). A day after John the Baptist pointed out Jesus as the Lamb of God to his disciples, Jesus went out and "found Philip" back in Galilee, and said, "follow me" (John 1:43). Philip did so, and also told Nathaniel about Him, saying, "We have found the one about whom Moses wrote in the law, and also the prophets, Jesus son of Joseph, from Nazareth" (John 1:45). The name "Philip" is of Greek origin, and it seems that he could speak the language (*The Complete Book of Who's Who in the Bible*). In fact, when certain Greeks came looking for Jesus in John's gospel, they came to Philip first (John 12:20–22). Though Philip was quick in following Jesus, he was not always quick to understand. He was the disciple who asked Jesus at the feeding of the five thousand how such numbers of people could possibly be fed (John 6:5–7). Philip also said to Jesus at the Last Supper, "Master, show us the Father, and that will be enough for us" (John 14:8).

The last we know from Scripture of Philip for certain is that he received the Holy Spirit on the Day of Pentecost. Traditions vary about his later life, ministry, and death.

Sts. Philip and James, pray for us!

St. Matthias
Apostle, First Century
Feast, May 14

St. Matthias was a faithful follower of Jesus and a witness to the key events of His ministry. He is mentioned in the Acts of the Apostles as having been chosen by lots to replace the traitor, Judas, as an Apostle (Acts 1:15–26).

According to the Acts of the Apostles, Peter, the leader of the Apostles, stood up before a large gathering of the faithful after Jesus' Ascension and declared that Judas must be replaced. He argued that the number of Apostles must be restored to twelve, and that the prophecy from the Psalms must be fulfilled: "May another take his office" (Acts 1:20). The community chose two candidates—Joseph Barsabbas and Matthias—and the lots fell to Matthias.

According to the tradition passed down through St. Cyril of Alexandria, St. Matthias had been one of the seventy-two disciples who Jesus sent out ahead of Him to preach the Good News. This seems plausible, because an essential role of the Apostles was to be personal witnesses of the original words and deeds of the man Jesus to the ends of the earth. There are conflicting traditions on where exactly Matthias preached the Gospel the rest of his days—whether he remained in Jerusalem or went out among the cannibals in Ethiopia—but it is believed that he earned the martyr's crown.

St. Matthias, pray for us!

St. Rita of Cascia
Religious, 1381–1457
Optional Memorial, May 22

Mother, widow, and nun, all in the most impossible of circumstances, St. Rita has become a saint to whom many people can relate. Rita's parents were overjoyed at her birth, since she came to them when they were advanced in years. Born at Roccaporena outside Cascia in the Umbria region of Italy, Rita was inspired by the nuns who used to visit, and she desired to become one of them herself. Her father, however, had promised her hand in marriage. Rita obeyed his wishes as God's will, and she was given in marriage at the age of twelve to Paolo Mancini. He was a watchman for the town, and also a member of a political faction that clashed violently with a rival faction. He was sometimes also violent to Rita at home, and she prayed for his conversion. Eighteen years into the marriage, Paolo was murdered by members of his rival faction, in the days when blood vendettas reigned among such groups and families. At the funeral, Rita publicly forgave the perpetrators and called for the end of the vendetta cycle.

Paolo left behind two teenage sons, who were strongly tempted through the influence of a friend to avenge their father despite their mother's wishes. Rita's heart was torn, and she prayed that, having already lost a husband, she would not lose her sons' souls over the sin of murder. An epidemic came upon the town later on, however, and her two sons both died of the illness—they were unable to carry out the vendetta, but had come to peace with God before their passing. Rita, though sorrowful, was relieved that her sons were on their way to heaven, not hell.

Now a widow and enduring the loss of even her sons, Rita sought out the Augustinian convent of St. Mary Magdalene, to which she had been drawn as a child. She was rejected because some of the nuns were members of the faction that was a rival to Rita's family, and they feared retribution. Given the impossible task of reconciling the clashing factions in the town as a condition of entry, she prayed fervently to her patron saints and was able to achieve peace and forgiveness among them. At last granted entry to the convent, Rita grew deeply in prayer and penance for the peace of the community and in charitable works.

About ten years into her religious life, while she was praying before an image of the crucified Lord, Rita was granted the wound of Christ on her forehead, which was visible to all. Additionally, one time she asked a woman to bring back a single rose from the old home of her parents. This was an impossible request because it was January, but sure enough, the woman miraculously found a red rose there and brought it to Rita. Rita was bedridden for the last four years of her life, sustained almost only by the Eucharist. At last, haven taken ill from tuberculosis, she died at the age of seventy-six. Her body remained incorrupt, and pilgrims continue to make pilgrimage to see her remains at Cascia to this day. Beatified in 1626 and then canonized in 1900, St. Rita has become a very popular saint to whom many can relate. She is the patron of impossible causes, difficult marriages, abuse victims, mothers, widows, and wounds.

St. Rita, pray for us!

St. Philip Neri
Priest, 1515–1595
Memorial, May 26

St. Philip Neri, known as the Apostle of Rome, was a beloved messenger of God's Word to common people, to the poor, and to youth. He was an important reformer during a time when the Church was in need of renewal, and his answer was a life of authentic holiness among the people.

Born in Florence in 1515, young Philip always had a good disposition and was known for his upright character, even earning the nickname "the good Pippo" (*New Advent*). In his teens, he was sent to help his father's rich cousin near Monte Cassino and was appointed his heir. Philip, however, was moved to prayer at a Benedictine chapel there and had a mystical experience that changed the course of his life. It was revealed to him that he was to be an Apostle to Rome.

So, Philip left his wealthy patron for Rome, not even knowing where he would stay, and he was taken in by an official there, Galecotto Caccia, who provided housing for him. Philip, however, chose the most austere of lifestyles, eating only once a day and then very meagerly. He hid his fasting in public, though, and would never refuse what was offered him if doing so would attract attention. He tutored Caccia's sons in gratitude for his generosity. Philip was an excellent tutor and moved them to holiness. This was the beginning of many years of fruitful teaching and conversations among the youth. Meanwhile, Philip took classes in philosophy and theology at the Sapienzia.

Rome, during the time of the Protestant Reformation in Europe to the north, was in a state of decadence, far from the ideals of the Catholic faith. The common people needed authentic spiritual engagement. Philip first went out to the hospitals, alone and then with others. Then he went out to the various gathering areas of the city simply to converse with the people. He was a great conversationalist. Known and loved for his humor, Philip made connections with people from all walks of life and brought the Gospel to life for them. He brought many sinners back to God. Philip would also gather the youth around him to instruct them in the faith. This was something that he loved to do, and it was sorely needed in the days when it was not commonly tended to, leaving room for other ideas to take sway.

Philip developed friendships within two other key reformers in the Church—St. Ignatius of Loyola and the cardinal St. Charles Borromeo. Philip established a confraternity of prayer for common laypeople, which met a great need for the people. The numbers kept growing, such that they had to always find larger meeting places.

Philip continued to experience great intimacy with God in prayer. Just before Pentecost in 1544, while praying for the gifts of the Holy Spirit, he was filled with an overwhelming portion of God's love. He saw a flame descending like a globe, and it filled his chest and made him shake as he fell to the floor. He reached for his heart, and there was a great swelling there (*New Advent*). Later, after his death, doctors performed an autopsy on him and found that his heart was very greatly enlarged, such that two ribs had broken to make room for it. When children gathered around him on cold days to hear his teaching, they said they could feel the heat that came forth from him. His heart would stir violently in prayer and during Mass.

Philip was still not sure whether to pursue the priesthood or simply to continue his unique apostolate as a layperson. His spiritual director, Fr. Persiano Rossa, however, invited him to holy orders, and he was ordained a priest in 1551. As a priest, he was invited to hear Confessions and he spent many long hours in the confessional, sometimes even being given the supernatural gift of reading the secrets of hearts. His Masses were very long because of his impassioned prayers. It gave him great joy to take an empty chalice, marveling how Christ would come down at the call of his own words (*Butler's Lives*).

Fr. Philip's organization became known as the Congregation of the Oratory, since they would ring a bell in calling the people to prayer. The impassioned preaching, stirring music, and witness to holiness attracted great numbers, and many were edified by their spiritual exercises. The Oratory introduced the Forty Hours devotion to Rome, which involved Eucharistic Adoration. Because Rome was a city that attracted many pilgrims, they also led devout pilgrimages to the Seven Churches and tended to the many pilgrims who visited the holy city. Ultimately, Philip had a room built over the church. He began to attract priests and seminarians to join him, and they received approval for their organization as a pontifical society of the apostolic life in 1575. The Oratorians spread, bringing great lights to the Church, including St. Francis de Sales and Blessed John Henry Newman in future years.

In his later days, Fr. Philip experienced many health issues, but these also led him closer to God. During his sufferings, he was even given a vision of the Blessed Virgin Mary. He prophesied his passing ten days before it happened. On that day, he could not wait for his soul to at last go to God. St. Philip Neri was canonized in 1622. He is the patron saint of Rome, of humor, and of the U.S. Special Forces.

St. Philip Neri, pray for us!

St. Charles Lwanga and Companions
Martyrs, d. 1886
Memorial, June 3

St. Charles Lwanga and his companions were martyred in southern Uganda in 1886 for standing up for Christian morality against a cruel and immoral tyrant.

Charles Lwanga was a chief official in the court of King Mwanga. The Society of Missionaries in Africa, known as the "White Fathers," converted a group of Africans to Christianity, including Charles Lwanga and other members of the court. King Mwanga at first welcomed the missionaries. But he was an immoral man, insisting on sexual favors from the young men and boys of his court. Charles Lwanga and his companions opposed this and kept boys away from being taken to him.

Realizing that Christian morality was undermining his rule and behavior, King Mwanga ordered his court to appear before him. Understanding the situation, Charles secretly baptized those companions who had not yet been baptized. Having already had several Christians killed, Mwanga told those who did not pray to stand with him and those who did pray to stand aside. Charles Lwanga and his companions stood to the side. When the enraged king asked whether or not they were Christians, these young men, all under the age of twenty-five, responded enthusiastically that they were.

The king ordered them to be put to death by burning. They were forced on a thirty-seven-mile death march to Namugongo, during which three were left to die along the way. The chief counselor vowed not to eat until one of the companions, named Andrew, was killed. Andrew told one of the executioners that he was ready to die, and thus not to let the chief counselor go hungry. So, the executioner killed Andrew on the spot. Even the chief executioner's own son was among the condemned. The chief executioner urged his son repeatedly to renounce Christianity and save himself, but he would not. Along the path to their execution, the companions marched past the dwelling of the White Fathers, who mourned for them. One young man said to the Fathers, "Why are you so sad? This nothing to the joys you have taught us to look forward to" (Catholic Online). At Mamugongo, Charles asked to build his own funeral pyre. He did so, and then lay down upon it. He burned there for a long time, but he was not heard to even moan. Then his companions were stripped, wrapped in reed blankets, and burned together on a pyre. They prayed until they gave up their spirits.

Far from extinguishing Christianity in the region, however, the bravery and prayers of the martyrs rose up great fervor for the faith. Though the White Fathers left the region for a time, they returned to find five hundred Christians and one thousand catechumens.

St. Charles Lwanga and Companions, pray for us!

St. Barnabas
Apostle, First Century
Memorial, June 11

St. Barnabas, the "son of encouragement," was among the first Christian missionaries and was the partner of St. Paul on his first missionary journey.

Given the name Joseph at birth, he was a Jew of the tribe of Levi, born on the island of Cyprus. He owned a piece of property, which he sold, giving all the proceeds to the Apostles to distribute to the needy, as did other early believers. The Apostles gave him the name "Barnabas," which means "son of encouragement," perhaps owing to the gift he had for encouraging others in the community, especially in a prophetic sense. His first mention in Scripture comes in the Acts of the Apostles, chapter three, in the context of the following idyllic portrayal of the life of the early Christian community:

> The community of believers was of one heart and mind, and no one claimed that any of his possessions was his own, but they had everything in common. With great power the apostles bore witness to the resurrection of the Lord Jesus, and great favor was accorded them all. There was no needy person among them, for those who owned property or houses would sell them, bring the proceeds of the sale, and put them at the feet of the apostles, and they were distributed to each according to need. Thus Joseph, also named by the apostles Barnabas (which is translated "son of encouragement"), a Levite, a Cypriot by birth, sold a piece of property that he owned, then brought the money and put it at the feet of the apostles (Acts 3:32–37).

According to tradition, Barnabas was one of the seventy-two disciples whom Jesus had sent out ahead of Him, two by two, to proclaim the Kingdom among the Jews (*Butler's Lives*).

Likewise, in the Acts of the Apostles, Barnabas is seen as a missionary, always going out with a partner.

Barnabas, ever the encourager, was the first Christian in the Jerusalem community to befriend Paul, despite his reputation for having been a persecutor of Christians in the past. We find this account in the Acts of the Apostles: "When he [Paul] arrived in Jerusalem he tried to join the disciples, but they were all afraid of him, not believing that he was a disciple. Then Barnabas took charge of him and brought him to the apostles, and he reported to them how on the way he had seen the Lord and that he had spoken to him, and how in Damascus he had spoken out boldly in the name of Jesus" (Acts 9:26–27).

Barnabas was stouthearted; after many Christians dispersed after Stephen's martyrdom, Barnabas was part of the remnant who stayed. He then was sent to Antioch as an emissary from the Church at Jerusalem to witness the powerful evangelization that was taking place there. We are told, "When he arrived and saw the grace of God, he rejoiced and encouraged them all to remain faithful to the Lord in firmness of heart, for he was a good man, filled with the holy Spirit and faith. And a large number of people was added to the Lord" (Acts 11:23–24).

Barnabas then went to Tarsus and brought Paul back to Antioch with him. There they began working in ministry together. A year later, the two were sent back to Jerusalem to provide supplies for relief during a famine that had been prophesied to happen (Acts 11:28–29). From Jerusalem, they were sent out on a greater mission (Acts 12:25). For this, they took along Barnabas's cousin John Mark. Paul and Barnabas preached the Word together in Cyprus, Pisidia, Iconium, Lystra, Pamphylia, Attalia, and Antioch.

Paul and Barnabas suffered much persecution and danger during their mission. They also worked many healings and mighty deeds in the midst of their hearers. In fact, the pagans at Lystra were actually convinced that Paul was the god Hermes, because he did most of the speaking, and that Barnabas, because he was mostly silent, was the high god Zeus. They were even about to offer sacrifices to them, but Paul and Barnabas tore their garments and insisted that they were merely men, carrying the saving message of Jesus Christ, who was the true God. Despite their protests against what the pagans were doing, however, Jews came and found Paul and stoned him for blasphemy, but he survived and continued with Barnabas (Acts 14:8–20).

Paul and Barnabas had much success in their mission, which was to both Jews and Gentiles. As such, it was one of the first large and successful missions to the Gentiles. We read in the Acts of the Apostles, "And when they arrived, they called the church together and reported what God had done with them and how he had opened the door of faith to the Gentiles. Then they spent no little time with the disciples" (Acts 14:27–28).

The community rejoiced, but some questioned whether the Gentiles must be first circumcised according to the Law of Moses in order to be saved. This led to what is called the "Council of Jerusalem" (Acts 15). Gathered with the Apostles at Jerusalem, Paul and Barnabas testified on behalf of the uncircumcised Gentile Christians that the Holy Spirit was truly with them. It was decided that Gentiles did not need to be circumcised in the New Covenant; they only needed to avoid association with idols and to be baptized in the name of the Lord Jesus Christ.

Paul and Barnabas, however, did not go out together on another missionary journey. Barnabas wanted to return, along with his cousin John Mark, to the churches they had founded.

But John Mark had abandoned them at Pamphylia, so Paul strongly objected to his being readmitted to their mission work. Paul, instead, went with Silas and did much great work in Greece and Asia Minor. Barnabas, who apparently still believed in John Mark, went along with his cousin to visit the churches again. John Mark later did become a very dependable support, even to Paul. Likely the writer of the gospel of Mark and a successful missionary, bishop, and martyr himself, perhaps John Mark needed the encouragement provided him by Barnabas to fulfill his true calling.

Traditions diverge on the specifics of Barnabas's later missionary work. The apocryphal epistle of Barnabas is attributed to him, although it was actually written after his lifetime in Alexandria. According to tradition, Barnabas died by being stoned on the Greek island of Salamis, thus receiving the martyr's crown at the end of his life. Though not one of the Twelve, like St. Paul, St. Barnabas is venerated by the Church under the title of Apostle.

St. Barnabas, pray for us!

St. Joan of Arc
Virgin, 1412–1431
Optional Memorial, May 30

St. Joan of Arc is a model of bravery, of someone who faithfully answered the call of God for the service of others. Her story has inspired countless generations both in the Church and in secular society.

Joan was born in the town of Dorémy in northeastern France. She had a happy childhood and was known to all as a good and charitable person. She used to care for the sick and would even give them her own bed if they had nowhere else to go. Her town, however, was subject to attack, since France had been submerged into civil war, and English conquerors, allied with the Burgundians, occupied important territories in France. At the age of fourteen, Joan began to hear heavenly voices. They told her that God had a plan for her to save France in battle. Later, these voices became visions, and Joan saw Jesus and numerous saints as they spoke to her. Though she protested that she was too young and had no military experience, the voices persisted.

The voices told her to present herself to a French ruler's officer named Robert Baudricourt at Vaucouleurs. Though he was at first dismissive of her, Joan won his interest by prophesying about imminent French setbacks, which only later did envoys come to report. At that time, Charles VII, whose power was clipped by the strong English and Burgundian presence, did not dare to accept the royal crown and he refused to place much effort into protecting his towns against the more powerful invading forces. His title remained as the Dauphin, the title for the heir to the French throne, and he spent his time with amusements at his court. Baudricourt brought Joan to the Dauphin, but his advisor ridiculed her. The Dauphin did agree, however, to bring her in, but he disguised himself so she could not know him except through supernatural means. She picked him out immediately. Impressed, the Dauphin sent for her revelations to be examined by theologians, and they recommended her to him.

At that, Charles VII put Joan to work in his army and gave her a position of command, working with his generals. As the voices had directed her and going into battle under an inspired religious banner, she captured the city of Orléans from the English. It was an important victory and began to turn the tide of momentum, providing a key stronghold for the French. Just as had been revealed to her beforehand, she was wounded by an arrow in the battle, but she recovered. Then she convinced the Dauphin to accept coronation as the rightful king of France. He did so with Joan at his side.

This was as far as the voices directed her for military campaigns. She made an unsuccessful raid on Paris, in which she was wounded, and then she suffered a defeat at Compiègne. There, she was captured when the French raised the drawbridge too soon, leaving Joan and her men stranded. Thus, in May 1430, she was imprisoned by the Bourgundians and became a personal prisoner of John of Luxembourg. Then in November, being that the French had done nothing to help her, she was sold to the English for £23,000. Her enemies, the English, hurried to find a way to have her executed within the boundaries of their law, so they brought charges against her of heresy and sorcery because of the voices she claimed to hear. Bishop Cauchon of Beauvais led the charges, hoping to secure the more important See of Rouen under the English (*Butler's Lives*).

According to legend, Joan made two attempts to escape the prison but was captured. She faced trial in February 1431 for the first time, facing theological experts without any representation. Her answers were recorded, and they have even since been quoted in the *Catechism of the Catholic Church*: "About Jesus Christ and the Church, I simply know they're just one thing, and we shouldn't complicate the matter" (no. 795). The judges, however, found ways to overlook her wise responses, entrapping her with difficult theological terms. They denounced her voices as diabolical and ordered her to recant. She refused at first, until she was led to a cemetery with a large crowd, where she did recant. But then when she was found again wearing men's clothes in prison, whether for protection or because that was all that was provided, she was declared a relapsed heretic and was sentenced to death. She was led to the marketplace at Rouen at 8 o'clock in the morning and tied to the stake. As the flames began to shoot up, she asked a Dominican priest there to hold up a crucifix before her eyes, and she called out the name of Jesus.

Joan of Arc died in 1431 at the age of nineteen. Her ashes were scattered into the River Seine. According to legend, only her heart was not burned. Twenty-three years later, Joan's mother and two brothers petitioned the Pope to reconsider her case. Having appointed a commission to the task, Pope Callistus III overturned the verdict at Rouen and exonerated Joan of Arc in 1456 (*Butler's Lives*). Held in high regard for centuries for her heroism and piety, she was at last canonized in 1920. She is the patron saint of France and of soldiers.

St. Joan of Arc, pray for us!

St. Justin
Martyr, ca. 100–ca. 165
Memorial, June 1

Justin Martyr was an early apologist, philosopher, theologian, and of course, a martyr. As an apologist, he provided strong reasoned defenses for the Christian faith against its detractors. He leaves us with three writings important to theological discourse—his two Apologies and his *Dialogue with Trypho the Jew.*

It seems that Justin was born a pagan around the year 100 in Palestinian Syria. He became interested in philosophy in order to learn about God and the meaning of life. In his *Dialogue with Trypho,* he describes his path in philosophy. He first became acquainted with Stoicism, but he learned nothing there of God. Then he studied under a peripatetic, but was put off when he demanded a fee. Next, he met a Pythagorean. For them, the world is ultimately about numbers, and Justin did not have the requisite training to be brought into their way of thought. Then he became acquainted with Platonism. Justin found some truth in Platonism and its belief in the soul, but he ultimately found fullness in Christianity. Impressed by the courage and conviction of the Christian martyrs, he became convinced of the moral beauty and truth of Christianity (*New Advent*). According to John's gospel, Jesus is the divine Word, or *Logos.* Justin was the first writer to likewise identify Jesus, the *Logos,* with the *logos,* or reason, sought by Greek philosophy.

In his *Dialogue with Trypho the Jew,* Justin defends Christianity against Jewish objections and also discusses Christian belief in the fulfillment of the Old Testament in Christ. In his *Apologies,* he writes to the Roman emperor to refute the slanderous charges against Christians made by the Romans. Christians were accused of cannibalism on account of the Eucharist, and atheism because they did not sacrifice to the Roman gods. In his *Apologies,* he gives a moving account of the early Christian Mass.

Justin and some of his own disciples received the martyr's crown and were beheaded for the faith. Justin refused to renounce Christianity, saying that one must never renounce truth for untruth.

St. Justin Martyr, pray for us!

Excerpt from the First Apology of Justin Martyr

And this food is called among us [the Eucharist], of which no one is allowed to partake but the man who believes that the things which we teach are true, and who has been washed with the washing that is for the remission of sins, and unto regeneration, and who is so living as Christ has enjoined. For not as common bread and common drink do we receive these; but in like manner as Jesus Christ our Saviour, having been made flesh by the Word of God, had both flesh and blood for our salvation, so likewise have we been taught that the food which is blessed by the prayer of His word, and from which our blood and flesh by transmutation are nourished, is the flesh and blood of that Jesus who was made flesh. For the apostles, in the memoirs composed by them, which are called Gospels, have thus delivered unto us what was enjoined upon them; that Jesus took bread, and when He had given thanks, said, This do in remembrance of Me, this is My body; and that, after the same manner, having taken the cup and given thanks, He said, This is My blood; and gave it to them alone (Ch. 66, New Advent).

St. Anthony of Padua
Priest and Doctor of the Church
Memorial, June 13

St. Anthony of Padua is a very popular saint. Known in his sainthood especially for intercession in finding lost objects, his earthly life was focused more on finding the lost and bringing them back to God through great preaching. His aspiration was actually for martyrdom, but instead he found joy through bringing the Word home through his sermons and homilies.

St. Anthony was born in Lisbon, Portugal, in 1195, to noble parents; he was christened as Fernando. His father was an officer in the king's army. He joined the canons of the Abbey of Santa Cruz in Coimbra, Portugal, where he set himself devoutly to the study of Scripture, the Church Fathers, and the Latin language. He was ordained to the priesthood, but he was captivated by another calling to a newly founded religious order—the Franciscans—which had recently established a monastery at Coimbra. The bodies of seven Franciscan friars had been brought back from Morocco; they had been martyred for spreading the faith. Fr. Fernando was filled with zeal and he desired to meet the same end. He joined the Franciscans, attracted also by their simplicity of life and witness to the Gospel. The convent was named after St. Antony of Egypt, an early inspiration to monastic life, so Fernando then took on the name Anthony. Friar Anthony's wish to be sent to Morocco was granted, but martyrdom never came. Instead, he became seriously ill on the voyage to Morocco and was sent back. But the ship did not return to Portugal; it landed in Italy instead. Anthony was taken in by the Franciscans there and given a new assignment in Italy, since he was still very sickly.

Once some Dominicans came to visit, prompting a question on who should preach to the brethren. All of the friars deferred, until Anthony was finally singled out to preach. He was only twenty-six years old, but he was filled with the Holy Spirit, who stirred his learning into an eloquence that moved the soul. Word of his fervent preaching spread among the brothers, and then was shared with St. Francis himself. St. Francis rejoiced at this gift and had Anthony sent for more instruction in theology to foster his gift. Always wary of knowledge as an occasion for pride, St. Francis exhorted Anthony to learn in a spirit of prayer and humility. Through his studies, St. Anthony became even more well-versed in Scripture, and in how to apply it to move the soul as the situation warranted. He became an eminent professor, teaching at several universities, but he never accepted any of the privileges, choosing instead to live as an ordinary friar (*Butler's Lives*).

Despite his educational background, St. Anthony preferred preaching to scholarship, drawing on his learning to move the sinner away from sin and to exhort the Christian to fervor. His voice was pleasing, his message was well-crafted, and his witness was genuine and profound. His sermons had a great effect on all sorts of people. The learned were intrigued by the way he spoke simple truths, and ordinary people felt that he spoke directly to their situation. He spoke in a very affected way that stirred the emotions, as well. He did not offend sinners, but advised them, and he tempered his teaching on God's wrath with God's mercy. St. Anthony was not merely a crafter of words, but he was a lover of truth who could masterfully direct the mind and heart in the way it should go. Conversions followed him wherever he went, as did miracles, and the crowds grew such that he had to preach out in fields and open marketplaces so everyone could hear. He was also a great confessor.

Once, Pope Gregory IX heard him preach, and he was very much impressed and inspired. He brought him in as his court preacher. His preaching in the papal court was dubbed the "jewel case of the Bible." St. Francis also put Anthony in charge of the brothers' instruction. This is how he came to be known after his death for intercession for finding lost objects. One story goes that St. Anthony had a hand-copied and personally annotated book of the Psalms that he used for the formation of the brothers. When one of the novices left the order, he stole St. Anthony's book and took it with him. St. Anthony prayed that the book would be returned. It was, and the novice also returned to the order (Catholic Online).

Another story speaks of St. Anthony's unique ability to stir the sinner to penance. There was an evil despot who was very much feared because he had no regard for human life, putting large numbers of people to death on suspicion of opposing him. St. Anthony, perhaps still desiring the martyr's crown, went to him and exhorted him to change his evil ways. Rather than give the usual order of death, the despot heard him favorably. The despot went back to doing evil after St. Anthony's passing, however, and was eventually captured by his enemies (*Butler's Lives*).

St. Anthony died in 1231 at the age of only thirty-five in Padua, Italy, a city that had become his new home and that mourned him greatly at his passing. St. Anthony's powerful intercession was sought after his death, and many miracles were attributed to him. Pope Gregory IX, who had known his preaching, canonized him in 1232, only one year after his death. St. Anthony is often portrayed holding the child Jesus, adoring Him. St. Anthony's body was exhumed more than three centuries after his death. His tongue alone was found incorrupt, in perfect form. In 1946, he was proclaimed a Doctor of the Church for his preaching by Pope Pius XII. St. Anthony is venerated as the patron saint for lost articles.

St. Anthony of Padua, pray for us!

St. Aloysius Gonzaga
Religious, 1568–1591
Memorial, June 21

Born to a princely Italian family, Jesuit scholastic St. Aloysius Gonzaga attained the heights of sanctity at a young age, dying at only twenty-three years old.

Aloysius was kept pure from a young age, forever keeping the purity of his baptismal garment unstained. His first words were the names of Jesus and Mary, since his pious mother taught them to him first. His greatest fault in his own eyes was when, at the age of seven, he repeated a word whose meaning he did not understand, but which turned out to be a bad word. Later in life, his confessors were confident that Aloysius had never committed a single mortal sin in his whole life. Aloysius loved reading and rereading the lives of the saints. In imitation of them, Aloysius devoted himself to constant prayer and strict mortifications. He practiced devotions, but he also learned mental prayer and contemplation on his own. Sometimes he would even spend the whole day in contemplation. He kept himself unstained from the vanities of the royal court. He would not command the servants but make gentle requests of them. Of all the scrumptious foods offered to him, he would choose whatever was least appealing. He practiced a very strict custody of the eyes, not even allowing himself to look upon women directly. The beautiful gowns of the ladies of the court had no effect on him. When offered a high title in the court, he renounced it. Aloysius desired to be regarded as nothing by the world (*Butler's Lives*).

Once he came upon a book about the Jesuit missionaries by St. Peter Canisius, and he desired to join the new order. His mother supported him in it, but his father had other plans for his future and opposed his vocation vigorously. He even threatened to beat him naked, but Aloysius said that he would rejoice in his sufferings for God. At last, his father relented, and even repented of his obstinacy. His father died only a short time after Aloysius entered the order.

At Rome, Aloysius underwent the long formation afforded to those entering the Society of Jesus, or the Jesuits. He followed every rule with the greatest care. He did not even attempt to speak to his uncle, a Jesuit, except at the proper times. Once Aloysius was wrongly accused of breaking a rule because of a misunderstanding and was made to publicly repent for it, and he did so.

Aloysius enjoyed great contemplation. Even at his classes, he appeared to be absorbed in prayer. His fastings and mortifications made him weak. At times, his spiritual directors ordered him to cease from his private prayer life apart from what was done in community. He obeyed, even though this was a very great difficulty for him. Once in prayer, it was revealed to him that he did not have much longer on the earth. This gave Aloysius great joy. Soon, an epidemic of the plague came over Rome, and the Jesuits helped the sick and the dying. Aloysius volunteered to go along, and he contracted the plague. It seemed he would recover, but he knew he would not. When his health took a sudden turn for the worse, he gave up his spirit, with his last word being the same as his first—the name "Jesus." Canonized in 1726, St. Aloysius Gonzoga is the patron saint of Catholic youth, as well as those who suffer from AIDS and those who care for those with AIDS.

St. Aloyisius Gonzaga, pray for us!

Sts. John Fisher and Thomas More
Martyrs, Sixteenth Century
Optional Memorial, June 22

Saints John Fisher and Thomas More were high officials in the English government, martyred by King Henry VIII for refusing to acknowledge him as the Supreme Head of the Church in England.

Both men were highly learned and well-respected and had ascended to the high echelons of the government. John Fisher, an eminent theologian and priest, became a bishop. He was a close advisor to Lady Margaret, the mother of King Henry VIII. Sir Thomas More, an eminent legal scholar, piously discerned the priesthood, but resolved that his true calling was marriage. He said he would prefer to be a good husband than a bad priest. His first marriage, to Jane Colt, was a happy one and brought him four children, but then Jane died. More soon after married a widow, Anne Harpur Middleton, who cared for his children. More became a key member of Parliament and was later made Chancellor of England by King Henry VIII. Both men, authors of important works, were staunchly Catholic, and they wrote in defense of the Church against the Protestant Reformation. Both also desired and wrote in favor of a reform of the Church from within.

Tribulations came when King Henry VIII divorced his wife, Catherine of Aragon, for failing to give him a male heir. He petitioned for an annulment from the pope to legitimize the divorce and his planned marriage to Anne Boleyn. There were no legitimate grounds for an annulment, however. Bishop John Fisher refused to encourage it or work out an annulment, and, in fact, he became a counselor to Catherine. Having heard of his stance on the matter, King Henry had Fisher arrested. He was released but later arrested again and ultimately arraigned for high treason when he refused to take the Oath of Supremacy. This oath included an allegiance to the future offspring of Anne Boleyn as the legitimate heirs to the throne and to King Henry as the Supreme Head of the Church of England. Pope Paul III made Fisher a cardinal, but King Henry refused to accept the hat from the pope's delegation, saying that instead he would send Fisher's head back to Rome (*New Advent*).

Meanwhile, Sir Thomas More attempted to quietly avoid taking the oath. Though he did not speak out against it, he resigned as Chancellor. More likewise failed to attend the coronation of Anne Boleyn, igniting the king's suspicions of disloyalty. More's reticence on the matter led to sanctions being placed on him, and later to his arrest. During his time in the Tower of London, More maintained his ever-jovial disposition, wrote letters to his family, read spiritual books, and also communicated with Cardinal Fisher. His interactions with Fisher were not looked upon kindly by the king. Ultimately, he was arraigned for high treason.

Both men were condemned to be drawn and quartered at Tyburn Hill, but the sentence was commuted to beheading at the Tower of London. St. John Fisher was beheaded in June of 1534, his saintly demeanor making much of an impact on the crowd. St. Thomas More was beheaded in July of that year, stating, "I die the king's good subject, and God's first." St. Thomas More is the patron saint of politicians, lawyers, adopted children, and difficult marriages.

Sts. John Fisher and Thomas More, pray for us!

St. John the Baptist (Nativity)
Solemnity, June 24

St. John the Baptist was the precursor of the Lord and the cousin of Jesus. Jesus said of him, "I tell you, among those born of women, no one is greater than John" (Luke 7:28).

The Solemnity of St. John the Baptist recalls a miraculous birth. Like the prophet Samuel, John the Baptist was born to a holy woman beyond childbearing age.

The gospel of Luke, after its prologue, begins with the announcement of the birth of John the Baptist. There we learn that his father "was a priest named Zechariah of the priestly division of Abijah; his wife was from the daughters of Aaron, and her name was Elizabeth" (Luke 1:5). The angel Gabriel came to Zechariah while he was serving in the Temple. Though he had a yearly period of service in the Temple, being chosen by lot to offer incense in the sanctuary was a very rare honor for him. We read in Luke's gospel:

> Then, when the whole assembly of the people was praying outside at the hour of the incense offering, the angel of the Lord appeared to him, standing at the right of the altar of incense. Zechariah was troubled by what he saw, and fear came upon him. But the angel said to him, "Do not be afraid, Zechariah, because your prayer has been heard. Your wife Elizabeth will bear you a son, and you shall name him John" (Luke 1:10–13).

Zechariah did not believe the angel's words, saying that his wife was too old to bear children. So, the angel said to him, "I am Gabriel, who stand before God. I was sent to speak to you and to announce to you this good news. But now you will be speechless and unable to talk until the day these things take place, because you did not believe my words, which will be fulfilled at their proper time" (Luke 1:19–20). When he came out to the people, he was unable to speak, making only gestures to them about what had happened. Elizabeth, at home, conceived and rejoiced that the Lord had removed her disgrace before men. The evangelist tells us that, despite the common belief that women who were barren were being punished for sin, Elizabeth and also her husband, Zachariah, were righteous before God.

The angel Gabriel then went to Mary to announce to her the birth of Jesus through the power of the Holy Spirit. He also told her the news of Elizabeth's miraculous pregnancy. We are told in Luke's gospel that Elizabeth was a cousin to Mary, and that she set out in haste from Nazareth in Galilee on the long journey south to the hill country of Judea, where Elizabeth and Zachariah lived. Elizabeth greeted Mary in a way reminiscent of how King David greeted the Ark of Covenant:

> When Elizabeth heard Mary's greeting, the infant leaped in her womb, and Elizabeth, filled with the holy Spirit, cried out in a loud voice and said, "Most blessed are you among women, and blessed is the fruit of your womb. And how does this happen to me, that the mother of my Lord should come to me? For at the moment the sound of your greeting reached my ears, the infant in my womb leaped for joy. Blessed are you who believed that what was spoken to you by the Lord would be fulfilled" (Luke 1:41–45).

Zachariah was still unable to speak at the time Elizabeth gave birth. When they came to circumcise him on the eighth day, their relatives wanted to name him Zachariah after his father, which was customary. They did not accept it when Elizabeth said, following what the angel said, that he was to be named John. Luke continues:

> So they made signs, asking his father what he wished him to be called. He asked for a tablet and wrote, "John is his name," and all were amazed. Immediately his

mouth was opened, his tongue freed, and he spoke blessing God. Then fear came upon all their neighbors, and all these matters were discussed throughout the hill country of Judea. All who heard these things took them to heart, saying, "What, then, will this child be?" For surely the hand of the Lord was with him (Luke 1:62–66).

From the announcement of his birth by the angel Gabriel to Zachariah, we have more insight into his way of life:

> "And you will have joy and gladness, and many will rejoice at his birth, for he will be great in the sight of [the] Lord. He will drink neither wine nor strong drink. He will be filled with the holy Spirit even from his mother's womb, and he will turn many of the children of Israel to the Lord their God. He will go before him in the spirit and power of Elijah to turn the hearts of fathers toward children and the disobedient to the understanding of the righteous, to prepare a people fit for the Lord" (Luke 1:14–17).

The prophesy that he "will be filled with the holy Spirit even from his mother's womb," along with the passage of how he leapt in utero at Jesus' arrival in Mary's womb, led to the tradition that John had been sanctified in the womb. In fact, this is the reason the Church celebrates John the Baptist's birth, which is marked about six months before Christmas, rather than his martyrdom in this solemnity; it is because it was taught by the saints that he was sanctified in the womb and that he emerged into the world in this way (*Butler's Lives*).

This special grace, though, is distinct from the Immaculate Conception of the Blessed Virgin Mary, who, according to Catholic dogma, was conceived free of Original Sin and all of its effects on her personality. John the Baptist would have been conceived with Original Sin, just as everyone else, but the grace he is said to have received at Jesus' visitation in Mary would have been similar to what Christians would later receive at their baptism, except he received it in utero and with a particular blessing for his life and ministry.

Drinking no strong drink, in the prophecy above, suggests that like the prophet Samuel, John might have been set apart for God according to the Nazarite vow, prescribed in Numbers 6. In the gospel of Matthew, we read of the adult John as a prophet: "John wore clothing made of camel's hair and had a leather belt around his waist. His food was locusts and wild honey. At that time Jerusalem, all Judea, and the whole region around the Jordan were going out to him and were being baptized by him in the Jordan River as they acknowledged their sins" (Matthew 3:4–6). This presentation of him is reminiscent of Elijah, who was prophesied to be a precursor to the Messiah.

All four gospels feature John the Baptist as the forerunner of Christ. John the Baptist was well-known in the region as a prophet. The first-century Judeo-Romano (non-Christian) historian Josephus also mentions the preaching of John the Baptist in positive terms, even echoing the popular belief that the later misfortunes of Herod Antipas were God's judgment upon him for having killed this good prophet.

John, as far as we know, was the first to perform baptisms. He likely meant baptism to be an internalization of the Jewish rituals of purification. Jesus then took on the practice, further endowing it with the power of the Holy Spirit. John said, "I am baptizing you with water, for repentance, but the one who is coming after me is mightier than I. I am not worthy to carry his sandals. He will baptize you with the holy Spirit and fire" (Matthew 3:11).

Jesus came to John for baptism, and although John was reluctant to baptize one greater than himself, Jesus told him to allow it "to fulfill all righteousness" (Matthew 3:15). The Holy Spirit settled on him in the form of a dove, and the Father's voice was heard saying, "This is my beloved Son, with whom I am well pleased" (Matthew 3:17). In this way, Jesus was marked and sent by God for His ministry among the people.

John's mission was to point the way to Jesus. He said, "He must increase; I must decrease" (John 3:30). Later, John denounced the ethnarch Herod Antipas for marrying his own brother's wife, Herodias, so Herod had him imprisoned at the fortress Machaerus on the desertous east bank of the Dead Sea. From prison, John sent messengers to ask Jesus for confirmation that He was, indeed, the Messiah. Jesus said, "Go and tell John what you hear and see: the blind regain their sight, the lame walk, lepers are cleansed, the deaf hear, the dead are raised, and the poor have the good news proclaimed to them. And blessed is the one who takes no offense at me" (Matthew 11:4–6).

When Herodias's daughter pleased Herod with a dance, he promised to grant her any request. She went to her mother, who told her to ask for the head of John the Baptist on a platter. She made the request, and though Herod was said to be distressed at the prospect, the martyrdom of St. John the Baptist came about in this way.

Canticle of Zachariah after the Birth and Naming of John the Baptist

> Blessed be the Lord, the God of Israel,
> for he has visited and brought redemption to his people.
> He has raised up a horn for our salvation
> within the house of David his servant,

even as he promised through the mouth of his holy prophets from of old:
salvation from our enemies and from the hand of all who hate us,
to show mercy to our fathers
and to be mindful of his holy covenant
and of the oath he swore to Abraham our father...
And you, child, will be called prophet of the Most High,
for you will go before the Lord to prepare his ways,
to give his people knowledge of salvation
through the forgiveness of their sins,
because of the tender mercy of our Gods
by which the daybreak from on high will visit us
to shine on those who sit in darkness and death's shadow,
to guide our feet into the path of peace (Luke 1:68–73, 76–79).

St. John the Baptist, pray for us!

St. Irenaeus of Lyons
Bishop and Martyr, d. ca. 202
Memorial, June 28

The Church Father St. Irenaeus was a Greek who learned the Christian faith at the feet of the martyr St. Polycarp, bishop of Smyrna, and the theologian Papias, both of whom received it from the Apostles. Lyons, a city in Gaul (modern-day France), had trade partnerships with Smyrna, so Irenaeus was sent to Lyons, where he was ordained a priest.

The bishop of Lyons was martyred, and Irenaeus was made the second bishop as his successor. Several generations after Jesus' Ascension, one of the forefront struggles in the Church was preserving the original teachings of Jesus and their right understanding and practice within the Church. Irenaeus took on the fight against heresy. When heresies arose in the Church, he would write letters to priests who went astray, to bring them back to the faith. He also sought unity within the Church, influencing the pope not to excommunicate those who insisted on a different date for Easter, but to tolerate them until proper explanation could be offered.

Irenaeus wrote perhaps the first work of systematic theology, *Against Heresies.* He became well-versed in the many errors of the day, and he refuted them in expert fashion, explaining the true faith. As the sure standard of orthodoxy, or right teaching, Irenaeus taught the doctrine of apostolic succession—that the teachings of Christ were handed on to the Apostles, who handed them on to the bishops, who further handed them on to their successors. So, to follow the true faith, one must follow the bishops. Against a heresy that rejected the Old Testament, Irenaeus argued that God, the Author of the whole of Scripture, recapitulated the Old Testament in the New. The first Creation is recapitulated in the New Creation; thus, Jesus is the New Adam, and Mary is the New Eve.

Irenaeus was very effective in evangelizing Lyons and its environs, and large numbers came to Christ. Persecution against the Christians, however, broke out under Emperor Severus. Christians were hunted down and martyred in large numbers. Irenaeus was among the many who suffered martyrdom, sacrificing the present life for the one of glory.

"The glory of God is the human person fully alive." —St. Irenaeus of Lyons

St. Irenaeus of Lyons, pray for us!

Sts. Peter and Paul
Apostles, First Century
Solemnity, June 29

Saints Peter and Paul were pillars of the early Church. St. Peter provided the Church with leadership, and Paul, with great evangelistic teaching. Both ended their days in Rome, where they suffered martyrdom on separate occasions. They are buried in Rome at their own respective major basilicas of St. Peter and of St. Paul, outside the Walls.

Together with his brother Andrew, Peter, originally named Simon, was one of the first disciples called by Jesus. They were fishermen, and they immediately left their nets and followed Jesus when He called them. After a miraculous catch of fish (Luke 5), Jesus called them to become "fishers of men" (Matthew 4:19). John's gospel tells us they were disciples of John the Baptist when they met Jesus (John 1). If he was for a time a disciple of John the Baptist in the wilderness, this indicates that, although Peter was married, he was able to take off some time from his labors to learn from the prophet.

Along with his follower's new mission, Jesus gave Simon a new name—Peter. There is no record in antiquity of anyone receiving this name, which means "Rock," prior to Simon. Along with his brother Andrew, Peter was among the Twelve, but he had further priority within that group. Together with James and John, Peter was also one of the three whom Jesus called to Himself during times of particular significance, such as the raising of Jarius's daughter, the Transfiguration, and the Agony in the Garden. Further, Peter is always named first in any list of Apostles throughout the New Testament because of his preeminence. Peter stepped forward when Jesus asked the disciples what they thought His identity was, and Jesus gave Peter a unique charge over the Church, which Catholics understand as establishing Peter as the first pope:

> He said to them, "But who do you say that I am?" Simon Peter said in reply, "You are the Messiah, the Son of the

living God." Jesus said to him in reply, "Blessed are you, Simon son of Jonah. For flesh and blood has not revealed this to you, but my heavenly Father. And so I say to you, you are Peter, and upon this rock I will build my church, and the gates of the netherworld shall not prevail against it. I will give you the keys to the kingdom of heaven. Whatever you bind on earth shall be bound in heaven; and whatever you loose on earth shall be loosed in heaven" (Matthew 16:15–19).

At the Resurrection, an unnamed disciple believed to be John waits for Peter to enter the empty tomb before him, presumably because of Peter's unique role (John 20). Although Peter had denied Jesus three times during His passion, the Risen Lord approached Peter about it, having him profess his love for Him three times. Jesus admonished him to "feed my lambs" and foretold his martyrdom (John 21).

Many of the stories in the gospels show a very human side of Peter, who was at times stubborn, slow to understand, and sometimes too bold or too fearful. After the descent of the Holy Spirit at Pentecost, it was Peter who, greatly strengthened by the Spirit, stepped forward to preach (Acts 2). His message was heard by the many Jewish travelers from around the world in their own languages, and "about three thousand persons were added that day" (Acts 2:41). When the Gentile but God-fearing centurion Cornelius sought baptism, Peter was given a dream about the admission of the Gentiles into the New Covenant, which showed that Gentiles were not expected to follow all of the prescriptions of the old Mosaic Law (Acts 10). Peter had Cornelius and his family baptized, and later Peter was a key figure at the Council of Jerusalem, where as much was decided for the whole Church (Acts 15).

Peter was imprisoned at Jerusalem, but was freed by an angel, who appeared to him at night (Acts 12). Peter later became the leader of the Church at Antioch and then finally at Rome, the capital of the Empire. During the persecution of Nero, Peter was inclined to flee, but tradition has it that the Lord appeared to him on the way, and Peter said to Him, "*Domine, quo vadi?*" or, "Lord, where are You going?" Jesus said, "I go to Rome to be crucified anew." So, Peter returned to Rome, where he was crucified, upside down since he considered himself unworthy to die in the same manner as the Lord. His remains were discovered in the mid–twentieth century where they were always traditionally thought to be—beneath St. Peter's Basilica in Rome. He wrote three epistles in the New Testament and is believed to be the apostolic authority upon which Mark rested for his gospel.

St. Paul, or Saul, was born a Jew of the tribe of Benjamin in Tarsus; he was also a Roman citizen (Philippians 3:5). He was finely educated in the Torah and was a Pharisee and zealous persecutor of the early Christians. He was an approving witness at the martyrdom of St. Stephen (Acts 8:1). While traveling to Damascus to arrest Christians, he was met by the Risen Lord in a vision; Jesus came to him in a great light. We read in the Acts of the Apostles:

> Now Saul, still breathing murderous threats against the disciples of the Lord, went to the high priest and asked him for letters to the synagogues in Damascus, that, if he should find any men or women who belonged to the Way, he might bring them back to Jerusalem in chains. On his journey, as he was nearing Damascus, a light from the sky suddenly flashed around him. He fell to the ground and heard a voice saying to him, "Saul, Saul, why are you persecuting me?" He said, "Who are you, sir?" The reply came, "I am Jesus, whom you are persecuting. Now get up and go into the city and you will be told what you must do." The men who were traveling with him stood speechless, for they heard the

247

voice but could see no one. Saul got up from the ground, but when he opened his eyes he could see nothing; so they led him by the hand and brought him to Damascus. For three days he was unable to see, and he neither ate nor drank (Acts 9:1–9).

The Lord came in a vision to a Christian named Ananias at Damascus, telling him to go to Saul. Ananias was frightened, but Jesus told him, "Go, for this man is a chosen instrument of mine to carry my name before Gentiles, kings, and Israelites, and I will show him what he will have to suffer for my name" (Acts 9:15–16). He prayed, and Saul's blindness was removed, and he accepted baptism. Saul then began preaching Jesus Christ in the synagogues of Damascus. Later, there was a conspiracy against him, and the Christians had to lower him out of the city walls in a basket to allow him to escape.

Early in his days as a Christian, Saul withdrew for three years into the Arabah Desert to reflect on the meaning of the New Covenant (Galatians 1). Perhaps it was there that he developed some of his deep and revolutionary teachings, such as the Church as the Body of Christ—perhaps reflecting on what Jesus had said: "Why are you persecuting Me?" when he was persecuting the Church. He then went to Jerusalem to present himself to Peter, the leader of the Apostles, to sanction his preaching (Galatians 1), where he was also befriended by Barnabas, a future partner in ministry (Acts 9:27).

Saul's name, Paul, seems not to have been a result of his conversion. It was likely part of a compound Greek and Jewish name, as was common. Saul was a Jewish name ,and Paul was a Greek name. He went by the name Paul especially in his missionary work among the Gentiles. He went on three missionary journeys, which took him, among other places, to Cyprus, Asia Minor, Greece, Macedonia, Jerusalem, Crete, and

Rome, where he was taken in captivity. He was the first to preach the Word in Europe. Paul writes:

> Five times at the hands of the Jews I received forty lashes minus one. Three times I was beaten with rods, once I was stoned, three times I was shipwrecked, I passed a night and a day on the deep; on frequent journeys, in dangers from rivers, dangers from robbers, dangers from my own race, dangers from Gentiles, dangers in the city, dangers in the wilderness, dangers at sea, dangers among false brothers; in toil and hardship, through many sleepless nights, through hunger and thirst, through frequent fastings, through cold and exposure. And apart from these things, there is the daily pressure upon me of my anxiety for all the churches (2 Corinthians 11:24–28).

Thirteen epistles in the New Testament are written by Paul. He wrote letters to many of the churches that he either founded or visited, and he also wrote to key leaders. These letters were read in the Church, and considered inspired, they were included in the canon of the New Testament. By most accounts, many of his epistles predate the gospels themselves, providing us with the earliest writings about Christ and the New Covenant. His writings provide us with an early and all-influential theology. He is also considered to be the apostolic authority behind Luke's gospel. Like Peter, Paul insisted that salvation does not come through the works of the old law, but through the grace of Christ in faith. In one of his epistles, Peter calls Paul his "beloved brother" and endorses his writings (2 Peter 3:15).

Rescued by Romans in Jerusalem from a Jewish mob, Paul, as a Roman citizen, appealed to bring his case to the emperor himself, so that he might witness to him (Acts 25). He was sent to Rome by ship. During his time in captivity, he continued writing his letters and witnessing to those around him. At Rome, he was finally beheaded during the persecution of Nero.

St. Peter and St. Paul were both essential pillars of the Church, influencing the Church all the way to the present day. Peter, the Rock and the Church's first pope, represented the authority of the Church, and Paul developed the meaning of Christ's coming in his writings and he spread the Word far among the Gentiles. Complementary in their ministry, they were united again in the place of their martyrdom—Rome.

Sts. Peter and Paul, pray for us!

St. Junipero Serra
Priest, 1713–1784
Optional Memorial (USA), July 1

St. Junipero Serra, who is honored in civil society with statues at the United States Capitol and the Golden Gate Park in San Francisco, was influential in the settlement of California in the future western United States. The driving passion of the "Apostle of California" was the evangelization of the native peoples in New Spain.

Junipero was born on a Spanish island in the Mediterranean region in 1713. He became a Franciscan friar and spent his first years of religious life and priesthood as a philosopher and a theologian. Fr. Serra became an eminent professor, but he was inspired by the stories of Spanish missionaries in South America. He left the world he knew, volunteering to sail to the Spanish colony of Mexico, never to return home. He landed in Vera Cruz, Mexico, in 1749. Such was his zeal that he refused the horse offered to him and walked the 250 miles to Mexico City. Fr. Serra became known for his crusty frontier bravery. In addition to the hardships of the terrain, he wore a hair shirt, imposed severe penances on himself, and spent most of his nights in prayer.

Fr. Serra became the leader of the Franciscan missions, and also the former Jesuit missions, and he did much to further them. Working his way north from the Baja Peninsula in present-day Mexico to Upper California in the present-day United States, he founded nine missions, including ones at Santa Clara, San Diego, and San Francisco, baptizing some six thousand persons (USCCB). He brought up the native converts in his mission communities, training them to live a Christian way of life.

Fr. Serra worked to apply the Gospel to the colonial institutions of which he found himself a part, making them at least more human-centered. He fought against many of the injustices of Spanish Conquistadors against the native peoples, whom he truly loved and whose salvation he longed for, also helping bring about the first legislation to protect them. But he did view the native populations in a paternalistic way, treating them more as children than as a free people.

Fr. Serra's passing in 1784 was greatly mourned by the native peoples, who knew his great love for them. His motto was, "Always forward, never back" (FranciscanMedia.org). Beatified by Pope John Paul II in 1988, St. Junipero Serra was canonized in 2015 by Pope Francis on his visit to Washington, D.C. He is the patron saint of California and of vocations.

St. Junipero Serra, pray for us!

St. Thomas
Apostle, First Century
Feast, July 3

St. Thomas was one of the Twelve personally chosen by Christ Himself. He was also called Didymus, which is a Greek name meaning "twin." He is mentioned only a few times in the gospels. Once was when he expressed a listless sorrow over the death of Lazarus, before witnessing Jesus raise him up (John 11:16). Most famously, Thomas was featured in a story in John's gospel about doubt and belief after the Resurrection. We read:

> Thomas, called Didymus, one of the Twelve, was not with them when Jesus came.
>
> So the other disciples said to him, "We have seen the Lord." But he said to them, "Unless I see the mark of the nails in his hands and put my finger into the nailmarks and put my hand into his side, I will not believe."
>
> Now a week later his disciples were again inside and Thomas was with them. Jesus came, although the doors were locked, and stood in their midst and said, "Peace be with you."
>
> Then he said to Thomas, "Put your finger here and see my hands, and bring your hand and put it into my side, and do not be unbelieving, but believe."
>
> Thomas answered and said to him, "My Lord and my God!"
>
> Jesus said to him, "Have you come to believe because you have seen me? Blessed are those who have not seen and have believed" (John 20:24–29).

According to tradition, Thomas was later directed by God to preach the Gospel in India. There, he was speared to death by the king, but he left behind a community of believers in India that thrives to this very day. St. Thomas is the patron saint of architects, construction workers, cooks, and Argentina.

St. Thomas the Apostle, pray for us!

St. Maria Goretti
Virgin and Martyr, 1890–1902
Optional Memorial, July 6

St. Maria Goretti, who died at the age of only twelve, is a model of purity, forgiveness, and fortitude in the face of great difficulties. Maria's father, Luigi, who lived outside Anzio in central Italy, was a struggling sharecrop farmer. The hardworking Luigi became ill and ultimately died from malaria, so Maria's mother, Assunta, and her siblings had to take to the fields to help provide for the family. Maria's duties were primarily at home, cooking, sewing, cleaning, and caring for her baby sister and other young children. Given the austerity of the family's situation, there was no opportunity for Maria to go to school. She did go for catechism instruction for First Communion, but she had difficulty because of her lack of education. She made her First Communion at the age of twelve, and she also grew deeply in prayer.

Unable to work the land by themselves, the Gorettis had to share part of their house and harvest with Giovani Serenelli and his eighteen-year-old son, Alessandro. Alessandro used to charm the Goretti children with his bird-catching abilities, but he later became vile and sullen, under the influence of pornographic materials (EWTN). He pined for the young but beautiful Maria, and he tried to seduce her. Maria, who was very much troubled by this situation, resisted his numerous advances, keeping the matter to herself in part because of his threats against her and her mother and because of the families' close ties.

One day, while she was at home tending to her chores, Alessandro came in and seized her by force, attempting to rape her. Alarmed especially for his salvation, Maria strongly resisted, saying, "No! No, Alexander! It is a sin. God forbids it. You will go to hell, Alexander. You will go to hell if you do it!" (EWTN). Enraged, he stabbed her eleven times, and when she started crawling away, he came back and stabbed her three more times before running out (Catholic Online). He was forced, however, to leave her virginity intact. Maria lay on the floor for some time until Alessandro's father, Giovanni, heard the cries of the children, and Assunta, Maria's mother, came in from the fields to check on the commotion.

Assunta, aghast, found Maria bleeding on the floor. At last, she asked her daughter who had done such a thing to her. Maria replied, "It was Alexander, Mama... Because he wanted me to commit an awful sin and I would not" (EWTN). Assunta tried to comfort Maria as she was carted off by a primitive ambulance to the nearest hospital, although every bump along the way exasperated her pains. At the hospital, she underwent surgery without anesthesia. The doctors held out little hope for her survival. One surgeon said to her, "Maria, think of me in paradise" (Catholic Online). A mob gathered outside the house shared by the Gorettis and Serenellis, waiting to lynch Alessandro. He was ultimately captured by the police, however, and brought to a fair trial. Before Maria died, within twenty-four hours of the attack, she forgave Alessandro. Looking on the crucifix given to her by her mother, Maria said, "I, too, pardon him. I, too, wish that he could come some day and join me in heaven" (EWTN).

Alessandro was sentenced to thirty years in jail. He was at first unrepentant and hostile, until Maria came to him in a dream. In the dream, she offered him lilies, but when he took them, they burned his hands. Alessandro was changed by this experience and had a true conversion of the heart. He was released after twenty-seven years, and he went to Maria's mother, begging for her forgiveness. Assunta said, "If my daughter can forgive him, who am I to withhold forgiveness?" (Catholic Online). Alessandro became a lay Capuchin Franciscan, spending his all the rest of his days at a Capuchin monastery and serving the brothers.

St. Maria Goretti, who is regarded as a martyr since she died for her faith, was canonized in 1950 by Pope Pius XII before a crowd of 250,000 at St. Peter's Square. Alessandro was among the pilgrims in solemn attendance, as was Maria's mother, Assunta, and several of her siblings. St. Maria Goretti is the patron saint of purity, rape victims, young women, and youth.

St. Maria Goretti, pray for us!

St. Benedict (of Nursia)
Abbot, c. 480–543
Memorial, July 11

Hermit, abbot, miracle-worker, and exorcist St. Benedict of Nursia is for the West the Father of Monasticism and the patron of Europe. His monastic rule, known as the Rule of St. Benedict, was very widely practiced for centuries into the present day, and was the basis for many other future rules in the religious life. It laid important foundations for Western civilization through the institution of the monastery, which has provided so much to the learning and spirituality of Europe.

Born in Nursia in central Italy around the year 480, St. Benedict was sent as a young man for a classical education. When he was scandalized by the immorality of the students, he absconded to the mountainous wilderness of Subiaco to live as a hermit, supplied by a monk named Romanus with a monastic habit and periodically with bread. There, St. Benedict gained mastery over his passions and did battle with the evil one. Word spread of his miracles, though, and people began to come to him. He was sought out to become abbot at Vicovaro after its previous abbot died, but the monks despised him because of his strict reforms. They poisoned his drink, but when St. Benedict made the sign of the cross over it, the glass shattered, and their plot was revealed.

St. Benedict left Vicovaro and established twelve monasteries around Subiaco, and the power of God was with him. When one of the monks became distressed after the blade of his sickle flew off into a lake, St. Benedict prayed and dipped the handle into the water, and the heavy blade floated up to the surface and joined with the handle. Also, when two young boys, Brother Marus and his younger brother, Brother Placid, were entrusted to the monastery, Brother Placid fell into the water and began to drown. St. Benedict, who was praying at the time, raised his awareness to the situation, and at that very moment Brother Marus ran over to save Brother Placid. Brother Marus recalled later that he must have literally been able to run on top of the water, because Brother Placid was in the middle of the lake.

A local priest Florentinus became jealous of St. Benedict because so many people were flocking to him. He gave St. Benedict a poisoned loaf, but after he left, the saint called forth a raven to dispose of the loaf where it would not be eaten. Then Florentinus sent seven naked dancing girls to tempt the monks in their courtyard. For the good of his monks, St. Benedict determined to personally withdraw from Florentinus's area so he would leave them alone to pursue the path of holiness. Meanwhile, God chose to strike down Florentinus, and he was killed when his building collapsed around him.

St. Benedict went to Monte Casino, where he built a monastery on the mountaintop in place of an old temple to Apollo. There was no water source at the site, but at St. Benedict's prayers, a spring emerged to supply the monks' needs. Also, during the construction, a certain rock became strangely immovable, but it became docile after St. Benedict made the sign of the cross over it. Underneath was found a pagan idol, but the idol continued its mischief when the monks dug it out and temporarily brought it to the kitchen of the monastery. The room broke into flame, but at St. Benedict's approach, the flames disappeared. Later, when St. Benedict was praying, the devil came and told him he would harass the monks that day. Sure enough, one of the monks was killed, crushed during the construction of a wall. St. Benedict had the body brought to him, and through his prayers, the monk was restored right then to life and good strength.

King Totila, an Ostrogoth, heard of St. Benedict's wonders and came to visit him. He played a trick, dressing one of his courtiers as himself. When the imposter arrived with an entourage, St. Benedict immediately perceived that it was not the king. After having received word about this, the king himself came to St. Benedict, who proceeded to admonish the king to change his evil ways, foretelling that he would die in ten years. King Totila's biographer recalled that he did have somewhat of a change after that encounter, but also that he did die ten years later.

St. Benedict had a twin sister, St. Scholastica, who was an abbess of nuns and a holy woman. The twins visited with one another once a year, but near the end of their lives, they had one last encounter to meditate together on the glories of heaven. In the evening, St. Benedict insisted on returning home, in observance with the rule of the monastery. But St. Scholastica prayed, and a terrible storm began, making his trip home impossible. Thus, the twins spent the whole night conversing about the mysteries of God. After he was able to return to his monastery, St. Benedict saw the soul of his sister rising to heaven like a dove. He later foretold his own death, as well, even having his monks open his grave, though he seemed in good health. St. Benedict died at the appointed time, and two monks separately reported seeing a mystical staircase rising to heaven to make way for the saintly abbot.

St. Benedict's rule provided structure for monastic life in the West and guided many saints to holiness. The rule was written as a guide to achieving holiness within a communal life, leading its followers away from selfishness and toward charity and perfection under the guidance of a superior. The day's work was sanctified by the chanting of the liturgy of the hours at regular points. The rule was thus known for its balance of prayer and work—*ora et labora*.

Pope St. Gregory the Great leaves us with the primary account of St. Benedict's life. St. Benedict was proclaimed the copatron of Europe by Pope Paul VI in 1964, and Pope Benedict XVI selected his papal name in part after him. Many of the faithful continue to seek the protection of St. Benedict, especially with the St. Benedict medal, against the forces of evil. (For further reading, see: *The Life and Prayers of Saint Benedict* by Wyatt North.)

St. Benedict, pray for us!

St. Kateri Tekakwitha
Virgin, 1656–1680
Memorial (USA), July 14

St. Kateri Tekakwitha was a Native American who grew to high levels of sanctity despite having only a few helps in the faith and much opposition. Born in 1656 in the Iroquois village of Ossernenon in present-day upstate New York, she was the daughter of a captive Christian Algonquin woman and a Mohawk chief. Her birth came just ten years after the martyrdom of St. Isaac Jogues, S.J., and his companions in the same village. She was given the Mohawk name Tekakwitha, which means "she who trips over things." Her whole family was wiped out by a smallpox epidemic when she was four years old. Tekakwitha alone survived, but she was left badly scarred on her face, which she used to cover with a blanket.

Tekakwitha was raised, then, by her uncle, who was also a Mohawk chief. While she was still a young girl, her uncle tried to arrange for her marriage to a young boy, but she resisted. Though she was not yet a Christian, she had stirrings toward the faith as taught in the village by the Blackrobes, or the Jesuits. And though she did not know yet of the life of women religious, she had a desire to preserve her virginity for God. Her uncle strongly disapproved of her interest in Christianity, although treaties with the French required that all villages with Christian captives be supplied with a presence from the Blackrobes (Franciscan Media).

At the age of nineteen, and over the strong protests of her uncle, she was baptized on Easter Sunday, taking the name Kateri, the Mohawk variation of Catherine, after St. Catherine of Siena. Becoming a Christian greatly lowered her social status, and she was essentially reduced to slavery. Kateri was ordered to work on Sundays, but she refused and forfeited receiving any food for the day. Refusing marriage was looked upon with great ridicule and suspicion, and it would surely lead to poverty. She was accused of sorcery, and when she would go out to the woods to pray, she was eventually accused of ensconcing with a young man.

266

Kateri escaped to a community of Christian native peoples at Kahnawake on the St. Lawrence River in Quebec, south of Montreal, some two hundred miles away. She arrived with a letter of recommendation from her priest, saying, "I ask you to please take charge of directing her; it is a treasure which we are giving you. Guard it well and make it bear fruit for the glory of God and the salvation of a soul which is certainly very dear to Him" (kateritekakwitha.net). At Kahnawake, Kateri received her Frist Communion and grew under wise direction from a priest and an old Christian woman. Learning of religious life in Montreal, Kateri had a desire to join, but she was advised to stay as she was. Kateri had long practiced harsh penances and grew weak in her body. Finally succumbing to illness, she died at the age of twenty-four. But before she passed on, her worn-out face shone with peace. The scars from the smallpox vanished, and she smiled gently. Healings and miracles were attributed to her from very early after her death. The cause for her canonization was opened by the American bishops in 1884. Beatified in 1980, St. Kateri Tekakwitha was finally canonized in 2012. She is the patron saint of ecology, the environment, people in exile, and Native Americans. She is honored with a memorial in the United States on July 14 and on April 17 in Canada.

St. Kateri Tekakwitha, pray for us!

St. Bonaventure
Bishop and Doctor of the Church, 1221–1274
Memorial, July 15

The holy and learned St. Bonaventure, known as the Seraphic Doctor, was an early Franciscan mystic, theologian, writer, administrator, and cardinal. Born in 1221 in Bagnoregio in central Italy, he was christened as John. As a young child, he became ill to the point of death. His miraculous healing was attributed to the intercession of St. Francis. By some accounts, John's mother took him to St. Francis and begged for her son to be healed. In young adulthood, sometime after St. Francis's death, John joined the new Franciscan Order and took the name Bonaventure, meaning "good fortune," perhaps looking back to his healing in childhood through St. Francis's prayers.

Bonaventure studied under the great Franciscan scholar Alexander of Hales, who helped him attain mastery of the Church Fathers and the scholastic theology of the current day with its focus on disputed questions. Bonaventure, a natural genius, excelled greatly in his studies, though he never strayed from humility. He focused in his theology on what was edifying to the soul and set aside anything of worldly hubris. He is said to have often gazed on a crucifix displaying the five wounds of Christ. One day he explained his approach to theology to St. Thomas Aquinas, a colleague at the University of Paris: "This is the source of all my knowledge. I study only Jesus Christ, and him crucified" (*Butler's Lives*). When he was awarded the degree of doctorate along with the Dominican scholar St. Thomas Aquinas, the two vied for leaving the place of greater honor for the other.

With good instruction from his mother, St. Bonaventure practiced piety and penance from a young age, and this kept him on the path for spiritual greatness (*Butler's Lives*). He also attended to the sick himself, even the more repugnant cases. Alexander of Hales said Bonaventure seemed as if unstained by the sin of Adam. Still, he considered himself unworthy and a great sinner. Before his ordination to the priesthood, he even kept himself from approaching the altar for Communion until an angel appeared and brought him the sacred Host miraculously. He then received Communion regularly with extraordinary joy. Bonaventure taught, "A spiritual joy is the greatest sign of the divine grace dwelling in a soul" (*Butler's Lives*). Later, and after careful spiritual preparation, he accepted ordination to the priesthood.

Bonaventure taught at his convent until he was awarded a professorship at the University of Paris upon the death of his mentor, John of Rochelle. The age requirement of thirty-five was waived for him; Bonaventure was thirty-three. He became known to King St. Louis of France, who brought him into his court for counsel and asked him to write a devotional book for him on Christ's Passion. At the age of thirty-five, Bonaventure was elected minister-general of the Friars Minor (the Franciscans). This came at a pivotal time in the order. There was much controversy at this time over how to practice Francis's commitment to simplicity and poverty, even while the order was increasing greatly in numbers and responsibilities. Bonaventure brought peace and compromise as best he could. He also sent out Franciscan missionaries to preach the Gospel to new lands and also oversaw the enshrining of the relics of St. Clare and St. Anthony.

Bonaventure became the official biographer of St. Francis, compiling the stories of his life and explaining their meaning. Providing an authoritative biography was important, because there were some who were misrepresenting Francis at the time and were falling into heresy. This was troublesome, not only for the Church, but also for the integrity of the Franciscan Order. Once St. Thomas Aquinas came to visit St. Bonaventure while he was writing the *Life of St. Francis*. Bonaventure was in ecstasy and was levitating above the ground. Aquinas said, "Let us leave a saint to write for a saint" (*Butler's Lives*). Bonaventure was also said to be in ecstasy while writing *The Journey of the Mind into God.* Though Bonaventure's path was through theology and learning, he did not consider that necessary for all. He wrote of St. Francis in his *Life of St. Francis*, "...albeit he had no instruction or learning in the sacred writings—yet, illuminated by the beams of eternal light, he searched the deep things of the Scriptures with marvelous intellectual discernment. For his genius, pure from all stain, penetrated into the hidden places of the mysteries, and, where the learning of a theologian tarrieth without, the feelings of the lover led him in" (XI, 1).

St. Bonaventure had both the feelings of the lover and the learning of a theologian. He did theological reflection on the experience of St. Francis, putting words to the mystery contained there. Francis saw all creation as one under God's fatherly care. For Bonaventure, all creation is symbolic of God and expresses Him. St. Francis spoke of "Brother Sun" and "Sister Moon." Bonaventure spoke of there being vestiges, or footsteps, of God seen in animals, plants, and rocks. Francis saw Christ in the leper and the poor. In scriptural terms, Bonaventure spoke of the human soul as being created in the image of God. Being in the image of God is marked for Bonaventure by being endowed with natural illumination; thus, for him, even our natural reason is inseparable from God. Francis, though, was granted special light, and this came, in Bonaventure's theology, from a higher illumination—the one that comes from our calling to be in not just the image, but also the likeness of God.

Toward the end of his life, Bonaventure was named as a cardinal and made bishop of Albano, near Rome. He was found outside Florence and was washing the dishes when the papal envoy arrived. Bonaventure could not immediately take the cardinal's hat from them with his hands, so he had them place it on the bough of a tree until he could properly come out. Soon afterward, Pope Gregory X ordained Bonaventure a bishop and called him to speak at the Second Council of Lyons, which he did. St. Thomas Aquinas, however, died during the journey to the council. Several months after Aquinas's passing, Bonaventure died, as well, on July 15, 1274, during his stay in Lyons for the council.

Together with St. Thomas Aquinas, Bonaventure was proclaimed Doctor of the Church in 1587 because of the significance of his writings for the Church. He was given the title of Seraphic Doctor, after the seraphs, the angels closest to God who burn with His love. A commentator writes of Bonaventure, "His expressions are full of fire, they no less warm with divine love the hearths of those who read them, than they fill their understanding with the most holy light" (Trithemius in *Butler's Lives*).

St. Bonaventure, pray for us!

St. Mary Magdalene
First Century
Feast, July 22

In the East called "Apostle to the Apostles," St. Mary Magdalene was the first witness to the Resurrection and the first to announce it to the Apostles. She had been a faithful disciple for some time, after having had seven demons driven out from her by Jesus.

Mary is likely from the town of Magdala in Galilee. She is mentioned by name in all four gospels, indicating that she was a significant and known disciple. Divergent understandings of Mary Magdalene's life have developed over the centuries, but the gospels do provide us with some plain facts about her life. From the gospel of Luke, we find that there were a number of women disciples who had been "cured of evil spirits and infirmities" (Luke 8:2). As Jesus went about with His disciples, these women "provided for them out of their resources" (Luke 8:3). Mary Magdalene, we are told, is one "from whom seven demons had gone out" (Luke 8:2).

Being that Mary Magdalene once had "seven demons," it seems likely that she had a "past," but the gospels do not plainly tell us what it was. Mary Magdalene has often been considered to be the sinful woman who anointed the feet of Jesus at the house of Simon the Pharisee at Bethany, as recounted in the synoptic gospels. Western Fathers tended to see the sinful woman and Mary Magdalene as one and the same, while Eastern Fathers saw them as different women from the beginning (*New Advent*). A loose textual argument can be made to support the Western tradition that she was this woman, because Luke's account of the story is followed by his introduction of the women disciples, including Mary Magdalene. Most scholars today, however, believe that the two women are distinct. Some people today even look to Mary Magdalene as a saint for those who suffer from false rumors, on the assumption that she has been misrepresented by history. Either way, Mary Magdalene is a model of one who wholeheartedly accepted Christ's invitation to redemption from the domain of the devil.

St. Thérèse of the Child Jesus, however, assuming Mary Magdalene to be the sinful woman who anointed the feet of Jesus, looked to her in that way as a model of repentance and love. Although St. Thérèse's confessor assured her that she herself had never committed a mortal sin, St. Thérèse struggled to love Jesus as much or more than Mary Magdalene. Jesus had said of the sinful woman who anointed His feet, "Her many sins have been forgiven; hence, she has shown great love. But the one to whom little is forgiven, loves little" (Luke 7:47). St. Thérèse reflected that perhaps, even though she had not committed great sins, she had been forgiven even more than the Magdalene, since she had been preserved by Jesus from more serious sins. St. Thérèse writes, "He wishes me to love Him, because He has forgiven me, not much, but everything. Without waiting for me to love Him much, as St. Mary Magdalen did, He has made me understand how He has loved me with an ineffable love and forethought, so that now my love may know no bounds" (*Story of a Soul*, Ch. 4).

Mary Magdalene's love for Jesus was great and not concerned for self. While most of the disciples abandoned Jesus at His crucifixion, Mark and John tell us that Mary Magdalene was one of the few women who remained with Him. This also makes her a witness of His death. Mark also tells us she was a witness to His burial (Mark 15:47). Though the witness of women was not as readily accepted in the first century, Jesus apparently chose Mary Magdalene as the one most fitting to whom to first reveal His Resurrection. Mark mentions her as the first witness of the Resurrection (Mark 16:1), and John recalls the encounter in detail, as follows.

In John's account, Mary Magdalene went to the tomb, weeping, early in the morning, but was greeted by two angels and then by Jesus, whom she thought to be the gardener: "Jesus said to her, 'Woman, why are you weeping? Whom are you looking for?' She thought it was the gardener and said to him, 'Sir, if you carried him away, tell me where you laid him, and I will take him.' Jesus said to her, 'Mary!' She turned and said to him in Hebrew, 'Rabbouni,' which means Teacher. Jesus said to her, 'Stop holding on to me, for I have not yet ascended to the Father. But go to my brothers and tell them, "I am going to my Father and your Father, to my God and your God."' Mary of Magdala went and announced to the disciples, 'I have seen the Lord,' and what he told her" (John 20:11–18).

Reflecting on this passage, Pope Francis says, "It is as she is stooping near the tomb, her eyes filled with tears, that God surprises her in the most unexpected way. John the Evangelist stresses how persistent her blindness is. She does not notice the presence of the two angels who question her, and she does not become suspicious even when she sees the man behind her, whom she believes is the custodian of the garden. Instead, she discovers the most overwhelming event in the history of mankind when she is finally called by her name: 'Mary!'" (General Audience, 05/17/17, Vatican.va).

In 2016, during the Year of Mercy, Pope Francis elevated the memorial of St. Mary Magdalene to a feast, which is an honor reserved to the Apostles and those saints closely connected with salvation history. He presented her as an example of how God uses women in the work of evangelization and as a messenger of God's hope and forgiveness to the world.

Among other traditional areas of veneration, St. Mary Magdalene is the patron saint of penitents.

St. Mary Magdalene, pray for us!

St. James (the Greater)
Apostle, First Century
Feast, July 25

St. James the Greater had the privilege of being chosen by Christ to be one of the Twelve, as well as a part of a more intimate circle around the Master. St. James the Greater, not to be confused with St. James the Lesser, who was also an Apostle, was the brother of the Apostle John. James was probably older than John, because he was always listed first. They were the sons of Zebedee, a Galilean fisherman who had enough business that we are told he had hired assistants.

Jesus called James and John from their father's fishing boat on the Sea of Galilee, and they immediately left the nets and followed him (Mark 1:19–20). Jesus nicknamed the brothers "sons of thunder," because of their fiery demeanor. Jesus rebuked the sons of Zebedee when they wanted to call down fire upon an unrepentant Samarian town (Luke 9:54). He also rebuked them when they asked for the privilege of sitting at His left and right in His kingdom (Mark 10:35–40).

Together with their fishing partner, Peter, James and John made up another inner circle within the Twelve. Jesus called them to come alone with Him for important moments, such as the Transfiguration and the Agony in the Garden. James's ministry ended quickly, as he was the first Apostle to be martyred. We learn in the Acts of the Apostles that Herod, in an early persecution of the Christians, had James put to death by the sword (Acts 12:2).

The cathedral in Santiago de Compostela in Spain claims to house his remains, which were discovered in the ninth century. For centuries, it has been a popular pilgrim destination, at the end of hundreds of miles of trails on the *Camino de Santiago,* also known as the Way of St. James. St. James is the patron saint of pilgrims and of Spain.

St. James the Greater, pray for us!

Sts. Joachim and Anne
Parents of the Blessed Virgin Mary,
First Century B.C.
Memorial, July 26

Sts. Joachim and Anne, a sainted married couple, are venerated in the Church as the parents of the Immaculate Virgin Mary, and thus the grandparents of our Lord Jesus Christ. Though Sts. Joachim and Anne are not mentioned in Scripture, it can be assumed that a completely sinless child must have come from holy parents. If God preserved the Blessed Virgin Mary from the stain of Original Sin and kept her free of sin throughout her life, He must have also graced her childhood with special gifts. From early times, the couple has been venerated within the Church.

Apocryphal sources, though rejected from Scripture by the early Fathers and the Church, speculated on the lives of Mary's parents and provide us with a possible narrative for them. The accounts may be more pious legend than fact, but they tell a story of a faithful but childless couple that finally received the gift of a special child, whom they dedicated to God. The stories, which are similar to each other in the various apocryphal accounts, seem to be modeled on various Bible stories, and especially that of the birth of the prophet Samuel.

According to the apocryphal *Protoevangelium* of James, written in the second century, Sts. Joachim and Anne lived in Nazareth, where they were well off. Once, when Joachim went to Jerusalem for a feast, he was turned away from offering sacrifice to the Lord because he had no child and was thus thought to be cursed. He cried out to the Lord, going into the desert to fast for forty days and forty nights. His wife, Anne, or in Hebrew, Hannah, likewise cried out to the Lord and went into mourning. Chided by her handmaid, Anne put aside her clothes of mourning and put on a wedding garment as a sign of faith. She prayed a lamentation to the Lord, who heard her and sent the angel Gabriel to announce the good news. The Angel Gabriel said to her, "Anna, Anna, the Lord hath heard thy prayer, and thou shalt conceive, and shall bring forth; and thy seed shall be spoken of in all the world" (*Protoevangelium* of James, no. 4). Anne promised to dedicate the child to God, regardless of whether it would be male or female. Then the angel Gabriel went to Joachim and told him the same news. Joachim rejoiced and took ten female lambs from his flocks and sacrificed them to the Lord.

Anne conceived a daughter, Mary, who grew wonderfully and filled her parents' hearts with joy. At the age of only six months, the child Mary walked seven steps to her mother's bosom. Anne picked her up, held her to her heart, and said, "As the Lord my God liveth, thou shall not walk on this earth until I bring thee into the temple of the Lord" (no. 6). They brought her to the Temple to be blessed by the high priest and offered to God. They waited, however, until she was three before leaving her to be raised in the Temple. They set the child Mary on the steps of the Temple, and she did not turn back as a child normally would. We read of the child Mary: "The Lord sent grace upon her; and she danced with her feet, and all the house of Israel loved her" (no. 7). She is said to have remained in the Temple until she was betrothed to Joseph. According to the legendary account in the *Protoevangelium* of James, the priests selected Joseph the carpenter to be Mary's husband, praying and then choosing him by lots. Rods were used as lots, and a dove is said to have emerged from Joseph's rod.

These specific accounts are not factually sure, but what we do know is that God blessed and guided the parents of the Blessed Virgin Mary, the grandparents of Jesus. Today in Québec, St. Anne is honored most famously with the Shrine of St. Anne de Beauprès, where she is credited with many miracles.

Sts. Joachim and Anne, pray for us!

St. Martha
First Century
Memorial, July 29

Martha, together with her sister, Mary, and her brother, Lazarus, who lived at Bethany, were friends of Jesus. According to John's gospel, "Jesus loved Martha and her sister and Lazarus" (John 11:5). Martha is also mentioned by name in the gospel of Luke. She is known for her hospitality to Jesus and for her faith in the resurrection on the last day.

According to Luke's gospel, "As they continued their journey he entered a village where a woman whose name was Martha welcomed him" (Luke 10:38). Martha was very attentive to making preparations for the Master, but her sister, Mary, "sat beside the Lord at his feet listening to him speak" (Luke 10:39). Luke continues: "Martha, burdened with much serving, came to him and said, 'Lord, do you not care that my sister has left me by myself to do the serving? Tell her to help me'" (Luke 10:40). Jesus replied, "Martha, Martha, you are anxious and worried about many things. There is need of only one thing. Mary has chosen the better part and it will not be taken from her" (Luke 10:41–42).

Jesus did not rebuke Martha for serving, but for wanting Mary to serve, too, at a time when she needed to listen to His words. Martha and Mary later came to be understood to be symbolic of the two main types of religious life, namely active and contemplative life. Those who are active in service must be concerned for many things, but those who are contemplative have chosen the better part. Both, however, are needed. Most people, in fact, must be more like Martha than Mary, because life requires it of them.

Martha was a person of great faith. When their brother, Lazarus, became seriously ill, "the sisters sent word to him, saying, 'Master, the one you love is ill'" (John 11:3). Jesus remained where He was for two days, and meanwhile Lazarus died. Jesus went to Bethany, and this dialogue between Jesus and Martha ensued:

When Martha heard that Jesus was coming, she went to meet him; but Mary sat at home. Martha said to Jesus, "Lord, if you had been here, my brother would not have died. [But] even now I know that whatever you ask of God, God will give you." Jesus said to her, "Your brother will rise." Martha said to him, "I know he will rise, in the resurrection on the last day." Jesus told her, "I am the resurrection and the life; whoever believes in me, even if he dies, will live, and everyone who lives and believes in me will never die. Do you believe this?" She said to him, "Yes, Lord. I have come to believe that you are the Messiah, the Son of God, the one who is coming into the world" (John 11:20–27).

Jesus sent for Mary, and they went with all those mourning to the tomb of Lazarus. Jesus wept over Lazarus, in a genuine realization of human loss, but then ordered that the stone be removed from the tomb. John continues:

So Jesus, perturbed again, came to the tomb. It was a cave, and a stone lay across it. Jesus said, "Take away the stone." Martha, the dead man's sister, said to him, "Lord, by now there will be a stench; he has been dead for four days." Jesus said to her, "Did I not tell you that if you believe you will see the glory of God?" So they took away the stone. And Jesus raised his eyes and said, "Father, I thank you for hearing me. I know that you always hear me; but because of the crowd here I have said this, that they may believe that you sent me." And when he had said this, he cried out in a loud voice, "Lazarus, come out!" The dead man came out, tied hand and foot with burial bands, and his face was wrapped in a cloth. So Jesus said to them, "Untie him and let him go" (John 11:38–44).

About a week before His passion and death, Jesus came to Bethany again, which was on the Mount of Olives, to visit Martha, Mary, and Lazarus (John 12:1–11). Mary anointed Jesus' feet with costly oil, presumably in thanksgiving for the raising of her brother, Lazarus. Martha again was busy serving the Master and the guests, but she did not disturb Mary from sitting at the Master's feet and pouring out the costly oil upon Him. This time, Judas Iscariot, who was soon to betray Jesus, objected to the costliness of the oil, wishing he could have stolen the money if it had been given over for distribution to the poor. Jesus said to him, "Leave her alone. Let her keep this for the day of my burial. You always have the poor with you, but you do not always have me" (John 12:7–8).

St. Martha is venerated as the patron saint of cooks, housewives, servants, and waiters and waitresses (francsicanmedia.org).

St. Martha, pray for us!

St. Ignatius of Loyola
Priest, 1491–1556
Memorial, July 31

St. Ignatius of Loyola was born in the castle of Loyola in Spain to noble parents. His father was the lord of Ognez and Loyola. Ignatius, or Inigo, was raised in the king's court to one day become a military officer. Though familiar with religion, he was not focused so much on pleasing God as pleasing his fellows. He was a youth of gallantry. His inclinations were generally good, though he was beset spiritually with some vice.

He tasted a degree of military success, but the army came to be greatly outnumbered by the French in Navarre in 1521. When the citadel was abandoned, Ignatius took up a position there to secure honor despite the inevitability of defeat. The French closed in, but Ignatius kept them at bay with maneuvers of his sword. He was taken down at last when his leg was badly injured by the blast and a ricochet from a nearby cannonball explosion. His men surrendered, and Ignatius was carried off as a prisoner of war. Though treated well, his leg was poorly and hastily set. It had to be reset, and Ignatius endured the pain, choosing not even to be held down. He was still impaired, however, and a protruding bone would make wearing tights unseemly, so he elected for yet another painful procedure in which part of the bone would have to be sawn off. He endured bravely despite the excruciating pain, but he was soon overcome with a fever and was thought to be near the end. He prayed to Sts. Peter and Paul, whose feast day it was, and he received a dream of St. Peter bringing him healing, and so it happened.

While recovering at the castle of Loyola, Ignatius asked for books on romance. None could be found, so he was given a book on Jesus and the lives of the saints. He was moved by the stories and inspired by their holy valor. Accustomed to boasting and to competing with the gallantries he would read about in books, he thought to compete with the extreme fasting and fortitude of the saints. It was the beginning of a change in him, but it was not final. On the one hand, he sought to pursue the hand of a certain lady in marriage, and on the other to radically pursue a life of penance in the Holy Land like the hermits of old. Developing what would become his Spiritual Exercises, he became aware of how these two impulses led him. The thought of gallantry gave him a sense of momentary pleasure, while the thought of radical holiness gave him an enduring peace. He chose the latter.

He took to the extreme to pursue holiness, imposing on himself very harsh penances and fasts and praying as much as seven hours a day. He visited the famed monastery of Monserrat, a community of monks set on the crags of a mountainside and a Marian apparition site, and there hung up his sword before an image of the Blessed Virgin. He ate very little and wept at great length for his sins. Ignatius let his hair and nails grow out so that he became a laughingstock, and yet he accepted this as a penance and to grow closer to God. Now and then, however, people would see the great spiritual wisdom that was growing in him.

Ignatius went through an intense period of scrupulosity, during which time he did not feel forgiven for his sins, nor did he feel that he had even confessed them properly. He was pressed to the brink of despair and refused even to eat, hoping to die. Ignatius began eating a week later at the command of his spiritual director, and he was then filled with great peace of soul, which brought an end to his scrupulosity.

Desiring very much to go to the Holy Land and live there like Christ and the early hermits, he set off on foot for Venice to set sail for the Holy Land. On board the ship, the sailors wanted to drop him off on a deserted island since he had been exhorting them so strongly to change their ways, but they were prevented from landing. Ultimately, the ship disembarked in Joppa, and he walked four days from there to Jerusalem.

Visiting the holy sites filled him with fervor, which he ever cultivated. He desired to stay in the Holy Land, but the Church authorities would not allow him to do so. So, after ensconcing twice back to his favorite site on the Mount of Olives to see Christ's footprint, he began the long journey back to Europe.

Ignatius would catechize children, turn sinners away from the path of destruction, and give people spiritual advice. Twice, he was briefly imprisoned, suspected of heresy, since he had no recognized qualifications to teach the faith. Not content to please Jesus by himself, Ignatius burst with desire that Jesus be known and loved by others, as well. In prayer, he would sigh, "O my God! O my Lord! O that men knew thee!" (*Butler's Lives*).

So, he began to take care of his appearance—not for vainglory, as he had in his youth, but for God's glory—and to pursue an education that would lead to the priesthood. At first, he had to embrace the humiliation of being in classes with young boys, studying the basics of Latin and enduring their mockery. Later, he took up studies at the University of Paris. He continued his arduous life of prayer and penance and performed works of charity for the sick—even those with infectious diseases. His peculiar but sincere ways led to his having followers. His detractors, however, sent bad reports about him to the administration, and he was summoned for a public beating. Ignatius explained his case to the administrator. The administrator led him out for the beating, but instead proclaimed Ignatius's innocence to the student body and begged his forgiveness.

Ignatius desired to turn sinners back from their ways. Once, when a man was on his way to see a prostitute, Ignatius waded completely into a frigid pond and called out to the man that he was doing penance so that he would turn from his ways. Later, in Rome, after he had founded his order, Ignatius set up a refuge for prostitutes who wanted to turn from their ways. Some warned him that many of them might not be sincere, but he said it was worth the trouble even if he could prevent just one sin. He also set up a refuge for poor girls who were vulnerable to be taken into prostitution.

Ignatius celebrated his first Mass as a priest in 1538. After receiving approval from the pope for ordination along with several other companions, he chose to spend many months in preparation for his first Mass. He wept greatly at his first Mass to receive such a high honor.

Ignatius and his followers, including St. Francis Xavier, formed the Society of Jesus, or the Company of Jesus. The name meant they were soldiers for Christ. They were later pejoratively called Jesuits—a name they came to embrace. The Jesuits professed their first vows at the chapel of Montmartre in Paris in 1534. Later, they went to the pope, who heard them favorably, even though it seemed to him that there were too many religious orders at the time. They wanted to become a new type of order that was sent out for mission work. In addition to the usual vows of poverty, chastity, and obedience, they took a fourth vow, to go wherever the pope should send them. The need was great, in light of the recent Protestant Reformation and the opening up of new territories abroad for mission work. Jesuits underwent rigorous training and formation and were dedicated to combatting ignorance and heresy through Catholic education. They were ultimately recognized as an order in 1540. Their motto was *Ad majorem Dei gloriam*, or "to the greater glory of God."

At the request of the king of Portugal, the pope desired to send ten men to India from the Jesuits, but there were only seven Jesuits at the start. Ignatius sent two men, including St. Francis Xavier, who became the apostle to India. The Jesuits, however, grew quickly in numbers, and many others were sent out to new lands. When they went, he would tell them, "Go, brethren, inflame the world, spread about that fire which Jesus Christ came to kindle on earth" (*Butler's Lives*). Popes also sent for the Jesuits to take part in the Council of Trent. They wanted to elevate them to higher positions in the Church, but Ignatius insisted that Jesuits refuse such offices except at the insistence of the pope, in order to better pursue humility.

By the time of Ignatius's death in 1556, the Jesuits had grown to require twelve provinces, had established one hundred colleges, and had brought the Gospel with great success to new lands. Since that day, they have brought forth innumerable saints for the Church and today make up the largest Catholic religious order. St. Ignatius is the patron saint of the Society of Jesus, soldiers, and educators.

Suscipe Prayer of St. Ignatius

> *Receive, O Lord, all my liberty, my memory, my understanding, and my whole will. You have given me all that I have, all that I possess, and I surrender all to your divine will, that you dispose of me. Give me only your love, and your grace. With this I am rich enough, and I have no more to ask* (Butler's Lives).

St. Ignatius of Loyola, pray for us!

LIVES OF THE SAINTS
VOLUME III (AUGUST – SEPTEMBER)

Michael J. Ruszala

Foreword

Is Christianity true or holiness possible? The saints give witness through the authenticity of their lives. From every land, from every race, and from every vocation, holy men and women, young and old, have lit the path to the fullness of the Christian calling. The Church lifts up their example for all to see what God can do in one's life.

According to the Second Vatican Council, everyone is called to holiness, whether they are clergy or are served by them (*Lumen Gentium,* no. 39). In his 26 years as pope, St. John Paul II canonized some 482 saints. He further beatified 1,327 persons, in the final step before sainthood. Pope Benedict XVI and Pope Francis have continued to raise up many new saints as well.

John Paul II encouraged the crowds at World Youth Day in 2000, "Young people of every continent, do not be afraid to be the saints of the new millennium! Be contemplative, love prayer; be coherent with your faith and generous in the service of your brothers and sisters, be active members of the Church and builders of peace. To succeed in this demanding project of life, continue to listen to His Word, draw strength from the Sacraments, especially the Eucharist and Penance. The Lord wants you to be intrepid apostles of his Gospel and builders of a new humanity."

The saints show us that no matter who we are, where we're from, or what we've done, we are called to greatness and holiness, if only we open our hearts fully to God.

Introduction

How does one become a saint? According to Catholic theology, it starts with God and his plan. Each person is created with a plan, and that plan involves becoming a saint, though not everyone chooses to live fully for God. A saint, in the general sense, means any of the blessed in Heaven. It comes from the Latin word *sanctus*, which means 'holy.' To be holy is to be pure and good.

Yet it is not simply the purity and goodness of a child, but one that is full and mature and works with God's grace. This is virtue. Virtue comes from the Latin word *virtus*, which means 'strength.' Some children and adolescents have attained it, though some adults never have.

Morally good habits of the soul are called virtues. The foundational virtues, known as the cardinal virtues, are prudence, temperance, justice, and fortitude. These are natural virtues, but the higher, supernatural (higher than nature) virtues given by God's grace presuppose them.

'Grace' comes from the Latin word *gratia,* which means 'free,' referring to God's free gift. 'Grace' is a word used in translation from the New Testament. Actual grace refers to God moving a person to draw near to himself. Its purpose is to make way for sanctifying grace. Sanctifying grace is God's gift within the soul that makes the soul holy and pleasing to him. It is necessary for Heaven.

The gateway to the sacraments, and thus the ordinary way of first receiving sanctifying grace, is baptism. This is why many of the saints revered their baptism in various ways. It is the sacrament that makes one a child of God. All the other sacraments build upon and presuppose it.

In baptism, the soul is infused with the most basic and necessary supernatural virtues. These are called the theological virtues because they have God for their object. They are faith, hope, and charity (1 Cor. 13:13). Faith is in God and what he has revealed; hope is in his promise of Heaven; and charity is love for God above all and for our neighbor as ourselves. The greatest virtue is love, or charity, because it remains even in Heaven and all of the other virtues are ordered to it.

Sacraments, or signs from Christ that effect grace, further the life of holiness and make it possible. Confirmation strengthens the grace of baptism. Reconciliation can restore sanctifying grace lost through serious sin and always brings actual grace to do better. The Eucharist nourishes the soul and brings it closer to Christ.

In his Sermon on the Mount, Jesus gives eight Beatitudes for those who are pleasing to God:

Blessed are the poor in spirit,
for theirs is the kingdom of heaven.

Blessed are they who mourn,

for they will be comforted.

Blessed are the meek,

for they will inherit the land.

Blessed are they who hunger and thirst for
righteousness,

for they will be satisfied.

Blessed are the merciful,

for they will be shown mercy.

Blessed are the clean of heart,

for they will see God.

Blessed are the peacemakers,

for they will be called children of God.

Blessed are they who are persecuted for the sake of
righteousness,

for theirs is the kingdom of heaven.

Blessed are you when they insult you and persecute you and utter every kind of evil against you [falsely] because of me.

Rejoice and be glad, for your reward will be great in heaven. Thus they persecuted the prophets who were before you. (Mt. 5:3–12)

Moreover, one who lives the Christian virtues displays certain signs, called the fruits of the Spirit, which are listed in Scripture as "love, joy, peace, patience, kindness, generosity, faithfulness, gentleness, self-control" (Gal. 5:22–23).

Some Christians have become so thoroughly converted from ordinary selfishness to a life in Christ that they don't just demonstrate the virtues consistently; they live them out heroically. The Church recognizes some of these people and raises them up as saints. It only does this after they have finished their earthly life.

In the early Church, saints were simply recognized by the people and then by their leaders. Martyrs who died for the true faith had clearly given all and, thus, were saints. Other holy religious leaders came to be recognized as such by the people after their death, even if they had not died as martyrs. Ultimately, it was up to the bishop to grant a holy person the honors of the altar for which the people called. By the end of the first millennium, in order to standardize the process, the pope reserved to himself the right to canonize saints.

Today, the process begins in the diocese of the holy person. People bring a petition to the local bishop to investigate the life of a holy person. The bishop can grant this person the status of Servant of God. Then the cause can be taken to the Vatican's Congregation for the Causes of Saints. Upon favorable review, they give the person the title of Venerable.

The next step is for the pope to beatify the person, granting them the title of Blessed. Unless they were confirmed to be a martyr, this follows a miracle confirmed by the Vatican. Upon verification of a second miracle, the pope may canonize the person, or declare them a saint. The saint is proposed to all the faithful for emulation and veneration, as a sign of the glory of God's work in them. The faithful may also pray for their intercession. Given the belief in the Communion of Saints and the effectiveness of the prayers of the just, the faithful essentially ask the saints in Heaven to pray to God on their behalf.

Saints are often assigned to a traditional category. Some are designated as martyrs for giving up their life specifically for the faith. Others are designated as confessors as a result of being imprisoned for the faith. Some are designated as religious (such as brothers or sisters, monks or nuns), who follow the Evangelical Counsels (essentially, the 'advice of the Gospels') of poverty, chastity, and obedience. Some are abbots and abbesses, who were leaders of men or women religious. The clergy are listed among the deacons, priests, bishops, archbishops, and popes. Some saints are designated as virgins because they remained faithful in consecrating their virginity to God. Some are given the distinct honor of being declared doctors of the Church for their extraordinary defense or explanation of Church teaching, and some are remembered as apostles. Other saints are unique and fit into none of these traditional categories, but are nonetheless raised in their own right to the honors of the altar.

St. Alphonsus Mary Liguori
Bishop and Doctor of the Church, 1696–1787
Memorial, Aug. 1

St. Alphonsus Liguori, doctor of the Church and patron of confessors and moral theologians, is remembered for his sound moral teaching and for founding the Redemptorist order. He was born outside Naples in 1696 into the noble Liguori family. Alphonsus' father was a captain of the royal galleys and was married to a Spanish woman. His parents were devout, and he used to attend retreats with his father. Alphonsus' father had him schooled at home by tutors and also had him trained in harpsichord. His father had designs for him to become a lawyer. Alphonsus was very intelligent, talented, and passionate, and pursued legal studies with enthusiasm.

By election, he was awarded his doctorate in law from the University of Naples at the mere age of 16, though the minimum age was set to 20. He began practicing law at the age of 19 and continued practicing for several years without losing a case. At last, when he did lose a case in 1723 because he had overlooked a document, it was a very important case. Alphonsus was very much affected by this loss. Alphonsus was afraid that his oversight would be considered dishonest.

Until this point, Alphonsus, though a good person, was rather worldly. He used to attend parties and the theater, but now he was confronted with the fact that God was calling him to a higher standard. He considered the transitory nature of the world and began to fast and pray for what God wanted him to do.

Alphonsus visited the Hospital of the Incurables, as he was sometimes accustomed to doing, and there was given a mystical experience. He was surrounded by a great light and heard a voice say, "Leave the world and give thyself to Me" (*New Advent*).

Alphonsus hung up his sword before a statue of Our Lady. Though concerned about what his father would think, he resolved to become a priest, and his father finally consented. In 1726, he was ordained a deacon and then a priest. He became known as an excellent preacher and retreat-master. Three years later, he took up residence with Fr. Matthew Ripa, who had returned from missionary work in China and founded a college in Naples for missionaries to be sent to China. Though Fr. Liguori did not join his order, he developed a friendship there with an older priest named Fr. Thomas Falcoia, of the Congregation of Pious Works, who became very influential for him.

Fr. Liguori became interested in founding a new religious order, and Fr. Falcoia had likewise been trying to found one for both nuns and priests. One of the sisters in the convent connected with Fr. Falcoia—a novice named Sister Maria Celeste—had visions about the founding of a new order, which served as confirmation for this endeavor. A rule for the order was also revealed to her that was, essentially, what Fr. Falcoia already had in mind. Fr. Falcoia had it approved on theological grounds, but he encountered resistance from the community in adopting it. Fr. Falcoia was then appointed Bishop of Castellamare and left Fr. Liguori with the foundation of the new order. Fr. Liguori was able to secure a unanimous approval of the new rule by the convent in 1731, and the order was established in 1732 as the Congregation of the Most Holy Redeemer, who came to be known as the Redemptorists.

Much contention arose in the new order, however. There was dissension again over the rule among the priests and the nuns, and opposition to Fr. Liguori and Bishop Falcoia. Even Blessed Sister Maria Celeste left the order to found a new convent, but Fr. Liguori persevered for the rest of his days to support his new order, despite the continued controversies. Approval from Rome for the men's and women's congregations finally came in 1749 and 1750, respectively.

Fr. Liguori traveled about central Italy preaching missions, which is a key ministry of the Redemptorists. He was very faithful to his work, even vowing not to waste a single hour. He also established several houses for the Redemptorists.

One difficulty was that the various kingdoms in Italy had anticlerical policies and tried to force the new order to be secular rather than religious—that is, not to take the religious vows of poverty, chastity, and obedience. Some of the houses became rebellious to Fr. Liguori. In his old age in 1780, some within his order even tricked him into submitting his rule for approval to the government, who delayed and altered it. With some of the houses becoming rebellious, the pope allowed them to split off from his order and, thus, from his governance. Though the Redemptorist order thrives to the present day, the state of his order during his lifetime was a source of suffering for him.

Fr. Liguori also served as a teacher of theology and is especially remembered for his work in moral theology. It seems he gravitated to that field because of his formation as a lawyer. Fr. Liguori left us, too, with numerous books. During his day, there was a debate between moral theologians who were either too rigorous or too lax. Fr. Liguori took the middle course, offering his theory of 'Equiprobabilism.' Whereas Probablism asserted that one could opt for even the lesser argument, Fr. Liguori's Equiprobablism taught that the two arguments must at least be equally probable. Acting according to a lesser argument simply because it is convenient is morally wrong. His teachings became helpful to priests counseling penitents in the confessional.

In 1762, Fr. Liguori was made bishop of St. Agatha of the Goths, a small diocese outside of Naples that was in need of reform. Bishop Liguori instituted reforms of the seminaries, convents, and priests of the diocese. He taught the people, provided for their instruction in the faith, and served the needs of the poor. Bishop Liguori also made regular pastoral visits to the parishes, and he prayed and fasted for his people.

Meanwhile, he kept petitioning Rome to be allowed to resign because of old age and infirmity. His request was not granted for a number of years, when he thought he would soon die. Instead, Bishop Liguori suffered in health for several more years. Rheumatic fever left him paralyzed and with a neck bent forward severely so that he had to drink out of a tube. He continued, however, to care for his religious houses as he could and to celebrate Mass with special accommodations. At last, he entered eternity on August 1, 1787. Canonized in 1839, he was named a doctor of the Church in 1871. He is patron saint of confessors, moral theologians, and the lay apostolate.

St. Alphonsus Liguori, pray for us!

St. Pius of Pietrelcina (Padre Pio)
Priest, 1887–1968
Memorial, Sept. 23

Padre Pio is known for his many supernatural gifts—including miracles, special knowledge, visions, and bilocation—and for bearing the stigmata, or wounds of Christ. Canonized in 2002 as St. Pius of Pietrelcina, Padre Pio, or Father Pio, was born as Francesco Forgione in the small town of Pietrelcina, Italy, in 1887. His parents were devout peasants, and his childhood was immersed in the Catholic faith. From a young age, he was given to see supernatural beings such as angels and demons, and he conversed with Jesus and Mary. At the age of five, Francesco dedicated his life to God under the patronage of St. Francis, his namesake. Impressed with the Capuchin Franciscans who came to Pietrelcina to beg, he told his parents, "I want to be a friar ... with a beard" (EWTN).

As a teenager, he again expressed his desire to become a friar, and his parents supported him in his vocation. Francesco, however, had only three years of formal schooling since he had to labor to help support his family. The Capuchins told him he must further his studies before entering. Hiring a private tutor was beyond the family's means, so Francesco's father, Grazio, went to work in America and sent home the money to support his son's education. After further studies, Francesco was granted entry into the Capuchins at the age of 15 in 1903, taking the name Pius, or Pio. The practices at the monastery at Marcone were very strict, but Fra Pio embraced them.

Attacked by demons visibly and physically, Fra Pio became seriously ill and could hardly eat. He had to be sent home for a time, where he was still allowed to live as a friar and continue his studies. It was not clear whether he would even live to see his ordination day, but he was indeed ordained a priest in 1910 and celebrated his first Mass with tears of joy and special visions.

Because of his poor health, Padre Pio was sent back to Pietrelcina to live at home and serve there as a priest. Around the time of World War I, he was drafted into the medical corps of the Italian army, but he had to be sent home multiple times because of illness. Padre Pio was then assigned by the Capuchins to San Giovanni Rotundo.

Ever living in a world of visible angels and demons, Padre Pio was given further spiritual gifts in 1918. First, while hearing confessions on August 5 and feeling ill, he had to dismiss a boy from the confessional. Seeing a winged creature with a lance, Padre Pio felt his heart being pierced through. It was a mystical experienced called the transverberation of the heart. Then, on September 20, he again encountered the winged creature, but this time his hands, feet, and side were bloodied. Padre Pio then received the full stigmata, which remained in his body visibly until it was time for him to die, 50 years and 3 days later. The stigmata bled profusely, requiring constant bandaging, and caused him much suffering, which he offered to God. Though Padre Pio at first tried to hide the stigmata, he could not, and it aroused much attention and suspicion. Hs superiors ordered various tests to determine its nature.

The following year, news of the stigmata began to spread, and people began to flock to San Giovanni Rotundo to see Padre Pio and have him hear their confessions. He performed miracles and would tell penitents about sins they had withheld from him. His Masses lasted three hours because of his supernatural visions, and he would often hear confessions for 19 hours a day. Many people were converted though Padre Pio. He was even known to levitate in the air and to bilocate, or be present at the same time in two places in order to help someone in need.

Some people, however, were suspicious of Padre Pio. Complaints and false stories mounted against him, and the Vatican's Holy Office published a disposition against Padre Pio, forbidding him from blessing anyone from his window, showing anyone the stigmata, or communicating with his spiritual director. The faithful were also instructed not to believe in the supernatural origin of his stigmata. The Capuchins tried to transfer Padre Pio from San Giovanni Rotundo, and Padre Pio was resigned to whatever might come, but the townspeople rose up and would not allow him to leave. Later on, the Holy Office would even forbid him from corresponding spiritually with people, saying Mass in public, or hearing confessions. Finally, in 1933, Pope Pius XI said, "I have not been badly disposed toward Padre Pio, but I have been badly informed," and began to reverse the sanctions against Padre Pio until they were completely lifted (EWTN).

Out of concern for the many pilgrims at San Giovanni Rotundo and the lack of medical services available to the locals, Padre Pio enlisted the help of his followers in establishing a hospital in the town. The Home for the Relief of Suffering opened in 1956, and doctors and their families moved to San Giovanni Rotundo to be part of his ministry. A new church was built in San Giovanni Rotundo to accommodate the pilgrims, and it opened in 1963. Padre Pio established a network of prayer groups to help people in their spiritual life, and he adopted people as his "spiritual children." If they would commit to taking the spiritual life seriously, he would offer them his powerful intercession.

Padre Pio's health declined in his last years, and he died in 1968 at the age of 81, having been given a vision of the Blessed Virgin Mary. His funeral was attended by 100,000 people. He often gave people this advice: "Pray, hope, and don't worry." St. Pius of Pietrelcina is the patron saint of civil defense volunteers, adolescents, Pietrelcina, stress relief, and January blues.

St. Pius of Pietrelcina, pray for us!

St. John Mary Vianney
Priest, 1786–1859
Memorial, Aug. 4

St. Jean-Marie-Baptiste Vianney, as known in his native French, is the patron saint of parish priests and is commonly known as the Curé of Ars, or Pastor of Ars. Though he struggled in his seminary studies, he won over the small town of Ars for Christ through his priestly witness and presence. Spending long hours in the confessional, and known for his simple yet profound sayings on the faith, he attracted tens of thousands of pilgrims each year to his small town.

John was born in Dardilly, France, near Lyons, in 1786. He grew up during the French Revolution, when priests, religious, and their supporters were often subjected to the guillotine. John knew priests in hiding and was inspired by their bravery for Christ. Enlivened by his First Holy Communion, he wanted to become a priest. Because of the chaos of the French Revolution, John was not able to receive a proper education as a child. In 1806, after Catholicism had again been legalized, John entered a school for ecclesiastical students to study for the priesthood. Now older, he struggled there considerably, especially in Latin. But his teachers saw his piety, so they were willing to work with him despite his poor academics.

When Napoleon was in need of soldiers for his war with Spain, he lifted the exemption on conscripting seminarians in certain dioceses. John was drafted into the army, and his father was unsuccessful in offering a replacement for him. So John went to meet with his company, but he was delayed at prayer. A man offered to take him to them, but instead led him to a gathering of deserters. The mayor of the town convinced him to assume a new name and live there as a schoolmaster, which he did for 14 months, until his brother entered military service in his stead (*New Advent*).

John then returned to his studies and went to another seminary, where he likewise struggled with academics. Nonetheless, he was ordained a priest in 1815. He was assigned as an assistant to one of the priests, Fr. Balley, who had been a mentor and advocate to him. Three years later, when Fr. Balley passed away, Fr. Vianney was assigned as the priest for the remote hamlet of Ars, with its population of only 200.

Ars was a satellite of a nearby parish, and a priest had not been assigned there in years. It was a wayward town, and the faith was lax. Saddened by the state of the faith in Ars, Fr. Vianney started out with much prayer and fasting, kneeling constantly before the Tabernacle and offering up harsh penances. His preaching was simple and clear, focusing on the essentials of the faith and on salvation and God's love. Inviting the people to Reconciliation, he spent hours in the confessional. The Curé of Ars was a great director of souls, offering excellent advice to penitents. Sometimes he could even supernaturally reveal to the penitents secret sins that they had withheld. Fr. Vianney also had dramatic confrontations with the devil, who would harass him.

Fr. Vianney opened an orphanage for at-risk girls so they would not fall into professions of ill repute. He gave them wonderful catechetical instructions and filled the church with attendees. Through his prayers, he was able to obtain miraculous funds as needed for his orphanage. The orphanage, however, only lasted for a time, as Fr. Vianney closed it in 1847 because of numerous complaints that he had received.

Fr. Vianney truly transformed the town of Ars, and the faith of the people was renewed as never before. In 1823, the bishop made Ars its own parish and Fr. Vianney its pastor. Fr. Vianney told his congregation in the homily, "Ars ... is not Ars anymore!" (EWTN).

Fr. Vianney's homilies often drew from rural imagery and were illuminated with the fervor of his own faith. His direction in the confessional offered common sense advice in addition, at times, to prophetic knowledge. People came to him for advice about their vocations and about difficult situations. Even priests, religious, and bishops came to this simple priest for advice and Confession. He also had gifts for curing the sick. For three decades, about 20,000 people came to him every year from across Europe. When they came, they heard sermons with words like this, on the Eucharist:

> Our Lord is hidden there, waiting for us to come and visit him and ask him for what we want. He is there, in the Sacrament of his love, sighing and interceding unceasingly for sinners before God his Father. He is there to console us ... See how good he is! He adapts

himself to our weakness…. In heaven where we shall be triumphant and glorious, we shall see him in all his glory; if he had appeared before us now in glory, we should not have dared to approach him; but he hides himself like one in prison, saying to us, 'You do not see me, but that does not matter; ask me for all you want, and I will grant it you.'

Fr. Vianney tried several times to escape from Ars to become a monk, but the people would not let him go. Having worked hard and done much mortification in his life, Fr. Vianney died at the age of 73 on August 4, 1859. St. John Mary Vianney was canonized in 1925 by Pope Pius XI, who named him patron of parish priests in 1928.

St. John Mary Vianney, pray for us!

St. Dominic
Priest, 1170–1234
Memorial, Aug. 8

St. Dominic de Guzman, the founder of the Order of
Preachers, or Dominicans, was born in 1170 to a noble
family in Old Castile in north-central Spain. His father, Felix
de Guzman, was a royal warden, and his mother, Blessed
Juana de Aza, was a saintly woman. Juana was barren and
made a pilgrimage to Silos to pray that she could have a
child. Before conceiving Dominic, she received a dream in
which a dog leapt forth from her womb, bearing a torch in
its mouth to set the world on fire (Catholic Online).

As a child, Dominic was particularly inspired by his
mother's holy example and became a godly youth. He was
provided with a good education and ultimately attended the
University of Palencia, where he pursued advanced studies
in theology for some ten years. He was ordained a priest
and appointed a cathedral canon at Osma, where he was
raised to the rank of prior. He provided an example of
holiness to those in his charge, and he spent much of nine
years in contemplation (*New Advent*).

St. Dominic accompanied Don Diego, the bishop of Osma, on
a mission from the king to make marriage arrangements for
the king's daughter. St. Dominic and Bishop Diego passed
through the city of Toulouse in southern France and were
shocked to find how entrenched the Albigensian heresy had
become in those parts. Meanwhile, the princess died
unexpectedly, leaving St. Dominic and Bishop Diego with
some time to spare abroad. They resolved to set out for
Rome. The bishop wanted to ask the pope to release him of
his duties so he could preach the gospel abroad. The pope,
Innocent III, did not approve the mission for the bishop, but

did approve it for St. Dominic, whom he sent to Languedoc in southern France to join with the Cistercian monks in preaching to the Albigensians.

The situation was already far gone in Languedoc, where Albigensianism had taken hold of much of their society. The Albigensians were dualists in that they believed good and evil are both ultimates, with spirit coming from the good power while matter and the body are from the evil power. Consequently, they denied the power of the sacraments, which have a material dimension. Their leaders impressed the populace with fasting and self-denial. They even went so far as to praise those among them who committed suicide because they were supposed to have become liberated from the body.

St. Dominic noticed that the reason the people did not listen to the Cistercians was because they lived sumptuously and did not provide a good example of a life of self-denial. St. Dominic convinced them to change their lifestyle and follow his example. Together with St. Dominic's teaching, this led to an effective ministry. He focused especially on the very religious women who formed the bedrock of the Albigensian faithful. He converted many of them. Some desired to become nuns, so St. Dominic established a convent for them at Prouille. He made them into a religious order and wrote a rule for them. These nuns became the first Dominicans.

The times were violent, and religion was often a motive for war. Some of the Albigensians threatened the lives of Catholic priests, including St. Dominic, whom they could not defeat simply by argument. They killed a Cistercian legate, which provoked the Catholic prince Simon de Monfort to wage a crusade against them. St. Dominic was called in as a theological expert by the Inquisition, though he was known to advocate for mercy.

St. Dominic had long thought of founding a religious order to combat heresy, an idea that he had conceived some years before while at prayer. His friars were to be provided an extensive theological education to supply them with an arsenal to fight heresy. So St. Dominic went to Pope Honorius III and finally received approval for his new order. The pope promoted it with a bull that recommended and praised the new order, which he called the Order of Preachers.

The order flourished and spread throughout Christendom and beyond. During St. Dominic's time, the order was established not only in Spain, France, and Italy, but also in Germany, England, Norway, Finland, the Holy Land, and North Africa (*Butler's Lives*). The early Dominicans were courageous preachers, willing to bring the gospel even into hostile territories. Numerous Dominicans of their founder's time ultimately became martyrs for the faith. St. Dominic also established a friendship with St. Francis, the founder of the Franciscan order. The Dominicans and the Franciscans came to be called mendicant orders since they lived among the people, begging for their basic needs.

While he was in prayer, the Blessed Virgin Mary appeared to St. Dominic and revealed the Rosary to him as a weapon against heresy. St. Dominic made use of it in his preaching, and the devotion appealed to both the learned and the unlearned. 'Mary's Psalter' was made up of 150 Hail Marys, the same as the number of the Psalms in the Bible. Each decade starts with an Our Father and ends with a Glory Be. The prayers themselves, based on Scripture, are simple to learn, but the meditations on the Gospel during each decade can be as deep as the one praying is able to make them. The Rosary itself became a teaching tool, and the graces won by it from the Blessed Virgin Mary were said to be the cause of many victories.

Even while tending to the administration of the order, St. Dominic continued preaching. He was known to have worked numerous miracles as well, and even to have raised several people from the dead. He personally converted some 100,000 heretics (*New Advent*). At last, he became ill and died in 1234, at the age of 50.

St. Dominic, pray for us!

St. Teresa Benedicta of the Cross
(Edith Stein)
Virgin and Martyr, 1891–1942
Optional Memorial, Aug. 9

Carmelite nun and philosopher St. Teresa Benedicta of the Cross was born into a Jewish family as Edith Stein in Breslau, Germany, in 1891. She was always a very rational person, even reasoning to obey her parents as a child after being convinced that doing so was for her own good (EWTN). As a teenager, she became an atheist because she reasoned that people do not really believe in God since they live their lives as if he did not exist. Edith attended prestigious universities in Germany and received her doctorate in philosophy. She became an assistant to the philosopher Edmund Husserl, the founder of phenomenology, a modern philosophy of experience.

Edith converted to Catholicism after reading the autobiography of St. Teresa of Avila. Edith was impressed with St. Teresa's depth and authenticity, and she was baptized in 1922. Edith became a professor and an author of many philosophical books, also taking on the subject of femininity. She understood the greater life, however, to be that of contemplation. She entered a Discalced Carmelite convent at Cologne, taking the name Sister Teresa Benedicta of the Cross. Her time there, however, was cut short because of the threats of the anti-Semitic Nazi regime. In order to protect herself and her sisters, Sister Teresa asked to be transferred to a convent outside Germany. She was transferred to a convent at Echt in Holland in 1938, but unfortunately, the Nazis invaded Holland a few years later, and the targets of their persecution included Catholics with Jewish ancestry.

Sister Teresa was arrested and loaded onto a cattle train for the Auschwitz death camp. Only a few days later, she died there in the gas chambers—on August 9, 1942. St. Teresa Benedicta of the Cross was beatified in 1987 and canonized in 1998, both by Pope St. John Paul II.

St. Teresa Benedicta of the Cross, pray for us!

St. Lawrence
Deacon and Martyr, 225–258
Feast, Aug. 10

St. Lawrence was a young deacon and a highly celebrated early Christian martyr. He is said to have been chosen as an archdeacon of Pope St. Sixtus II, and to have proven very loyal in this capacity.

In 257, Emperor Valerian ordered a persecution of the Christians, demanding the death of all bishops, priests, and deacons. Pope Sixtus, bishop of Rome, was arrested and led to his execution. Deacon Lawrence followed behind, weeping. He cried out, "Father, where are you going without your son? Whither are you going, O holy priest, without your deacon? You were never wont to offer sacrifice without me, your minister. Wherein have I displeased you? Have you found me wanting to my duty? Try me now, and see, whether you have made choice of an unfit minister for dispensing the blood of the Lord" (*Butler's Lives*).

Pope Sixtus replied, "I do not leave you, my son; but a greater trial and a more glorious victory is reserved for you who are stout and in the vigor of youth. We are spared on account of our weakness and old age. You shall follow me in three days." Pope Sixtus suffered martyrdom by beheading.

The Church of Rome had a certain amount of wealth at the time and was charitable in its giving to the poor of the city and to other churches in need. Pope Sixtus gave Deacon Lawrence a final instruction to distribute the wealth to them. Deacon Lawrence, whose duty it was to care for the poor, kept a list of those in need in the city, and he did as he

330

was told. But Deacon Lawrence was caught by the Roman authorities, who were envious of the wealth of the persecuted Church. The Roman prefect demanded he show them the treasures. Deacon Lawrence replied, "The Church is indeed rich; nor hath the emperor any treasure equal to what it possesseth. I will show you a valuable part; but allow me a little time to set everything in order, and to make an inventory" (*Butler's Lives*).

Deacon Lawrence asked for three days, during which he gathered the poor and ill of the city helped by the Christians. Then he brought the prefect to them, displaying them as the riches of the Church. The prefect was angered and threatened Deacon Lawrence with torture and death. He replied, "What are you displeased at? The gold which you so eagerly desire is a vile metal and serves to incite men to all manner of crimes. The light of heaven is the true gold, which these poor objects enjoy. Their bodily weakness and sufferings are the subject of their patience, and the highest advantages; vices and passions are the real diseases by which the great ones of the world are often most truly miserable and despicable. Behold in these poor persons the treasures which I promised to show you; to which I will add pearls and precious stones,— those widows and consecrated virgins, which are the Church's crown, by which it is pleasing to Christ; it hath no other riches: make use then of them for the advantage of Rome, of the emperor, and yourself" (*Butler's Lives*).

The prefect was incensed and replied, "Do you thus mock me? Is it thus that the axes and the fasces, the sacred ensigns of the Roman power, are insulted? I know that you desire to die; this is your frenzy and vanity: but you shall not die immediately, as you imagine. I will protract your tortures, that your death may be the more bitter as it shall be slower. You shall die by inches" (*Butler's Lives*). The prefect ordered hot coals to be placed under a gridiron and had Deacon Lawrence stripped and chained over it so that he would die very slowly and painfully. Yet Deacon Lawrence kept his focus all the while on Christ and his heavenly crown as the hours passed. Then he made his famous jest, "Let my body be now turned; one side is broiled enough." His wish was granted. After praying for the city of Rome, his earthly life expired. Years later, the Christian Emperor Constantine built a basilica over the place of his burial. The St. Lawrence River in Canada, which forms part of the U.S. border, is named in honor of this early martyr. St. Lawrence is the patron saint of Rome, students, miners, tanners, chefs, the poor, and firefighters (Catholic Online).

St. Lawrence, pray for us!

St. Clare
Virgin, 1194–1253
Memorial, Aug. 11

St. Clare, the first Franciscan woman religious, was born in Assisi in 1194 to a wealthy and noble family. Her parents were devout, and she had a love for religious things from a young age. As a child, she would use pebbles and stones to count off her Our Fathers and Hail Marys and had a desire to devote herself wholly to God. As a teenager, she heard St. Francis' teaching and felt called to follow his way of life. Her parents had plans for her to marry, but she refused. At the age of 18, she escaped from her parents' home, accompanied by another woman, and met St. Francis and his followers at the Portiuncula chapel, where he received her. She laid her rich outer coat on the altar, put on a course sackcloth, had her hair cut off, and went about barefoot.

When her friends and relatives found out, they came to take her back. She resisted and clung to the altar, lifting back her veil to show them her cut hair. A few days later, Clare's younger sister, who took the name Agnes, joined in her new life. St. Francis put them up at first in the Benedictine convent of St. Paul, until more noble women joined Clare in the religious life. At first, St. Francis served as their superior, but then he left their charge to Clare, who became their abbess. They came to be called "the Poor Ladies of San Damiano."

Clare was very harsh in her penitential practices. She wore a hair coat, slept on the ground, fasted very strictly, prayed constantly, rose early, and retired late. During Lent, she would take only bread and water. Her sacrifices, however, were out of love, and she always showed a cheerful disposition. Clare always lived more rigorously than the other sisters and fought to preserve the rule of strict poverty in the order. Pope Gregory IX wanted to limit their rule of poverty, but Clare persuaded Pope Innocent IV to uphold its strictness. In fact, when Clare inherited her parents' estate, she sold it and gave the money to the poor, not even saving anything for her convent.

Clare loved the Eucharist and believed in the power of its protection. When Assisi was being attacked by a large number of Moors enlisted by Emperor Fredrick II, Clare and her sisters were in danger, even more so because their convent was outside the city walls. Clare prayed for safety and heard a voice saying, "I will always protect you" (*Butler's Lives*). She took the Eucharist in a monstrance and held it up, and the attacking soldiers fell back as if they were being assailed by an unseen enemy. They left Assisi and harmed no one there that day.

Clare was known to work many healings and miracles, though she tried to conceal her gift. She came to be known for her wisdom and was visited by two popes—Innocent IV and Alexander IV.

Yet Clare was often sickly, and she eventually succumbed to her illnesses, at the age of 59. She was canonized just two years later by Pope Alexander IV, and ten years later, her order changed its name to the "Order of St. Clare." They are known as the Poor Clares. In 1958, Pope Pius XII declared St. Clare the patron saint of television since when she was too ill to attend Mass, she could see it on the wall of her cell.

She is also the patron saint of eye disease, goldsmiths, and laundry.

St. Clare of Assisi, pray for us!

St. Maximilian Mary Kolbe
Priest and Martyr, 1894–1941
Memorial, Aug. 14

St. Maximilian Kolbe is known as the Martyr of Charity. He died at the Auschwitz concentration camp in Poland, offering his life in place of a husband and father selected to die. A Polish Conventual Franciscan friar, St. Maximilian Kolbe is remembered for his devotion to Mary and for promoting Marian consecration.

St. Maximilian Kolbe, who was christened as Raymond Kolbe, was born in Poland in 1894. His childhood was a typical one, to the extent that his mother once said to him, "I don't know what's going to become of you!" (Franciscan Media). This began to change around the age of ten, when Raymond had an extraordinary dream. In it, the Blessed Virgin Mary appeared to him, offering two crowns—one white, representing perseverance in chastity, and the other red, representing martyrdom. She asked him which he would take. He replied that he would accept both.

Though he felt the tugging of the priesthood on his heart, Raymond also had an interest in becoming a soldier. He was prevented, however, from pursuing the path of the soldier. Instead, he joined the Conventual Franciscan Order, where he was given the name Maximilian. He was ordained a priest in 1910 and also earned doctorates in theology and philosophy. Ever the soldier at heart, and filled with devotion to Mary, he founded the Militia Immaculata, an organization of prayer, work, and penance for Catholics to fight religious indifferentism and bring the world under Mary's maternal care. At the vanguard of the technology of the time, he even published a magazine, the *Knight of the Immaculata,* which he distributed to readers among his million-strong membership, circulating well over 100,000 copies per issue. Attracting as many as 760 friars, Fr. Maximilian established a Franciscan monastery at Niepokalanow, Poland, to headquarter the Militia Immaculata and publish its magazine. He established another monastery at Nagasaki, Japan.

Fr. Maximilian wrote his own total consecration to Mary, which he also promoted. The consecration was an entrustment of one's life and spirituality entirely to Mary, to do with as she will. He also pondered the question of Mary's identity as the Immaculate Conception, asking, "Who are you, O Immaculate Conception?" He came to the realization that Mary, the Spouse of the Holy Spirit, is the created Immaculate Conception, while the Holy Spirit is the uncreated Immaculate Conception. The Holy Spirit is eternally conceived of the love of the Father and the Son. Mary is an expression of the Holy Spirit, and thus her human free will is perfectly aligned to the will of God. Thus, in all things, she was enabled to say, "May it be done to me according to your word" (Luke 1:38).

Kolbe and his friars were initially arrested when Niepokalanow was captured by the Nazis during the invasion of Poland in September 1939. He was released, but refused to sign the racist Deutche Volksliste, which would have granted him rights on par with a German, recognizing his race as a valuable one to the Nazis. Meanwhile, Fr. Maximilian used the monastery at Niepokalanow to shelter 1,500 Jews. He also suffered from tuberculosis. In February 1941, the Nazis arrested Fr. Maximilian during a roundup of leaders and closed down the monastery. He was sent first to Pawiak prison but then to Auschwitz in May. There he was known as prisoner 16670 and was subject to beatings, lashings, and other abuse.

In July, ten prisoners escaped Auschwitz. In response, the Nazis determined to select ten men from the camp to be starved to death as a deterrent to would-be escapees. When a man named Franciszek Gajowniczek was chosen, he cried out for his wife and children. Fr. Maximilian offered to take his place, and his offer was accepted.

The ten men were locked in a bunker and deprived of food and drink. Fr. Maximilian ministered to his fellow inmates while in the bunker and was often seen praying on his knees. After two weeks, only Fr. Maximilian was still alive. The guards entered to give him carbolic acid as a lethal injection, and he calmly offered his left arm. He died on the eve of the Assumption, August 14, 1941, at the age of 47.

Fr. Maximilian was beatified in 1971 by Blessed Paul VI and canonized in 1982 by Pope St. John Paul II, who recognized him as a true martyr. Franciszek Gajowniczek, the man for whom Kolbe died, attended his canonization at St. Peter's Square. St. Maximilian Kolbe is recognized beyond Catholicism, and even outside of religious contexts, as a hero of World War II. His statue can be found at Westminster Cathedral in London. Moreover, he was honored in Germany with a postal stamp and in Poland with a year dedicated by the government to his honor. St.

Maximilian Kolbe is the patron saint of drug addicts, prisoners, families, and the pro-life movement.

St. Maximilian Mary Kolbe, pray for us!

St. Bernard of Clairvaux
Abbot and Doctor of the Church, 1090–1153
Memorial, Aug 20

St. Bernard of Clairvaux is known as the Last of the Fathers and as the Mellifluous, or Honey-bearing, Doctor, because of the sweetness of his teachings. St. Bernard was born to noble Burgundian parents outside of Dijon in France. A holy man uttered a prophecy that the child would become great, so his parents had him well-educated from a young age, and he excelled in literature and in the ways of God.

As a young man, Bernard became drawn to the monastery of Cîteaux, which had been founded recently, in 1098, by Robert of Molesmes. While many monasteries had become more lax and opulent, Cîteaux, the first Cistercian monastery, followed a strict observance of the Rule of St. Benedict. So impassioned was Bernard for growth in virtue that 30 other young noblemen followed him in joining Cîteaux. After three years of formation, Bernard was sent out to found a new monastery at a place he named Clairvaux, or Clear Valley. He was joined by numerous companions, as well as his brothers and father. The strict reform of monasticism spread far beyond Clairvaux. Bernard founded at total of 163 monasteries throughout Europe, which expanded further in turn (*New Advent*).

Above all, Bernard was a man of contemplation, which he cherished dearly. For him, preaching was necessary for the sake of others, but contemplation was the highest and sweetest path. He pursued God with passion and ardor, in response to how God pursued him. Bernard wrote numerous mystical works, including his *Commentary on the Song of Songs.* There he wrote on the gradual approach to intimacy with God in terms of the kiss of the feet, the kiss of the hands, and the kiss of the mouth. He addressed both the love of God for the soul and the fruitfulness of the soul from the love of God. Bernard wrote numerous other works, too, including *On Loving God.* Bernard was particularly fervent in his love of the Blessed Virgin Mary, and he provided lasting influence in promoting Marian devotion within the Church. Bernard was also gifted with miracles and mystical experiences.

Bernard's period of history was a time wanting for learning and refinement, but he provided light for the Church through his teachings and his work for reform within the Church. He helped influence other, non-Cistercian monasteries to become stricter and also won the respect of popes and bishops. Bernard became an advocate for the Church in matters with the state and was called upon to be a mediator in various important Church matters. The pope commissioned Bernard to preach a new crusade in response to trouble in the Holy Land. Bernard was successful in bringing together the forces, but the crusade itself failed because of the sinful actions of those who waged it. This caused Bernard much sorrow in his later years. Bernard died at Clairvaux on August 21, 1153. Canonized in 1174, he was proclaimed a doctor of the Church in 1830.

Largely on account of the St. Bernard breed of dogs, famous for remarkable mountain rescues under the guidance of monks at the St. Bernard Pass in the Alps between France and Italy, St. Bernard of Clairvaux is regarded as the patron saint of skiing, snowboarding, hiking, backpacking, and mountaineering.

St. Bernard of Clairvaux, pray for us!

St. Pius X
Pope, 1835–1914
Memorial, Aug. 21

St. Pius X, who reigned as pope from 1903 to 1914, is remembered for his holiness and humility. Padre Pio had a particular admiration for him as a pope uniquely modeled after the humble heart of Jesus. He was only the second pope elected after the fall of the Papal States, and he helped solidify a new direction for the papacy in later years—one more of pastoral guidance than of regal dignity.

Unlike many of his predecessors, Pope Pius X was not born from nobility, and he spent years as a parish priest among the common people. Born to parents of common stock in Venice in 1835, he was given the name Guisseppe Sarto. His father was a mail carrier. The family was poor enough that Guisseppe used to carry his shoes to school so as not to wear them out. He was a good student and excelled in his studies. Winning a scholarship to seminary, he was ordained a priest in 1858 and assigned to pastoral and parochial duties, which he performed for many years. He took particular interest in catechesis for adults and in care for the sick, though he also taught in seminary.

He was assigned as bishop of Mantua in 1884, where he was particularly active in the care of his flock. He focused on the formation of priests through reform and care for the seminary, and he also adapted to the current situation of schooling in Italy by providing religious instruction for public school students. During this time, many of the powers of the papacy were in dispute with the Italian government. Pope Leo XIII held a secret consistory of the cardinals in 1893, during which he named Bishop Sarto as a cardinal. The Italian government refused to recognize the

Pope's authority to do so without a nomination from the Emperor of Austria and, as a reprisal, prevented as many as 30 bishoprics in Italy from being filled (*New Advent*). When the government at last conceded, Cardinal Sarto assumed his position as Patriarch of Venice, where he likewise improved the seminary, adding a faculty of canon law.

When Pope Leo XIII died in 1903, Cardinal Sarto was elected pope, taking the name Pius X in continuity with the recent line of popes with that name. He took as his papal motto "To Restore All Things in Christ." Pope Pius X opted for more simple attire as pope and even filled the papal palace in 1908 with refugees from an earthquake that had devastated the city of Messina. He is credited with the beginnings of papal support for modern liturgical reform. In a time when people shrunk from approaching the Blessed Sacrament because of unworthiness, Pope Pius X promoted frequent reception of Communion for the lay people so as to make the grace of receiving Jesus in Communion more accessible. He also lowered the age at which children could receive First Communion to the age of reason, which is about 7 years old. To promote a more active participation in the liturgy, he promoted the use of Gregorian chant, with its simple plainchant melody that the people could join. Pope Pius X also effected a reform and update of canon law and established numerous new dioceses, including in the United States.

Concerned with false teachings of the day that were creeping into Church circles, Pope Pius X took a strong stance against a heresy he called 'Modernism.' This heresy, forms of which were already widespread among liberal Protestant scholars, could speak the language of traditional Church doctrine while at the same time discounting the objective reality of God's Revelation. It saw religion as a kind of natural inner impulse, reinterpreting the meaning of the faith and essentially equalizing it with other kinds of opinions and beliefs. Pope Pius X decried this heresy in his papal syllabus *Lamentabili* and then wrote an Oath Against Modernism that all priests and seminary professors were required to take. Moreover, he established Councils of Vigilance in each diocese to monitor the spread of the Modernist heresy.

Greatly distressed at the approaching belligerence in Italy leading up to World War I, Pope Pius X suffered a heart attack and died on August 20, 1914, at the age of 79. St. Pius X was canonized in 1954 by Pope Pius XII.

St. Pius X, pray for us!

St. Rose of Lima
Virgin, 1586–1617
Optional Memorial, Aug. 23

St. Rose of Lima overcame many obstacles to live a prayerful and penitential life at her home in colonial Peru. Canonized in 1671, this young Spanish colonist was the first saint from the New World to be canonized.

She was born Isabel Flores de Olivia but was called Rose soon after her birth because of her beautiful complexion. At her Confirmation, she officially took the name Rose. Her beauty, in fact, would become a trial for her since even from childhood, she wanted to belong only to God and to offer sacrifices to him. She desired only to have spiritual beauty.

Rose invented many harsh penances for herself. As a girl, she was given a garland of flowers by her mother to wear as a headdress. Rose used it to conceal a pin that pricked her head so much that the garland was difficult to take off at night. Later, she would wear a silver crown with nails pointed inward. (Silver was a common metal at that time in Peru.) Rose also maintained a garden, in which she positioned crosses and grew bitter herbs to eat as a penance. She would often take only two hours for sleep so she could spend all the time possible praying. Rose especially loved adoring the Blessed Sacrament, and she received Holy Communion every day.

When she became old enough to attract suitors, many young men became interested in Rose because of her beauty, and men often would stare at her. She became concerned for their purity and did not want to become an occasion of sin, so Rose cut her hair short and rubbed indigenous pepper on her face to create blotches and swelling. Her parents tried to force her to marry, and she underwent much persecution from her friends and family because of her way of life and her refusal to marry. As a child, she was always perfectly obedient to her parents, but in this, there was much tension, and her parents strongly disapproved of her lifestyle.

Rose persisted, however, and her father finally gave her a room of her own. It became her cell, and she cloistered herself inside. But later on, her parents lost their house because of overspending, so Rose was taken into the home of a pious family in the city—the house, in fact, of a government official. Rose worked in gardening and needlework for the family to earn her keep.

She became inflamed with the love of God because of her great openness to God's will in her life. Christ once appeared to her and called her his spouse (*Butler's Lives*). Rose died at the age of only 31. The government provided her with a state funeral, which was attended by many, and miracles were soon attributed to her intercession.

St. Rose of Lima is the patron saint of embroiderers, gardeners, florists, those ridiculed because of their piety, and those who suffer family problems (Catholic Online). The Roman Calendar currently celebrates St. Rose of Lima on August 23, but in Peru and certain other Latin American countries, she is celebrated on August 30.

St. Rose of Lima, pray for us!

St. Bartholomew
Apostle, First Century
Feast, Aug. 24

Bartholomew is listed as one of the Twelve Apostles in Matthew, Mark, Luke, and Acts. As such, he would have accompanied Jesus as a witness to his words and deeds, learning at the feet of the Master himself. The name Bartholomew means 'son of Tolomai.' He is often listed together with Philip, and some scholars believe him to be the same as Nathaniel, who John's gospel tells us was from Cana in Galilee. Jesus paid Nathaniel a great compliment by saying, "Here is a true Israelite. There is no duplicity in him" (Jn. 1:47).

Nothing else is mentioned about Bartholomew in the Bible except what is common to all the Apostles. According to tradition, however, he preached the gospel in India and then in Armenia, where he was martyred, possibly by being flayed alive. St. Bartholomew is the patron saint of Armenia.

St. Bartholomew, pray for us!

St. Louis
1214–1270
Optional Memorial, Aug. 25

King Louis IX of France was among the few monarchs canonized for winning the heavenly crown. Louis was 8 years old when his father became king and 12 years old when his father, Louis VIII, died, leaving him to become king. Louis' mother, Blanche of Castile, ruled as regent until he was 21. She raised him well and with piety, telling him, "I love you, my dear son, with all the tenderness a mother is capable of; but I would infinitely rather see you fall down dead at my feet, than that you should ever commit a mortal sin" (*Butler's Lives*). This stuck with him.

Born and baptized at Poissy outside Paris, Louis showed favor to the place, often bestowing special royal generosity there in honor of his baptism. Crowned at the cathedral at Rheims at the age of 12, Louis took the grace and blessing of his coronation and oath before God very seriously. Perfidious men brought an army against him after his coronation to steal his crown, but young King Louis, his mother, and his army kept them in check. The years of his minority were often troubled by these pretenders. One of them at last surrendered to the king, who showed him mercy by sending him into exile in Palestine.

King Louis spent several hours a day in prayer and kept the Divine Office. When others chided him for his lengthy prayer time, he pointed out how other kings spent their leisure time in games, shows, and hunting. He showed the utmost reverence in church. He banished forever from his presence anyone who used foul language in front of him, and he was harsh in enforcing the laws against blasphemy. King Louis found ways of mortifying himself despite the

357

luxuries of the court by avoiding the choicer foods, by wearing a hair shirt under his garments, and by allowing himself to be scourged. When it was time for him to marry, he chose Margaret of Provence because of her virtue.

King Louis was a friend of the poor as well. He kept a list of poor people and typically served about one hundred per day from the royal table, often personally. He had hospitals built and would also go out to visit the poor and the sick, even dressing the lepers. His favorite saint and model was St. Francis of Assisi, and he may have been a Third Order Franciscan, if only in spirit. King Louis also heard the cry of those who suffered injustice, and he reformed the judicial system. He banned the old practice of trial by ordeal in favor of examination of witnesses, and he introduced the presumption of innocence until proven guilty.

France was united in peace during the time of King Louis IX. He was steadfast in upholding treaties and agreements, and he was often chosen as a mediator in international affairs. He respected the rights of the Church, insofar as it truly served the Body of Christ. He avoided war whenever possible and forbade wars among his vassals. King Louis also constructed numerous cathedrals and other building projects during his time.

King Louis led two crusades —the Seventh and Eighth Crusades—because of encroachments in the Holy Land. Though neither crusade was successful, Louis showed great bravery and skill in battle and in planning war. He never feared death because death only meant winning the crown of martyrdom. During the Seventh Crusade, he was captured in battle and kept hostage in Palestine for four years. His captors were impressed by his moral courage. They at last released him in exchange for one of his cities and a sum of money. Also during the Seventh Crusade, the Latin emperor of Constantinople, Baldwin II, gave him a relic believed to be the true Crown of Thorns in thanks for his generosity to the Christians of the region. Ultimately, King Louis built the famous and beautiful *Sainte Chappelle* in Paris to house the holy relic. He also spent much time there in prayer, beneath its breathtaking stained-glass windows.

During the Eighth Crusade, the ships of King Louis were found off Tunis, awaiting the arrival of his brother, the king of Sicily. While waiting there on the shore, King Louis and many of his men suffered dysentery. King Louis thus died outside Tunis while on crusade. His youngest son, John Tristan, also died there of dysentery.

Before he died, King Louis gave this admonition to his eldest son Philip, who was to succeed him:

> My son, before all things I recommend to you that you love God. Be always ready rather to suffer all manner of torments than to commit any mortal sin. When sickness or any other affliction befalls you, return thanks to God for it, and bear it courageously, being persuaded that you deserve to suffer much for having

served God ill, and that such tribulations will be your gain. In prosperity give thanks to God with humility, and fear lest by pride you abuse God's benefits, and so offend him by those very means by which you ought particularly to improve yourself in his service. Confess your sins frequently, and choose a wise and pious ghostly father, who will teach you what to follow, and what to shun; let him be one that will boldly reprehend you, and make you understand the grievousness of your faults.

Hear the divine office devoutly,—meditate affectionately what you ask of God with your mouth; do this with more than ordinary application during the holy sacrifice of the mass, especially after the consecration. Be bountiful, compassionate, and courteous to the poor, and relieve and favor them as much as you can. If anything trouble your mind, reveal it to your ghostly father, or to some other grave and discreet person; for by the comfort you will receive you will bear it more patiently. Love to converse with pious persons; never admit any among your familiar friends but such as are virtuous and of good reputation; shun and banish from you the vicious. Make it your delight to hear profitable sermons and discourses of piety. Endeavor to gain the benefit of indulgences, and to get the prayers of others. Love all good, and abhor all evil.

Wherever you are, never suffer any one to detract or say anything sinful in your presence. Punish all who speak ill of God or his saints. Give often thanks to God for all his benefits. In the administration of justice be upright and severe; hear patiently the complaints of the poor, and in all controversies where your interests are concerned, stand for your adversary against yourself, till the truth be certainly found out....

Love and honor the queen your mother, and follow her counsels. Make no war, especially against Christians, without great cause, and good advice. If necessity force you to it, let it be carried on without damage to those who are not in fault, and spare the innocent subjects of your enemy as much as possible. Use all your authority to hinder wars among your vassals. Be scrupulous in the choice of good judges and magistrates. Have always a great respect for the Roman Church, and the pope and honor him as your spiritual father.... (*Butler's Lives*)

St. Louis was canonized in 1297. He is the patron saint of barbers, grooms, and the Secular Franciscan Order, and the city of St. Louis, Missouri, is named after him.

St. Louis, pray for us!

St. Monica
332–387
Memorial, Aug. 27

St. Monica, the mother of St. Augustine, brought her son back to the Church through many years of tears and prayers.

Monica was born to Christian parents in North Africa and was raised with the help of a maid-servant of the highest character. This maid-servant would not let the children drink too much water or drink between meals, lest they develop a liking later on for consuming too much wine. But sometimes when the young Monica would go to the cellar to pour wine for her parents, she would drink some herself—even whole cups. She became a little affected by the wine, and one time the maid-servant caught her and scolded her. Monica realized her fault and repented. This experience helped her become morally aware, and she soon afterward accepted baptism.

Monica was given in marriage to a pagan, Patricius, an upstanding citizen in Tagaste in North Africa. Especially through her example, Monica did her best to bring her husband to the Christian faith, and after many years he did, but only one year before he died. Until then, Monica suffered much and had to endure his fiery temper, as well as that of his mother, who lived with them. She also suffered from his infidelities. Monica refused to complain, and when other women complained about their husbands' mistreatment of them, she would stop them.

Monica and Patricius had three children: Augustine, Navigius, and Perpetua. Piously raised by Monica, Navigius became a monk and Perpetua became a nun—later an abbess. Augustine became a rhetorician and a scholar. Augustine was brilliant, though unruly, and took an interest in classical learning, having been sent for an education at a young age. Patricius applauded his son's learning because it would help him get ahead in the world. But through the influence of his peers, Augustine was turned against the Catholic faith and was overcome by the vice of pride. Though preparations had been made for him to be baptized while ill, he recovered and did not go through with the baptism.

Patricius died when Augustine was 17, having converted to Catholicism, repented, and been baptized. Augustine had an interest in Christ but was persuaded to join the heresy of the Manicheans. He even enjoyed stumping Catholics over their faith. Monica cried for him more than over a son who had died, and she refused to let him live in her house and eat at her table. Augustine took a mistress, with whom he developed a lasting relationship. They had a son, Adeodatus, but they could not marry since she was of a low social class.

Monica wept, prayed, and fasted. At last, she was granted a dream that gave her encouragement. In the dream, she was standing on a wooden rule. Monica was very sad in the dream, but an angel comforted her saying, "Your son is with you." Then she saw Augustine join her in standing on the wooden rule. Monica later told Augustine about the dream, but at first he insisted that it meant that she, too, would become a Manichean. She responded quickly and

364

confidently that the angel had said, "Your son is with you," not the other way around. This made an impression on Augustine, though he persisted in his ways for another nine years (*Butler's Lives*).

Monica continued to pray and fast for Augustine. She also visited numerous learned priests, persuading them to speak with her son. Finally, a bishop gave her comfort, prophesying to her, "Go: continue as you do. It is impossible that a child of such tears should perish."

Augustine set off for Rome to teach rhetoric. Monica was opposed to this because she believed it would reinforce him in his ways. Augustine became very sick in Rome, but it seems he recovered miraculously due to Monica's prayers. Augustine then went on to Milan to teach rhetoric. There he met St. Ambrose, the bishop of Milan, who was a great scholar and rhetorician. Augustine was highly impressed by St. Ambrose, who dissuaded him from the errors of the Manicheans. He did not immediately convert to Catholicism, though he told his mother that he had abandoned Manicheism. Monica continued her prayers and vigils. Augustine ultimately opened himself to God's tug on his soul through further spiritual experiences, and he was baptized at Milan together with friends.

Monica was overjoyed and treated all his newly baptized friends as family. Monica made arrangements for Augustine to marry a good Catholic girl so he would be affirmed in the Catholic faith. But she was even more overjoyed when he expressed to her his intention to live a life of celibacy for the sake of Christ.

Monica said that since her son Augustine had become Catholic and had dedicated his life to the service of God, there was nothing more for her to do on earth. Monica caught a fever in Ostia in Italy and instructed, "Lay my body here." Her other son, Navigius, said she ought to be buried at home. But she replied, "Lay this body anywhere; be not concerned about that. The only thing I ask of you both is, that you make remembrance of me at the altar of the Lord wheresoever you are" (*Butler's Lives*).

Thus, Monica died blessedly at Ostia in the presence of her sons, and they buried her there. Augustine later became a founder of monasteries, a priest, bishop of Hippo, a great theologian, a saint, and one of the greatest of the doctors of the Church. He wept for his mother bitterly because she had wept so much for his salvation, and he recalled her faithfulness in his memoirs, the *Confessions*. St. Monica's body was later translated to Rome in 1430 by Pope Martin V, where it was venerated by the faithful. St. Monica is the patron saint of married women, alcoholics, difficult marriages, disappointing children, victims of unfaithfulness, and victims of verbal abuse, and is the namesake of the city of Santa Monica, California.

St. Monica, pray for us!

St. Augustine
Bishop and Doctor of the Church (354–430)
Memorial, Aug. 28

St. Augustine was one of the greatest and most influential theologians in the history of the Church. After converting to Catholicism, he became a monk and later a priest, a bishop, and an eminent preacher and writer. He was born in 354 in Tagaste, in the Roman province of Numidia in North Africa. He is known as St. Augustine of Hippo, after the name of the North African city over which he presided as bishop for the last 34 years of his life.

Augustine's father was Patricius, a pagan who converted to Christianity on his deathbed, and his mother was St. Monica, a devout Christian. Patricius saw great talent and potential in his son and had him educated well in hopes of making him into a wealthy lawyer. Augustine later recalled his school days in his famous autobiography, the *Confessions.* As a young pupil, he often had to be disciplined with a rod, but he ultimately became very intellectual. His erudition led him into the vice of pride, though Augustine later reflected that this was not something that concerned his worldly masters. Steeped in classical Roman and Greek philosophy, Augustine became an accomplished orator and rhetorician in the classical tradition and became a teacher of rhetoric (*Butler's Lives*).

Though Augustine was almost ready to be baptized when he became seriously ill, he recovered and never received the sacrament until he chose to ask for it many years later. As a young man, Augustine got into mischief and strayed from the morals given to him by his mother. In his late teens, he took in a concubine, whom he could not marry, and fathered a son, Deodatus, with her. Around that time,

368

he became intrigued with the arguments of a learned Manichean and abandoned the Catholic faith for Manicheism. The Manicheans were dualists, believing that there were two equal deities—one good, who created the things of the spirit, and one evil, who created the things of the material world. The Manicheans sought to liberate the spirit (from what they believed to be an evil body) through secret knowledge offered in incremental levels of initiation. Augustine remained in this heresy for years and delighted in sparring intellectually with simpler Catholics.

Augustine's mother Monica was distraught for many years over her son's fall into heresy and prayed and fasted for him constantly, with many tears. At last, her prayers were answered. After having him introduced to many priests, she finally arranged for him to meet St. Ambrose, bishop of Milan, while Augustine was teaching rhetoric in Italy. Augustine found Ambrose intellectually intriguing, and Ambrose was able to demonstrate the errors of the Manichaeans to Augustine. Augustine did not convert to Catholicism immediately, not wanting to give up his immoral lifestyle just yet. He prayed, "Grant me chastity, but not yet!" He questioned whether he would even be able to remain chaste since the fire of lust burned so strongly in him.

Then Augustine encountered God's mercy in prayer. He was in a garden, contemplating what to do, when he heard the voice of a child say, *"Tolle, lege"* ("Take up and read"), as if it were part of a children's game. He found a Bible and opened it to the first page he landed on. Augustine was cut to the heart when the first passage he read was: "Not in revelling and drunkenness; not in chamberings and impurities, not in strife and envy; but put ye on the Lord Jesus Christ, and make not provision for the flesh in its concupiscences" (Rom. 13:13). Augustine put aside his concubine and resolved to convert to the Catholic faith. His mother Monica was overjoyed. She offered to find him a good Catholic wife but was delighted to learn that he intended to live a life of celibacy for God. Monica became ill and died soon afterward, but she was happy in the conviction that her work on earth was complete.

Augustine returned to his home of Tagaste in North Africa, where he sold his possessions and gave everything he had to the poor. He lived a life of prayer, fasting, and the work of a theologian. Other men flocked to him and his way of life, so he founded a monastery. Augustine never intended to become a priest, but while visiting Hippo, there was a public outcry that the bishop there, Valerius, should ordain him. And so it happened in 391 (*New Advent*). Valerius also gave him church land with which to found another monastery and later appointed Augustine as his successor as bishop of Hippo.

Augustine wrote prolifically and debated with heretics with great success, truly evangelizing the flock of his diocese. Manicheans, Donatists, Pelagians, and Arians were the main groups of heretics that threatened the unity of faith at Hippo. Augustine took special interest in bringing Manicheans back to the Catholic faith since he had been one of them. The key philosophical foundation of Manichaeism is dualism—that good and evil are both equal, necessary, and ultimate powers. Against this, he taught that God's goodness is the first impulse of the will, but that creatures' free will opens the possibility to choosing a lesser good. This brings about the possibility of evil, through the choice of lesser goods over higher goods. Augustine was so successful in his public debates with Felix, the Manichean champion in Hippo, that Felix conceded Augustine's argument and converted to the Catholic faith (*New Advent*).

The Donatists caused a schism by refusing to acknowledge the validity of sacraments and ordinations performed by priests or bishops who had denied the faith during persecutions. A certain society of Donatist monks was even violent toward Catholic leaders, sometimes causing serious injury. Against the Donatists, Augustine argued that the Church welcomes sinners for the sake of leading them to salvation. Even its ministers may number among the sinners being led onward. The sacraments effect grace from Christ *ex opere operato,* by the act being performed, not because of the holiness of the minister.

Augustine also sparred with the Pelagians, who taught a rigorism such that only Christians who apply themselves to the path of perfection are given grace. In other words, grace, God's 'free gift,' must be earned. Against this, Augustine taught that even the first desire for God is given freely by God's grace. Original sin is inherited from Adam, in whom all humanity is represented. The concupiscence, or disorder of the passions, is an effect of original sin. It makes it so that we cannot attain Christian perfection on our own natural power before God's grace.

At the time of Augustine's passing, he was engaged in debate with the Arians, since the Vandals who besieged Hippo were Arian. The Arians believed that Christ is only a creature, though the firstborn of all creatures. Augustine became ill and died during the siege at Hippo at the age of 76, having presided as bishop of the city for 34 years.

St. Augustine wrote a great many books, including his *Confessions, The City of God, On Christian Doctrine, On Free Choice of the Will*, and *On the Trinity.* He is known as the Doctor of Grace, and no other post-biblical theologian is cited by the *Catechism of the Catholic Church* more than St. Augustine. Augustine was also greatly respected and studied by the Protestant reformers.

St. Augustine, pray for us!

Excerpt from the Confessions of St. Augustine

Late have I loved you, beauty so old and so new: late have I loved you. And see, you were within and I was in the external world and sought you there, and in my unlovely state I plunged into those lovely created things which you made. You were with me, and I was not with you. The lovely things kept me far from you, though if they did not have their existence in you, they had no existence at all. You called and cried out loud and shattered my deafness. You were radiant and resplendent, you put to flight my blindness. You were fragrant, and I drew in my breath and now pant after you. I tasted you, and I feel but hunger and thirst for you. You touched me, and I am set on fire to attain the peace which is yours. (10.27)

The Passion of St. John the Baptist
First Century
Memorial, Aug. 29

Since he was sanctified in the womb, St. John the Baptist is one of the few holy persons memorialized on their nativity. The Solemnity of the Nativity of St. John the Baptist is celebrated on June 24. On August 29, however, we memorialize the passion and death of the one of whom Jesus said, "Among those born of women, no one is greater than John" in the period of the Old Covenant (Lk. 7:28).

John, who was the cousin of Jesus, was chosen as the precursor to the Messiah, who would "make straight his paths" (Mk. 1:3). Ever in humility to the greater One who was to come, he went out to the wilderness and preached a baptism of repentance on the banks of the River Jordan. People from all walks of life came out to hear him preach, and he exhorted them to change their ways. John the Baptist admonished the Pharisees, the Sadducees, tax collectors, and soldiers. Wearing camel's hair and a leather belt and eating only locusts and wild honey, he preached to the crowds, saying, "You brood of vipers! Who warned you to flee from the coming wrath? Produce good fruits as evidence of your repentance; and do not begin to say to yourselves, 'We have Abraham as our father,' for I tell you, God can raise up children to Abraham from these stones" (Lk. 3:7–8).

One of those to whom John preached was the powerful ruler Herod Antipas. Herod Antipas was tetrarch of Galilee and Perea. His father, Herod the Great, had been king, but the Romans divided his territory after his death among his sons and denied them the title of king. Herod Antipas' half-brother, Philip the Tetrarch, was the ruler of the

Transjordan. Philip's wife was Herodias, who was the niece of Herod Antipas. While Antipas and Philip were traveling in Rome, Antipas became romantically involved with Herodias. When they returned home, Antipas divorced his wife, Phasaelis, the daughter of King Aretas of the Arabs, and caused her to flee. Meanwhile, Herodias left her husband, Philip, and went to Herod Antipas.

John the Baptist exhorted Herod Antipas to repent for having married his brother's wife and to change his ways. Instead, he had John arrested and kept in the fortress Machaerus, a desert stronghold on the Dead Sea, as we learn from Josephus. We read in the Gospels that John's arrest caused Jesus much distress. When John's disciples visited him in prison, they told him of Jesus' wonders, and he sent them to Jesus to ask for reassurance that the latter was, indeed, the Messiah. Jesus gave this answer: "Go and tell John what you have seen and heard: the blind regain their sight, the lame walk, lepers are cleansed, the deaf hear, the dead are raised, the poor have the good news proclaimed to them. And blessed is the one who takes no offense at me" (Lk. 7:22–23).

Herod Antipas would visit John's cell and was intrigued by his preaching. At his birthday celebration, however, Antipas was enchanted by the erotic dance of Herodias' daughter Salome, who was his great-niece. He offered to grant her any request, up to half of his kingdom. The adolescent girl went to her mother, Herodias, who despised John the Baptist for condemning her marriage to Antipas. Herodias had her daughter ask for the head of John the Baptist to be brought out immediately on a platter. The Gospels tell us that Herod Antipas was distressed at the request but ordered that it should be done. John's disciples then went and took the body for burial. Thus, John died to uphold the sanctity of marriage.

John the Baptist was greatly respected by the Jews. Herod Antipas and his fortress Machaerus were later conquered by King Aretas of the Arabs, the father of Phasaelis, the wife Antipas had driven out. Antipas and Herodias were at last exiled to Gaul. The Judeo-Romano historian Josephus reported that it was commonly believed Antipas' woes were due to God's judgment against him for putting the prophet John the Baptist to death.

St. John the Baptist, pray for us!

St. Gregory the Great
Pope and Doctor of the Church, ca. 540–604
Memorial, Sept. 3

Pope St. Gregory the Great, called the first medieval pope by historians, was one of the most influential popes of the first millennium.

Gregory was born to a leading Roman family in the days after the fall of the Roman Empire. His father even served for a time as prefect of Rome. During his childhood, the population of Rome was decimated by a plague, and later the city was sacked by the Ostrogoths. Gregory's family owned estates in Sicily and survived these upheavals by retreating there during those crises. Gregory was well-educated and excelled in his studies. At the age of 33, he was made prefect of Rome, as his father had been. As part of his position, he was required to wear the glorious robes of state. At 35, however, he transformed his late father's estate into a monastery. He lived the monastic life strictly and also enforced strict observance on the monks under his care.

Having noticed some English slaves in the marketplace and finding that their people were still pagan, Gregory desired to go to England as a missionary. He even received permission from the pope to do so, but the Roman people would not let him leave, so beloved was he in Rome. Pope Pelagius, however, selected him as an ambassador to Constantinople and then recalled him to serve as his personal secretary. When the pope died, Gregory was unanimously elected by the clergy, senate, and people to take his place (*Butler's Lives*). Preferring the monastic life, Gregory protested, but the people clamored for him to accept.

As pope, Gregory was attentive to the great needs of the city. He was generous in providing for the poor and would personally go out among them. He also required the clergy to go out and serve the poor, even replacing clergy in their posts if they refused. During a famine, he redirected the harvest from the farms owned by the Church in Italy to feed the hungry masses free of charge.

During his time, there were many needs not only in Rome but in other regions as well. As the successor to Peter, Gregory understood his role as stretching beyond the city to the Universal Church. He wrote many pastoral letters to the other churches and heard cases involving clergy, even bishops, in those other churches. Pope Gregory always signed his letters "Servant of the Servants of God," a tradition which the popes thereafter have retained. He combated heresy and paganism throughout the Universal Church by sending out missionaries and preachers from among the monasteries that he supported near Rome. Among these was St. Augustine of Canterbury, who became the apostle to the English. England and Spain both owe their Christian origins to Pope Gregory's apostolic concern. Pope Gregory wrote the biography of St. Benedict, the Father of Western Monasticism, and the missionaries he sent out established monasteries throughout Europe, implementing the Rule of Benedict.

Pope Gregory also reformed the Mass, bringing lasting changes, including the current place of the Lord's Prayer. He is usually considered the father of Gregorian Chant, a form of plainchant that follows the text of the liturgy and which became an integral part of the Roman Mass for centuries.

Pope Gregory suffered from gout in his old age and died in 604. The patron saint of musicians, singers, teachers, and students, he was also proclaimed a doctor of the Church for his many wise writings and sermons (Catholic Online). Pope St. Gregory I was given the title 'the Great' by public acclamation.

St. Gregory the Great, pray for us!

St. Peter Claver
Priest, 1580–1654
Memorial, Sept. 9

Spanish Jesuit priest St. Peter Claver was an apostle to African slaves in the New World. After entering the Jesuit order and completing his studies, Fr. Claver was given his assignment in the colonies. The slave trade was already well-established, and Peter could not abolish it despite papal statements condemning it. Trained by Père Alfonso de Sandoval, who labored for 40 years among the African slaves, Fr. Claver wholeheartedly embraced his mission. Like his predecessor, he called himself "slave of the negro slaves forever."

Fr. Claver would embark on the terrible slave ships and interact with the slaves, showing them his goodwill in the midst of their dreadful conditions. A third of the slaves typically did not even survive the journey from the west coast of Africa to the New World, and they were afflicted with illnesses, fear, malnourishment, and beatings—all in dark, squalid, cramped conditions. Fr. Claver would speak kindly to them and distribute treats to them to try to boost their spirits. With the help of various African translators, he would also preach the gospel to them, with its message of dignity and God's love. He would follow up on them when they left the ship and advocate for better treatment for them (*New Advent*). He also trained catechists to teach them, and he refused the hospitality of plantation owners, lodging instead in the slave quarters.

Fr. Claver was based out of Cartagena, in modern-day Colombia, where he had a church from which he continued his ministry to African slaves. During his lifetime, he baptized some 300,000 African slaves. He encountered much resistance and hardship because of the racism and prejudice of the colonists, as well as hostility from the slave traders and government officials, whose colonies relied on the slave trade for productivity in the mines.

But when Fr. Claver died after years of illness and neglect, the government provided him funeral honors at state expense. He had at last won the respect of many without regard to race. St. Peter Claver is the patron saint of African Americans, African missions, Colombia, comedians, communication workers, and interracial justice (Franciscan Media).

St. Peter Claver, pray for us!

Sts. Cyril and Methodius
St. Cyril, Monk (ca. 826 / 827 – 869) and St. Methodius, Bishop (815 – 885)
Memorial, Feb. 14

Sts. Cyril and Methodius, brothers by birth and by spirit, are remembered as the apostles of the Slavic peoples. Born in Thessalonica to noble parents, the two had to overcome many obstacles — particularly political ones involving tensions between East and West — to bring the gospel into the lives and culture of the Slavic peoples. Concerned with bringing the Bible and the liturgy to the Slavs in their own language but in written form, the brothers are credited with inventing the alphabet that became the Cyrillic alphabet of today, used in Russia and several other Eastern European countries.

Cyril and Methodius are both names taken by the brothers at religious profession (*Butler's Lives of the Saints*). Cyril's birth name was Constantine and Methodius' was Michael. Their father was a high official in the imperial government. The future St. Cyril was at first a philosopher, studying under the most eminent Eastern scholars at Constantinople. During that time he was also ordained as a deacon. The future St. Methodius was governor of a Slavic colony of the Eastern Empire. Methodius, however, decided to become a monk and was elected abbot. Cyril, having gained a reputation for his erudition, withdrew to live a life of prayer and asceticism on the Bosphorus. Known as "the Philosopher," he was found and brought back to serve as a teacher and scholar at Constantinople.

Emperor Michael III sent Cyril to evangelize the Khazars on the far side of the Black Sea, and he made a great many converts. Then the prince Rastislav of Moravia (now in the Czech Republic), interested in tempering the Western influence of German missionaries, petitioned Constantinople for missionaries to teach the Slavic people in the own language. Photius, Archbishop of Constantinople and former teacher to Cyril, recommended Cyril and Methodius since they knew the Slavonic language. At the time, many in the Western Church insisted only on the use of Latin for both the Bible and the liturgy, even in Eastern lands. Cyril and Methodius were readily welcomed since the people were glad that they made use of their own language for sacred matters. Nonetheless, controversy swirled among influential Western churchmen, and the German bishop would not ordain any priests for them.

So Cyril and Methodius, having found the relics of Pope St. Clement I in a church in Crimea, went to Rome to present the relics to Pope St. Nicholas I and win his favor. The Holy Father is said to have summoned them to an audience. The pope died before they arrived, but his successor Adrian II likewise was favorable to the brothers. They impressed him very much with their efforts at bringing the faith to the Slavs in their own language. Pope Adrian also greatly appreciated receiving the relics of such an early and revered Bishop of Rome. Pope Adrian announced that he would consecrate the brothers as bishops and the Slavic converts who accompanied them as priests. Then as bishops, the brothers would be able to ordain priests as desired.

But it happened to be the time of Cyril's passing. He was a priest but not as yet a monk. He was consecrated as a monk at this time, and only then took the name by which we know him — Cyril. We do not know if there was actually an opportunity for the pope to consecrate Cyril a bishop before his death. His brother Methodius was, however, consecrated a bishop by Pope Adrian himself, who insisted that Cyril be buried with honor at Rome. Then Methodius and his priests returned to the land of the Slavs. He later became archbishop of Sirmium, a restored ancient see. Support from the Bishop of Rome and high rank, however, did not prevent other churchmen from trying to stall the progress of the Slavic liturgies and Bibles.

Svlatopluk, a prince, usurped his uncle Rastisalv's power and took a hostile stance towards Methodius, who had rebuked him for his sinful ways. Methodius was imprisoned for two years, falsely charged with intruding on another bishop's territory. Pope John VIII had Methodius freed, but he was at first suspicious when Methodius was again denounced for heresy. But upon summoning Methodius and hearing directly from him about the matter, he exonerated him and praised his work. Still obstructed in his efforts at home, Methodius spent much of his latter days translating the Scriptures into the Slavic languages, making use of the alphabet that his brother Cyril in particular had pioneered. When he died, he was greatly mourned by the people. But then his chief opponent, Wiching, who used to go so far as to forge papal documents against Methodius, became bishop and suppressed the Slavonic liturgy and translations of the Bible, even exiling Methodius' supporters. A later pope also forbade the Slavonic liturgy and Bibles, which previous popes had approved. But Methodius' supporters kept them alive, and they became of great influence in the future Eastern Orthodox and Eastern Catholic churches.

Today, Sts. Cyril and Methodius are celebrated in both Catholicism and Eastern Orthodoxy. Utilizing the highest ordinary use of papal teaching authority, Pope St. John Paul II wrote an encyclical *Slavorum Apostoli* in 1985 to recall the lessons of Sts. Cyril and Methodius. He sets up their example of unity between East and West and their presentation of the unchanging gospel in new cultural ways — what he calls "inculturation" (no. 21). John Paul II, the only Polish pope, regarded the apostles of the Slavs as his own spiritual fathers. The Eastern Orthodox, moreover, venerate them with the title of "Equal to the Apostles."

There are a number of days on which the two have been commemorated both throughout history and by the various Eastern churches. Pope Leo XIII likewise dedicated an encyclical to Sts. Cyril and Methodius in 1880. There he raised their observance, previously only celebrated in certain local Catholic churches, to the calendar for the universal Catholic Church. The date chosen was February 14, the date of St. Cyril's death. Sts. Cyril and Methodius are venerated as the patron saints of ecumenism and co-patrons of Europe, together with St. Benedict of Nursia.

Sts. Cyril and Methodius, pray for us!

St. John Chrysostom
Bishop and Doctor of the Church, ca. 349–407
Memorial, Sept 13

St. John Chrysostom, Archbishop of Constantinople and doctor of the Church, was a great preacher, theologian, writer, and confessor for the faith. Chrysostom means golden-mouthed and was a title given to him during his lifetime. A major Eastern liturgy celebrated by certain Eastern Orthodox and eastern Catholic churches is attributed to him and given his name. He was one of the original three great doctors of the Eastern Church, together with St. Basil the Great and St. Gregory Nazienzen.

St. John Chrysostom was born in Antioch around 349 to a wealthy father and a pious mother. He was given an excellent education at Antioch with the aim of a legal career. John was later educated in rhetoric by a famous pagan rhetorician, Libanius, in Athens. Back in Antioch, John was deeply drawn to the holiness of Bishop Meletius and became a monk, practicing strict asceticism and balancing prayer with labor. At Antioch, he also became a lector, deacon, and then priest, serving among the people and exercising his talent for preaching. St. John Chrysostom began his prolific career of theological writing at Antioch as well. He was held in high regard by the people and by Bishop Meletius.

Political divisions at Constantinople made it suitable for an outsider to be named as archbishop of that capital city of the Eastern Roman Empire. The emperor was advised to select John Chrysostom, who then emerged as the new Archbishop of Constantinople. He learned about the city and its ways and found much in need of moral reform. He disciplined corrupt clergy and dismissed scandalous ones.

Archbishop John Chrysostom was loved by the people because of his support of the poor, his reputation for holiness, his courage, his erudition, and his rousing preaching, which was appreciated by the learned and unlearned alike. Chrysostom continued to write prolifically, especially on moral and doctrinal issues.

The city was abuzz with the business of the government and with the pride and extravagance of those in power. St. John Chrysostom was expected to join complacently in this lifestyle. Instead, he cut back the luxuries of the archbishop's household and continued to live as a monk, preaching against the vanities of the world. He also preached against the hypocrisy of the rich people who liked to appear generous and devout while ignoring the dire needs of the poor. Though he maintained good relations with some of the wealthy and powerful, he would not submit to any of their iniquitous schemes, so he lost favor with them.

Archbishop Chrysostom was accused of many false charged and exiled, but then was called back to Constantinople amidst the cheers of the people. Empress Eudoxia, however, was offended again by Chrysostom's care for the church, so she had him exiled once more. Then, when a fire in the city destroyed the cathedral and senate, it was blamed on Chrysostom's supporters. Even the pope came to Chrysostom's defense, but at last, he was sent on a death march to the far reaches of the Empire and died of exhaustion. His last words were "Glory be to God for all things" (*New Advent*).

St. John Chrysostom, pray for us!

Excerpt from St. John Chrysostom

> *Do not be ashamed to enter again into the Church. Be ashamed when you sin. Do not be ashamed when you repent. Pay attention to what the devil did to you. These are two things: sin and repentance. Sin is a wound; repentance is a medicine. Just as there are for the body wounds and medicines, so for the soul are sins and repentance. However, sin has the shame and repentance possesses the courage.* (Aleteia.org, "10 Quotes from Saint John [Golden-Mouthed] Chrysostom")

St. Cornelius (Pope) and St. Cyprian (Bishop)
Third Century
Memorial, Sept. 16

Saints Cornelius and Cyprian were third-century leaders who guided the Church during times of persecution, and both died as martyrs for the faith. Cornelius was the pope of Rome, and Cyprian was bishop of Carthage in North Africa, as well as a key supporter of Pope Cornelius in the challenges he faced.

The Roman emperor Decius ordered a persecution of the Christians, especially their leaders. Pope Fabian was martyred in 250 during this persecution. Cornelius was duly elected as his successor. Cornelius, however, was opposed by the first antipope, Novatian, who was established by three bishops even after Cornelius' valid election.

The point of contention was how rigorous the Church should be toward the relapsed—those who had denied the faith and had sacrificed to idols in order to save their lives. There were many heroic martyrs of all walks of life who endured unspeakable tortures during those times, but not everyone accepted martyrdom. Many regretted having scarified to idols and having denied the Christian faith. Some even went back and accepted martyrdom. But others returned to the Church only after the persecution waned.

According to Novatian, who had been a losing candidate for the see of Rome, the sin of these relapsed Christians was so grave that it was unforgivable by the Church. They could not be admitted back to the ranks of the faithful but only to a life of penance. They must remain forever in a separate section in the church, reserved for penitents, and could not be given Communion as long as they lived. Only God could forgive them, but the Church could not.

Pope Cornelius, however, countered that it was heresy to deny the power of the Church to forgive sins, which is a basic belief of Catholic Christians. He admitted the relapsed back to full Communion with the Church, but only after rigorous penance and a lengthy period during which they were assembled with the other penitents at church. Finally, however, they were to be admitted back to full membership in the Church and were to be granted Holy Communion.

The controversy regarding who was the true bishop of Rome swirled all about the universal Church. Cyprian, bishop of Carthage, helped secure key support for Pope Cornelius by uniting the African bishops behind him. Cyprian's writings remain important in Church history. One of his most famous works was *On the Unity of the Catholic Church*. There he wrote, "He cannot have God as a father who does not have the Church as a mother" (no. 5). Cyprian also argued in this work that the unity of the Church rests on Peter and his successors and that those who reject his successor separate themselves from the Church. He quoted Matthew 16, in which Jesus says to Peter, "I say to thee thou art Peter, and upon this rock I will build my church" (quoted in no. 4). To show the Church's power to forgive sins, he quoted John's gospel, in which Jesus says to the Apostles, "if you forgive the sins of anyone, they will be forgiven him; if you retain the sins of anyone, they will be retained" (quoted in no. 4).

History remembers Cornelius as the true successor of Peter as bishop of Rome. A synod of bishops reaffirmed Cornelius as such. Novatian was excommunicated, but he nonetheless retained many of his followers and continued his schismatic church, which lasted even past his death.

Another persecution broke out, and Cornelius was exiled by the emperor in 253, after just over two years as pope. He is believed to have died under harsh conditions in exile. The inscription found on his tomb in the Catacombs reads, "Cornelius, Martyr." Bishop Cyprian went into hiding. Meanwhile, an opponent set himself up in Cyprian's place in Carthage. He readmitted all the lapsed without requiring penance. Cyprian, by his decision as bishop, had only allowed those who had sacrificed to idols to receive Communion on their deathbed and required a lengthy time of penance from those who had only signed papers claiming to have made sacrifice. So Cyprian and Cornelius both took a middle path between those who were too strict and those who were too lenient toward the lapsed.

Cyprian was forced into exile during the persecution of Emperor Valerian and refused to give up the names of his priests. He continued to provide support for the Confessors—those who were suffering persecution for the faith. Several years after the martyrdom of Cornelius, Cyprian heard news of the martyrdom of another pope, Sixtus II. He understood from this that the empire would not be satisfied with exile much longer. So he returned to Carthage to be martyred in his own city. He was beheaded in the year 258 at Carthage. He is regarded as the most significant African father after St. Augustine.

St. Cornelius and St. Cyprian, pray for us!

Excerpt from On the Unity of the Catholic Church *by St. Cyprian*

The spouse of Christ cannot be adulterous; she is uncorrupted and pure. She knows one home; she guards with chaste modesty the sanctity of one couch. She keeps us for God. She appoints the sons whom she has born for the kingdom…. He can no longer have God for his Father, who has not the Church for his mother. If any one could escape who was outside the Ark of Noah, then he also may escape who shall be outside of the Church. The Lord warns, saying, *He who is not with me is against me, and he who gathers not with me scatters.* He who breaks the peace and the concord of Christ, does so in opposition to Christ; he who gathers elsewhere than in the Church, scatters the Church of Christ. The Lord says, *I and the Father are one*; and again it is written of the Father, and of the Son, and of the Holy Spirit, *And these three are one* (Ch. 5, New Advent).

St. Andrew Kim Tae-gon, St. Paul Chong Ha-sang, and Companions
Martyrs, Nineteenth Century
Memorial, Sept. 20

Thousands of Christians gave their lives in a persecution that broke out in Korea between 1839 and 1867, giving seed to a strong church that arose there. St. Andrew Kim Tae-gon, the first native Korean Catholic priest, and St. Paul Chong Ha-sang, an influential Christian who was yet to be ordained, are the chief representatives of about a hundred Korean martyrs—men, women, and children—who have been officially canonized.

The first Korean Christians were baptized by Japanese Christians in the late sixteenth century, and Christian books were introduced to Korea from China in the seventeenth century (Franciscan Media). French priests secretly tended to the Korean Christians as they were able. The Christians there called themselves "Friends of the Teaching of God of Heaven" to emphasize equality among believers in opposition to the set class system in Korea. They also put aside ancestor worship and accepted ideas that had originated abroad. Thus, many of the rulers of Korea saw Christianity as a threat to Confucian culture, and persecutions came in waves.

St. Andrew Kim Tae-gon was born in Korea in 1821. His family converted to Christianity, and he was baptized at the age of 15. St. Andrew Kim's father, St. Ignatius Kim, was martyred for the faith not long after the family converted. St. Andrew Kim made the long journey to China to study for the priesthood. Within a year of his ordination and the start of his ministry among his own people, he was captured and martyred together with a group of 20 other Christians. St. Andrew Kim was tortured, and then beheaded, outside

Seoul on the banks of the Han River in 1846. He was 25 years old.

St. Paul Chong Ha-sang was born to a high-class family that also converted to Christianity. While he was still a boy, his father and older brother were martyred. St. Paul Chong Ha-sang was influential in the conversion of many to Christianity. He successfully appealed to the pope to establish a diocese for Korea and to send priests. The bishop himself provided St. Paul Chong with training and was to ordain him soon when a persecution broke out. St. Paul Chong was captured and called to trial in 1839. His written defense of Christianity impressed the judge, who nonetheless followed the king's orders. St. Paul Chong was tortured and then crucified on a cart at the age of 45.

The Church in Korea thrived despite, and even because of, the persecutions. It was largely a lay-led church, with many Korean Christians having little or no access to a priest. Religious freedom was finally granted in 1884. St. Andrew Kim Tae-gon, St. Paul Chong Ha-sang, and companions were beatified by Pope Pius XI in 1925 and canonized in Seoul, South Korea, by Pope John Paul II in 1984. Pope Francis beatified an even larger list of Korean martyrs during his visit to South Korea in 2014.

I urge you to remain steadfast in faith, so that at last we will all reach heaven and there rejoice together.

– St. Andrew Kim Tae-gon

St. Andrew Kim Tae-gon, St. Paul Chong Ha-sang, and companions, pray for us!

St. Matthew
Apostle and Evangelist, First Century
Feast, Sept. 21

St. Matthew was one of the Twelve Apostles called by Jesus to be witnesses and leaders. Referred to as Levi before his calling, he was a Jew, the son of Alphaeus, and likely was given the compound name of Matthew and Levi by his parents.

Levi was previously a tax collector at Capernaum. He sat at the customs booths and levied taxes, perhaps on the fish caught in the Sea of Galilee and other goods for the ruler Herod Antipas—and thus, ultimately, for the Romans. As a tax collector, he would have become wealthy from what he had extorted for himself on top of the required taxes, and he would have been hated by the Jews not only for theft but also for treachery because of his political associations. Moreover, he would have been ritually unclean from his association with Gentiles because of his job.

Nonetheless, when Jesus saw Levi at his tax booth, he called out to him, "Follow me" (Lk. 5:27). Levi must have been very dissatisfied with his past life and ready for a change, because he immediately left everything, followed Jesus, and threw a large banquet for him at his house. This prompted the scribes and Pharisees to scold Jesus, saying, "Why do you eat and drink with tax collectors and sinners?" (Lk. 5:30). Jesus replied, "Those who are healthy do not need a physician, but the sick do. I have not come to call the righteous to repentance but sinners" (Lk. 5:31-32).

Matthew is traditionally believed to be the writer of the Gospel that bears his name. As a tax collector, he would have been well-educated and, thus, versed in Greek. As a Jew, he would have been knowledgeable regarding the Old Testament and Jewish customs, as is clear from the Gospel. The Gospel of Matthew appears to have been written especially for Jewish believers in Palestine. It is the longest Gospel and has a special focus on Jesus' fulfillment of the Old Covenant. In his Gospel, Matthew shows Jesus as the New Moses, giving the New Law, especially as presented in the Beatitudes. The Gospel of Matthew also shows Jesus as the New David, ushering in the 'Kingdom of Heaven,' a phrase unique to Matthew's gospel. The traditional symbol for his Gospel is the winged man.

According to most traditional accounts, Matthew suffered a martyr's death, but sources do not agree on the place or manner of his death (*New Advent*). He is the patron saint of bankers.

St. Matthew, pray for us!

St. Vincent de Paul
Priest, ca.1580–1660
Memorial, Sept. 27

St. Vincent de Paul, known as the Apostle of Charity and Conscience of France, was born in Pouy in Gascony around 1580. He was from a peasant family that worked the land, but he pursued an education to raise up himself and his family. He aspired to the priesthood, hoping to be appointed to an office from which he could send money home to support his family members.

Vincent was ordained to the priesthood when he was about 20 and was very ambitious, making trips to Rome in hopes of a high appointment and pursuing the possibility of inheriting property. His attempts, however, were of little avail. Then, in 1605, while traveling by sea, he was captured by Tunisian pirates, made a slave, and brought to Tunis. His master was a Frenchman, and Vincent converted him. The two escaped back to France in 1607 (*New Advent*).

Vincent continued his studies first at Avignon and then at Rome before returning to France. He was appointed almoner to Queen Marguerite of Valois, distributing alms to the poor. After serving briefly as a parish priest, Fr. Vincent was commissioned by the powerful Gondi family. He tutored the children of Philippe-Emmanuel de Gondi, became the spiritual director of Madame de Gondi, and ran missions on their estates for the peasant workers. Fr. Vincent returned to parish work, where he organized assistance to the poor and attracted the help of other priests to the cause.

The Gondi requested his services again to help with the poor on their estates. Fr. Vincent became interested in the galley convicts, over whom Monsieur de Gondi had charge as general of the galleys. The condition of the prisoners on the galley ship was frightful, and they were far from God. It was the confession of a dying convict that most deeply moved Fr. Vincent, causing him to abandon his ambition and spend his energies on the poor of France. He went to Paris to visit the galley convicts. Then, as royal almoner to the galleys of Louis XIII, he also went to Marseille and Bordeaux to visit the convicts there. He would tenderly care for their needs, preach to them, and win many over for God.

With the help of Madame de Gondi, Fr. Vincent founded the Congregation of Priests of the Mission to serve the faith of the country people by putting on missions for them and by instituting seminaries to train priests to serve them. In the years after the Protestant Reformation, priests were in short supply and in need of formation. The fruit he had borne through his missions could only be sustained with the help of priests. So St. Vincent put on retreats and conferences for priests to form them in the essentials of their calling. Though he started with conferences of only ten days, he expanded them gradually to several months—and then again to several years. They developed into an early seminary system as called for by the Council of Trent. He first established a seminary at the College des Bons-Enfants in Paris with the help of Cardinal Richelieu and ultimately had 11 seminaries by the end of his life.

Fr. Vincent sought women to assist with the needs of the many poor people serviced by his missions. Together with St. Louise de Marillac, this led to the formation of a congregation of sisters called the Daughters of Charity. Later, when he was called by the Archbishop of Paris to organize efforts for the poor, he established another group, called the Ladies of Charity, for laywomen. Many upper-class ladies joined the cause to help the poor but did not know how to perform the various humble duties required, so they brought their servants to help and to show them. These women served the needs of very large numbers of poor. For example, with the help of the Ladies of Charity, St. Vincent housed 40,000 vulnerable people in one of his institutions, even providing them with work opportunities. He also was able to provide relief from the sufferings of the 30 Years' War and ransomed 1,200 captives seized by the Barbary pirates off North Africa.

Fr. Vincent maintained his connections with the wealthy and powerful, bringing their attention to the poor and encouraging them to give away the resources with which they were blessed. He was a frequent guest of King Louis XIII and his court. Fr. Vincent died on September 27, 1660, at peace and awaiting his reward. St. Vincent de Paul was canonized in 1737. He is the patron saint of charitable societies.

St. Vincent de Paul, pray for us!

St. Wenceslaus
Martyr, 907–935
Optional Memorial, Sept. 28

St. Wenceslaus was the duke of Bohemia and died protecting the liberty of the Church. The son of Wratislaw, Duke of Bohemia, he was born in 907 near Prague. His grandfather was the first Christian ruler of Bohemia, and his father, too, was a Christian ruler. However, his mother, Drahomira, was pagan. Wenceslaus' pious grandmother, St. Ludmila, took on his education and formed him to revere the Christian faith. Meanwhile, his younger brother Boleslaus followed his mother in paganism.

After Wratislaw's death, Drahomira became regent. She outlawed Christianity and persecuted the Church. Churches were closed, priests were exiled, and people were forbidden to teach the Christian faith. Her order resulted in the massacre of many Christians who refused to abandon their faith. Drahomira also set her sights on Ludmila for training Wenceslaus, the heir to power, in Christianity. Ludmila received word that Drahomira was going to have her killed, so she set her affairs in order and made a good confession. The assassins found her lying prostrate in church in prayer, and they strangled her with her own veil.

A coup by Christian forces took control and put Wenceslaus in power as Duke of Bohemia. Wenceslaus restored the Church and spent his days upholding justice and peace. He was very devout and spent much of the night in prayer. Wenceslaus also personally loved to pick the grapes and grain that would be made into the bread and wine consecrated at Mass.

Once, a rival army under Radislaus, prince of Gurima, met Wenceslaus' army for battle to challenge his reign over Bohemia. Before battle, Wenceslaus went out to negotiate with Radislaus. Wenceslaus challenged him to a duel to decide the matter rather than allow so many to die. His enemy accepted his challenge, expecting to overpower him easily. But during the duel, the enemy saw two strong angels defending Wenceslaus, and he surrendered to Wenceslaus' terms.

Wenceslaus did not marry because he had made a vow of celibacy. When Boleslaus' son was going to be born, Drahomira thought the time was right to have Boleslaus seize power from his brother. Thus, Boleslaus conspired against Wenceslaus, inviting him to a festival Mass. On the way, nobles allied with Boleslaus fell upon Wenceslaus before Boleslaus himself killed his brother with a lance.

Wenceslaus reigned in Bohemia for 14 years. His place of burial was honored by the Christian population as a holy site and was known to be a place of miracles, such that Boleslaus had to relocate it to the church of St. Vitus in Prague. Holy Roman Emperor Otto I, who had held great respect for Wenceslaus, went to war against Boleslaus to avenge his death. After a few years, the emperor was able to bring Boleslaus into submission. Otto also posthumously granted Wenceslaus the title of king. Culturally, he is remembered in the Christmas carol "Good King Wenceslaus," which recounts the saint's charity for the poor. St. Wenceslaus is the patron saint of Bohemia, Prague,

412

and the Czech Republic. In fact, the Czech Republic marks his feast day with a public holiday.

St. Wenceslaus, pray for us!

Sts. Michael, Gabriel, and Raphael
Archangels
Feast, Sept. 29

The Epistle of Jude uses the word 'archangel' to speak of the highest rank of angels and specifically mentions Michael as an archangel (Jude 9). Michael, Gabriel, and Raphael are the only angels mentioned by name in the canonical Scriptures. Traditionally, Michael, Gabriel, and Raphael have all been viewed as archangels. Supporting this is what Gabriel said to Zechariah: "I am Gabriel, who stand before God" (Luke 1:19). The Book of Enoch, not recognized in the canon of the Bible, lists a total of seven archangels, including Michael, Gabriel, and Raphael, and Jewish tradition has also honored these angels together.

The name Michael means "Who is like God." He is first mentioned in the Book of Daniel in the Old Testament, where he is mentioned as the protector of Israel and as a "great prince" (Daniel 12:1). Michael appears in the New Testament in Revelation. There we find that Michael did battle with Satan and cast him and his angels out of Heaven (Revelation 12). Traditionally, his role is understood as fighting against Satan, rescuing souls from Satan's power, protecting God's people, and bringing souls to God for judgment (*New Advent*). He is the patron saint of grocers, soldiers, doctors, mariners, paratroopers, police, and those who suffer from illness (Catholic Online).

The name Gabriel means "the Strength of God." He is mentioned in the Book of Daniel in the Old Testament, where he brought a message from God. Gabriel had the important role in the New Testament of bringing word of the birth of Jesus to the Blessed Virgin Mary and word of the birth of John the Baptist to his father Zechariah, a priest.

Zachariah, who was offering incense at the Temple, did not believe Gabriel's message, and as a result, he was made mute until the time of his son's birth. By contrast, Mary accepted God's message through Gabriel and responded, "Behold, I am the handmaid of the Lord. May it be done to me according to your word" (Luke 1:38). The name of the angel who appeared to Joseph in Matthew's gospel is not mentioned, but it is traditionally thought to be Gabriel. St. Gabriel is the patron saint of messengers, telecommunication workers, and postal workers (Catholic Online).

The name Raphael means "God has healed." He is only mentioned by name in the Book of Tobit, where he figures prominently. He journeys with Tobit's son Tobiah to Media, resolving the problems of the family. He keeps Tobias safe while he brings back the family money and effects the healing of Tobit's blindness through smearing the gall of a fish on his eyes. Raphael also finds a good, God-fearing wife for Tobias, bringing her own misfortunes to an end and chasing away the demon that harassed her. Though not mentioned by name in the New Testament, Raphael is traditionally thought to be the angel who stirs the waters of the pool of Bethesda in John's gospel, where Jesus heals a man who had lain there 38 years without anyone lifting him into the waters (John 5). St. Raphael is the patron saint of travelers, the blind, bodily ills, happy meetings, nurses, physicians, and medical workers (Catholic Online).

Prayer to St. Michael the Archangel

St. Michael the Archangel,
defend us in battle.
Be our defense against the wickedness and snares of the Devil.
May God rebuke him, we humbly pray,
and do thou,
O Prince of the heavenly hosts,
by the power of God,
thrust into hell Satan,
and all the evil spirits,
who prowl about the world
seeking the ruin of souls. Amen. (EWTN)

Saints Michael, Gabriel, and Raphael, pray for us!

St. Jerome
Priest and Doctor of the Church, 342–420
Memorial, Sept. 30

St. Jerome was an early Church Father, doctor of the Church, priest, and hermit, and is remembered especially for his classic translation of the Bible into Latin.

St. Jerome was born in Dalmatia, in modern-day Croatia or Slovenia, as Eusebius Sophronius Hieronymus. His parents were wealthy Christians, and Jerome was well-educated in classic Greek and Latin literature and rhetoric. Jerome was a man of fiery passion. In his youth, he let his passions take control, falling into immorality. He traveled Europe in pursuit of learning and culture.

Providentially, Jerome came under the good Christian influence of a relative named Bonosus, with whom he went to Triers, in modern-day Germany. There his passion for Christian piety, first given him by his parents, was rekindled. Through ascetic practices, he applied himself to the pursuit of virtue, not only to the perfection of the mind as before. Going to Aquileia in Italy, Jerome cultivated Christian friendships with notable monks and scholars, who supported him in his new life. He was also influenced in the practice of asceticism by the *Life of St. Anthony*, which had rather recently been written by St. Athanasius and which burgeoned the monastic movement in its early days. Later, at Rome, Jerome received the "sacrament of regeneration," in which he confessed his sins (*Butler's Lives*).

Jerome went into the desert in Syria to fast and pray. There he had a dream of the judgment seat of Christ. Christ asked Jerome who he was, and Jerome replied that he was a

Christian. The Judge told Jerome that this was a lie—that he was really a Ciceronian. He then handed over Jerome to a severe beating by the angels. Jerome was greatly affected by this dream and often pondered death and judgment to guide his behavior and thoughts. Pondering the last judgment, and even the flames of Hell, also helped Jerome with his temptations to impure thoughts, which were a constant struggle until he was able to mortify his flesh through harsh penances.

The Christological controversies were in full swing at the time, and Jerome wrote to Pope Damasus in Rome about the situation and to ask for clarification. While at Antioch in Syria, the patriarch insisted on ordaining Jerome as a priest. Jerome believed his calling was to the ascetic and monastic life, but he accepted ordination on the condition that he would not be assigned pastoral duties. Jerome then went to Constantinople, where he was taught Christology by St. Gregory Nazianzen, who was a champion in Christological orthodoxy. Later, Jerome went to Palestine to dwell as a hermit, settling in a cave near the Church of the Nativity, at the spot where Christ was born.

Pope Damasus remembered Jerome and sent for him to become his personal secretary, so Jerome went to Rome to serve the pope. In Rome, he promoted the ascetic life and also drew female disciples who wanted to learn about the new movement. Jerome had enemies since he was fiery and witty in his denunciation of abuses, and his enemies created false stories about his involvement with one of the women,

St. Paula. After Pope Damasus died, Jerome was vulnerable to their pressure, so he left Rome and sailed east.

Jerome traveled to Syria, where he established a monastery, and then to Palestine, where he established a hospital for pilgrims. He went to Egypt, where he visited the prominent monasteries. Wherever he went, Jerome studied under the great and saintly minds of the day and often confronted heresies, defending the true faith.

At the time, there were various translations of parts of the Bible into Latin, the language of the Roman world, but there were many errors and additions in the translations. It was difficult to know the authentic meaning of the text without reading Hebrew and Greek. Jerome was proficient in both of the latter languages and was endowed with God's Spirit. Knowledge of Hebrew was particularly rare, but he had learned it from a Jewish Christian and had studied it quite assiduously despite its challenges. Jerome spent years in his cave at Bethlehem prayerfully and authentically translating the Scriptures, with comparisons to the previous translations and with the necessary corrections.

The result was the Latin Vulgate Bible. 'Vulgate' means 'common speech,' hence its application to the translation of the Holy Scriptures into a commonly spoken language. It stands as the preeminent Catholic translation of the Bible. Pope St. Gregory the Great later recognized it as such, and much later, in the sixteenth century, the Council of Trent refused to recognize the authenticity of any translation other than the Vulgate. The Second Vatican Council, in the 1960s, reaffirmed the preeminence of the Vulgate but authorized other translations from the original languages, so long as they were made with comparison to the Vulgate and approved by the Church.

In addition to translating the Scriptures, Jerome wrote important commentaries on their spiritual meaning. In his old age, he was adversely affected by the encroachments of barbarians into the civilized world, but he died naturally in the year 420. A doctor of the Church, St. Jerome is the patron saint of archaeologists, translators, librarians, students, and biblical scholars.

St. Jerome, pray for us!

LIVES OF THE SAINTS
VOLUME IV (OCTOBER – DECEMBER)

Michael J. Ruszala

Foreword

In the Church, there is a patron saint for almost everything and a festival almost every day. Saints are models and guides for every walk of life. Memories of some saints remain from generation to generation, but other saints are remembered by those on earth for a more limited time or in a more particular place. The index of the classic *Butler's Lives of the Saints,* for example, serves as a reminder that there are myriads of "official" saints with whom hardly anyone is still familiar. In Heaven, surely, there are countless more "unofficial" saints who worship before the throne of God, and this is why the Church celebrates a Solemnity of All Saints on November 1.

In the Apostles' Creed, we state our belief in the "communion of saints." The saints in Heaven are not isolated in their worship of God. They are together a family of God, not only with the other saints in Heaven, but also with us on earth, their younger siblings in faith. This is why, from the earliest days, Christians sought the prayers of the holy martyrs. The saints in Heaven care for those on earth and offer intercessions for them before God. Popularly, the faithful in different states of life, places, and situations came to associate with certain saints. This way, they could also focus on particular saints, learn from them, and ask for their intercession. This book enables readers to learn more about saints and to find those who speak to their particular situation in some respect.

Introduction

October 4 was always a special day at my alma mater, Franciscan University. Morning classes were let out early that day, and there was always a feeling of excitement in the crisp autumn air. Crowds of students and groups of friends flocked to the field house for the Mass for the feast of their patron, St. Francis of Assisi, celebrated with the Franciscan friars who ran the University. The University chapel wasn't large enough to hold the thousand students, faculty, and staff who attended each year. Dozens of golden Communion cups and ciboria were prepared. Readers and other student ministers felt especially honored to be able to serve on this day. Mass started with a long, solemn procession, with the hymn "All Creatures of Our God and King" led by the student music ministry and joined enthusiastically by the congregation, who stood in front of the tightly packed rows of folding chairs that student workers had set up the night before. Stories of St. Francis dotted the friars' homilies all year round, but the homilist especially expounded on Franciscan spirituality on this day, the feast of Our Holy Father Francis, the Poverello of Assisi. After Mass, the throngs filed out together in long lines, mostly to the cafeteria for lunch. Special events were also planned throughout the whole weekend in commemoration of the feast, and at least one student actor went around dressed like the saint.

Such is the feeling of devotion and fellowship in celebrating a beloved patron saint. The Church celebrates the saints all year round, marking seasons and festivals. Somewhere around the world, a community is almost always celebrating a patron saint. This book, The Lives of the Saints: Volume IV (October – December), brings to completion a series of four volumes on the lives of the saints, covering the memorials, feasts, and solemnities of the whole Church year, in addition to several of the many optional memorials. This last volume brings with it some of the most beloved of the saints, including St. Therese of the Child Jesus, the Holy Guardian Angels, St. Francis of Assisi, St. Cecelia, and St. Nicholas.

St. Therese of the Child Jesus
Virgin and Doctor of the Church, 1873–1897
Memorial, Oct. 1

St. Therese of the Child Jesus is also known as St. Therese of Lisieux or the Little Flower. She died in a cloistered convent at the young age of 24 but became one of the most popular saints of the twentieth century after her highly relatable and inspirational spiritual autobiography was published following her death. St. Therese only considered herself a small flower in God's garden, but Pope St. John Paul II declared her a doctor of the Church in 1997 for her insights on the Little Way to Heaven.

St. Therese was born Marie Therese Martin in Lisieux, in Normandy, France. Her parents, Louis and Zelie, were very devout. Louis discerned the priesthood, and Zelie discerned becoming a nun, but they were both turned away. They then found and married each other, discerning this to be God's will, but they were so pure in their chastity that they would not even dance. Of the five daughters they had who survived childhood, all chose to become nuns—such were the values instilled in them from a young age. In fact, in 2015, Louis and Zelie Martin became the first married couple to be canonized as saints.

Zelie gave birth to four other children, though they did not survive past childhood. Zelie, in fact, died in childbirth when Therese was only four. In her autobiography, *The Story of a Soul*, St. Therese recalls some of her childish antics and possessive love of things, but the death of her mother left her with an early impression that life on earth is only for a time. Therese became very shy and sensitive following her mother's death. Even as she grew older, the slightest comment could make her cry. She also became ill and almost died in childhood, but she saw the statue of

Mary in her room smile and was miraculously restored to health.

Therese learned on her own how to meditate on the things of God, but she had what she called her "complete conversion" at the age of 13, on Christmas Eve, when she overheard her father comment that she was getting a little old to leave her shoes out for presents in the morning. She ran to her room to cry, but found the crucifix there and noticed how Jesus suffered. Touched by grace, she offered up her suffering for poor souls. She then made a habit of offering small sufferings for souls in need. Her first case was that of a condemned criminal about whom she read in the newspaper. She prayed and fasted for him, and then was consoled to learn that he had kissed the crucifix before going to the guillotine. It was a sign to her that God had used her prayers and sacrifices to offer grace to this soul in need. She nourished her prayer life with spiritual reading and the good company of her sisters, who were also serious in pursuing the spiritual life.

Therese desired earnestly to enter the cloistered convent of the Discalced Carmelites at Lisieux. Her older sister and caregiver Pauline had entered there, but Therese's longing was deeper than simply to join her sister. She asked her father for permission to enter Carmel. His response was tender to giving up his young daughter but open to God's will for her growth. She was still too young, though, to enter according to the rules, and the superior and the bishop would not grant her permission to enter at only 15. When Louis brought his daughters on a pilgrimage to Rome, Therese took the opportunity to speak about the matter to Pope Leo XIII himself during an audience, even though it was forbidden to speak to the pope. The pope responded that it would happen if God willed it. Soon enough, her bishop granted her request to enter Carmel at only 15, after a few months of waiting.

Young Sister Therese was not treated well by all of the nuns. One especially was very particular about the tasks she gave Sister Therese, and in her eyes, Sister Therese could do nothing well. The nun even assigned her the worst of motives. Sister Therese, however, saw this as an opportunity to offer sacrifice. The greatest sacrifice in that situation was to offer a kind smile, and when tending to the needs of an elderly sister, she imagined assisting Jesus himself.

Therese took the name Sister Therese of the Child Jesus. She grew in the life of prayer and later became a novice mistress, guiding other young women entering the convent into the ways of religious life and spiritual perfection. Two older sisters and a cousin were also sisters in the convent at Lisieux, and another of her sisters joined later, after Louis passed away. Her eldest sister, Marie, became the mother superior. Some of the nuns gossiped about their family bonds and suspected favoritism, though Therese, for her part, took care to treat her own sisters as she would any other religious.

Sister Therese developed a cough and was ultimately diagnosed with an advanced case of tuberculosis, for which little could be done. Mother Marie, her sister, knowing her deep spirituality, ordered her to write an autobiography. She did so, and it became the widely loved *Story of a Soul*, in which she spoke of God's mercies to her. Though she was never a great sinner, she took even her small sins of childhood seriously and saw that it was God, in fact, who had preserved her from falling into more serious sins. She taught her Little Way—that the shortcut to Heaven is in doing small things with great love. Not believing herself strong enough to do the great and heroic acts of the saints she had read about, like her namesake St. Teresa of Avila, she relied on Jesus to do the work. This, ultimately, was all that was needed after all. Everything was grace. She desired to become a missionary to convert souls in faraway lands but realized that instead, her work was to pray for priests serving there, offer sacrifices for them, and write them encouraging letters.

Sister Therese suffered much at the end and died at the age of only 24, promising to send down a shower of roses from Heaven. She was canonized in 1925 and is the patron of France, florists and gardeners, the missions, and sufferers of tuberculosis and AIDS. Those who pray her novena often look for roses as a sign of answered prayers.

St. Therese of the Child Jesus, pray for us!

Excerpt from The Story of a Soul *by St. Therese*

> Our Lord... showed me the book of nature, and I understood that every flower created by Him is beautiful, that the brilliance of the rose and the whiteness of the lily do not lessen the perfume of the violet or the sweet simplicity of the daisy. I understood that if all the lowly flowers wished to be roses, nature would lose its springtide beauty, and the fields would no longer be enamelled with lovely hues. And so it is in the world of souls, Our Lord's living garden. He has been pleased to create great Saints who may be compared to the lily and the rose, but He has also created lesser ones, who must be

content to be daisies or simple violets flowering at His Feet, and whose mission it is to gladden His Divine Eyes when He deigns to look down on them. And the more gladly they do His Will the greater is their perfection.

I understood this also, that God's Love is made manifest as well in a simple soul which does not resist His grace as in one more highly endowed. In fact, the characteristic of love being self-abasement, if all souls resembled the holy Doctors who have illuminated the Church, it seems that God in coming to them would not stoop low enough. But He has created the little child, who knows nothing and can but utter feeble cries, and the poor savage who has only the natural law to guide him, and it is to their hearts that He deigns to stoop. These are the field flowers whose simplicity charms Him; and by His condescension to them Our Saviour shows His infinite greatness.

The Holy Guardian Angels
Memorial, Oct. 2

The Holy Guardian Angels are pure spirits entrusted by God to guide human beings in their journey toward Heaven. The memorial of the Holy Guardian Angels honors their protection and guidance.

According to St. Thomas Aquinas, whereas the seraphs, who are wholly wrapped in the worship of God around his throne, are the highest the rank of angels, the angels entrusted to human beings are the lowest rank. Some theologians, however, have disagreed, arguing that any angel can be assigned as a guardian angel (*New Advent*). Guardian angels are believed to be able to provide direction by influencing the imagination, countering demonic powers, and affecting external events, though they cannot force anyone's free will. The guardian angel aims to lead the person to Heaven, and is said to even remain with him or her in Heaven should the person arrive there.

It is believed that God entrusts an angel to each human soul, but the Church has never officially defined a doctrine concerning guardian angels. It has, however, sanctioned their celebration in the liturgy. Pope Pius V elevated the observance of guardian angels from an early local tradition to the Roman calendar in 1608, assigning it to October 2 since this was the first open date after the feast of St. Michael the Archangel.

The Bible affirms that God sends angels to help human beings. In the Old Testament, God said to Moses, "Now, go and lead the people where I have told you. See, my angel will go before you" (Ex. 32:34). In the Psalms, we read, "For he commands his angels with regard to you, to guard you wherever you go. With their hands they shall support you, lest you strike your foot against a stone" (Ps. 91:11–12).

Jesus himself directly affirmed the existence of guardian angels in Matthew's Gospel, saying, "See that you do not despise one of these little ones, for I say to you that their angels in heaven always look upon the face of my heavenly Father" (Mt. 18:10). In the Acts of the Apostles, Peter is freed from prison by an angel sent to protect him (Acts 12).

The belief in guardian angels has been affirmed throughout Church history. St. Jerome wrote, "[H]ow great the dignity of the soul, since each one has from his birth an angel commissioned to guard it" (St. Jerome). St. Padre Pio was familiar with guardian angels and could see them. He wrote this advice concerning guardian angels to one of his spiritual daughters:

> Have great devotion, Annita, to this beneficent angel. How consoling it is to know that we have a spirit who, from the womb to the tomb, never leaves us even for an instant, not even when we dare to sin. And this heavenly spirit guides and protects us like a friend, a brother.

> But it is very consoling to know that this angel prays unceasingly for us, and offers God all of our good actions, our thoughts, and our desires, if they are pure.

> Oh! For goodness' sake, don't forget this invisible companion, ever present, ever disposed to listen to us and even more ready to console us. Oh, wonderful intimacy! Oh, blessed companionship! If only we could understand it! Keep him always before your mind's eye. Remember this angel's presence often, thank him, pray to him, always keep up a good relationship. Open yourself up to him and confide

your suffering to him. Be always afraid of offending the purity of his gaze. Know this, and keep it well present in your mind. He is easily offended, very sensitive. Turn to him in moments of supreme anguish and you will experience his beneficent help.

Never say that you are alone in the battle against your enemies; never say that you have no one to whom you can open your heart and confide. It would be a grave injustice to this heavenly messenger. (Letter to Annita, 7/15/1913, quoted on Aleteia.org)

Holy Guardian Angels, pray for us!

Prayer to the Guardian Angel
Angel of God
My guardian dear
To Whom His love
Commits me here
Ever this day
Be at my side
To light and guard
To rule and guide. Amen.

St. Francis of Assisi
1182–1226
Memorial, Oct. 4

St. Francis of Assisi is one of the most universally loved saints of all time. He is often regarded as one of the most Christlike of the saints, or even a kind of 'second Christ.' St. Francis is the founder of the second-largest religious order, the Franciscans, which has produced many saints over the ages, and he is also Pope Francis' namesake.

St. Francis was born in 1182 in Assisi, in Italy, to a wealthy cloth merchant named Pietro Bernadone and his wife, Pica, who was from Provence in France. Francis was christened Giovanni, but his father, who loved traveling in France, renamed him Francis. His parents were worldly, and young Francis was very jovial and loved to attend parties. He became popular, investing his time in frivolities and becoming known for his humor, charm, and chivalry. Still, he noticed the plight of the less fortunate and took an interest in helping them.

At the age of 20, Francis went to war for his city, Assisi, against the city of Perugia. He was captured, however, and was imprisoned for a year in Perugia. During that time, Francis became ill and began to think about the things of God. God began to speak to him in dreams during that time. When he was released, Francis was more open to God's will, but he still intended to return to war and pursue glory. Then God came to him in a dream and asked him, "Francis, who can do better for thee, the lord or the servant, the rich man or the poor?" (Bonaventure, *The Life of St. Francis* 1.3). Francis chose the Lord and returned home.

Around that time, Francis came across a leper, who stretched out his hand for alms. Francis shrunk away at first, out of fear of catching the disease, but subsequently ran up to him and kissed his hand. Then the leper disappeared. Francis would later say, "When thou seest a poor man, O Brother, a mirror is set before thee of the Lord, and of His Mother in her poverty. In the infirm, do thou in like manner think upon the infirmities that He took upon Him" (8.5).

While visiting the chapel of San Damiano and praying before the crucifix, he heard Jesus speaking to him from the crucifix: "Francis, go and repair My House, which, as thou seest, is falling utterly into ruin" (2.1). Taking the words literally, Francis devoted himself to rebuilding the chapel at San Damiano, which was in disrepair. He sold goods from his father's merchandise to raise money for the repairs and worked under the direction of the local priest. Fearing Francis' father, the priest would not accept the money, so Francis simply threw it out on the ledge, counting it as nothing.

Francis' change in behavior and newly disheveled appearance earned him insults from others, as well as the wrath of his father, who even sent men to capture Francis and end this disgrace to the family. Francis then became his father's prisoner, but his mother, though she did not approve of his new life, freed him. Afterward, Pietro turned his wrath on his wife, Pica, so Francis returned and confronted his father. His father wanted him to return, but he would not. Pietro wanted Francis to leave the province, but he would not. So Pietro sought to reclaim the money from the goods Francis had sold to raise money for the church, and took Francis before the bishop to disinherit him formally. Francis took off all his garments and returned them to his father, saying, "Hitherto I have called thee my father on earth, but henceforth I can confidently say 'Our Father, Which art in heaven,' with Whom I have laid up my

444

whole treasure, and on Whom I have set my whole trust and hope" (2.4). The bishop began to weep and clothed him in his own outer garment.

At Mass one Sunday, Francis listened attentively to the gospel and considered it literally for himself: "Do not take gold or silver or copper for your belts; no sack for the journey, or a second tunic, or sandals, or walking stick" (Mt. 10:9-10). Francis desired wholeheartedly to follow this, so from then on, he strictly embraced what he called "Lady Poverty." A man named Bernard joined Francis in his way of life, and the two entered a church and prayed for three scriptures to give them a rule by which to live. St. Bonaventure, St. Francis' biographer and future successor as minister general, recounted, "In the first opening of the book was discovered that saying: 'If thou wilt be perfect, go and sell that thou hast, and give to the poor.' In the second: 'Take nothing for your journey.' And in the third: 'If any man will come after Me, let him deny himself, and take up his cross, and follow Me'" (Bonaventure 3.3). They adopted this for their rule, and soon more men joined them.

Before long, Francis had to expand upon the rule and go to the pope for approval for his new order. At that time, there was a restriction on new orders being introduced, but Pope Innocent III was given a dream in which St. Francis was holding up St. Peter's Basilica as its support. Thus, the Holy Father approved the new order, called the Order of Friars Minor, which was then composed of 12 friars, paralleling the 12 Apostles of Christ. A few years later, Brother Francis received St. Clare, a young noblewoman from Assisi, into following his way of life. Though he first placed her in a nearby convent, she later became the superior of the Franciscan order for women.

In all of their ways, Francis and his brothers sought to live out the purity of the gospel. The brothers would preach in the marketplace and beg for their daily needs, relying on God's providence in all things. So great was Brother Francis' austerity that St. Bonaventure wrote of how "he restrained his sensual appetites with such strict discipline as that he would barely take what was necessary to support life" (5.1). Brother Francis considered himself a sinner; he accepted ordination as a deacon so he could preach in church but refused priestly ordination since he considered himself unworthy.

Brother Francis worked numerous miracles, many of which closely resembled the wonders of Christ in the Gospels. St. Bonaventure tells us that "he rejoiced in railings, and was saddened by praise" (6.1). Regarding all creation as brother and sister under one Heavenly Father, he called his body "brother ass." Even animals are said to have shown an awareness of the holiness of St. Francis and listened, as it were, to his words and instructions. He preached to a flock of birds, calling on them to praise the Creator. Fishes danced about his boat and would not leave before receiving his blessing. When animals caused trouble for people, he would speak to the animals and they would be at peace.

Brother Francis sent brothers to Morocco to convert the Saracens in the midst of wartime. Some of the Saracens were deeply moved by the brothers and their willing acceptance of poverty for the love of God. Brother Francis himself went to speak to a sultan to convert him and thus end the war. The sultan, who could have had Francis killed on the spot, was very impressed with Francis, but refused to convert out of fear of his own people. Later on, several Franciscan missionaries were martyred in Morocco.

Two years before he died, Brother Francis was praying on Mount La Verna when he saw a winged man coming down from Heaven with the marks of crucifixion. Light came out from the wounds and pierced Francis' body, leaving him with the stigmata—the marks of the wounds of Christ on his hands, feet, and side. There were even black protrusions, like the nails, in his hands and feet, which made it difficult for him to walk without being carried. He bled a great deal, and his blood became a healing balm, even healing animals that touched it. Brother Francis' state was a cause of humiliation to him since he preferred to hide his mystical unity with Christ.

At last, Brother Francis' infirmity, due to his harsh treatment of "brother ass," brought his earthly life to a close. Even then, he said, "Let us begin, Brethren, to serve our Lord God, for until now we have made but little progress" (14.1). When his time came, he lay on the ground naked so that he might go to God with nothing but himself. He consoled the brothers and encouraged them in virtue before he passed at the age of 44. He was canonized only two years later by Pope Gregory IX. St. Francis of Assisi is the patron saint of animals, ecology, Italy, merchants, messengers, metal workers, and archaeologists (Franciscan Media).

St. Francis of Assisi, pray for us!

The Prayer of St. Francis

Though St. Francis is most likely not the writer of the popular Prayer of St. Francis, the prayer captures the essence of his spirituality quite well:

> *Lord, make me an instrument of Your peace;*
> *Where there is hatred, let me sow love;*

Where there is injury, pardon;
Where there is doubt, faith;
Where there is despair, hope;
Where there is darkness, light;
And where there is sadness, joy.

O Divine Master,
Grant that I may not so much seek
To be consoled as to console;
To be understood, as to understand;
To be loved, as to love;
For it is in giving that we receive,
It is in pardoning that we are pardoned,
And it is in dying that we are born to Eternal Life.

Amen.

St. Teresa of Jesus (of Avila)
Virgin and Doctor of the Church, 1515–1582
Memorial, Oct. 15

St. Teresa of Jesus, also known as St. Teresa of Avila, was a Spanish mystic and a foundress of the Discalced Carmelite Order, a strict reform of the Carmelites. She became the first woman doctor of the Church, together with St. Catherine of Siena.

Teresa was born to a pious family in Avila, Spain, in 1515. As a child, she developed a great interest in the lives of the saints, even convincing her brother to join her in seeking martyrdom from the Moors. Her father found out, however, and put an end to it. When she was a teenager, Teresa's mother died, but her father did his best in guiding her on the path of holiness. Concerned by her vain interest in chivalrous novels, Teresa's father sent her to the Augustinian convent at Avila for an education from the good sisters. While there, Teresa was often very sickly, and this caused her to think more on the interior life and the things of God. Returning home, she was inspired by the ascetical writings of St. Jerome and resolved to join the Carmelite nuns at Avila. Leaving her father's house without his permission, she received his approval only after entering the convent.

As a young nun, Sister Teresa progressed in mental prayer and meditation, but the connections she kept to the world seemed to hamper her. Though she was allowed to converse in the parlor of the convent with visitors from the outside world, these visitors from her relations filled her mind with the worldly things she had entered the convent to be freed from, and her prayer life began to suffer. Sister Teresa's superior warned her about this, but she only made a change after Jesus himself appeared to her and expressed his displeasure with her behavior. She then closed the door on the things of the world and never looked back.

Sister Teresa began to be visited often by Jesus, Mary, saints, and angels. She had visions and inner locutions, which came without the aid of the senses. This is partly why Jesus called her to shut out the world so completely. Sister Teresa was even given a vision of Hell, in which she keenly realized how the vanities of her youth could have ultimately led her to eternal perdition and interior despair. Remembering this painful vision enabled her to more readily reject sin and vanity.

Sister Teresa sought mystical union with Jesus earnestly and with great longing. Along the way, she encountered much difficulty from small imperfections within and also from a dryness in prayer, called desolation. She sought the help of numerous holy spiritual directors—some more helpful than others—and read many spiritual books to try to understand her calling. In her autobiography, St. Teresa identified four stages of mystical prayer: meditation, the 'prayer of quiet,' union, and rapture. She also wrote an important spiritual book, *The Interior Castle,* in which she envisioned the soul as a castle of seven mansions through which we make our way to union with Jesus, who is its center. She is also remembered for her spiritual classic *The Way of Perfection.* St. Teresa of Avila found great spiritual kinship with St. John of the Cross, who likewise pined for union with God through stages, which he taught were marked by the growing pains he described as the "dark night of the soul." Sister Teresa was also known to levitate in the air sometimes during her ecstasy in prayer. Once, she held on to some railing to prevent herself from floating higher, telling Jesus she didn't want people to mistake her for a holy person. Sister Teresa also received what is called the transverberation of the heart, a mystical experience that left her heart pieced for love of God (*New Advent*).

Sister Teresa was made superior of her convent and brought about strict reforms, including restricting visits with outsiders in the parlor. The pope wanted to bring about a reform of the convents, which had become somewhat lax and in some cases were filled with women who entered for worldly reasons, so he appointed Mother Teresa of Jesus as a prioress. The nuns under her charge were very resistant to her reforms, but she slowly won them over through her humility and love. She also established strict convents for men with the help of St. John of the Cross and others. She ultimately founded 16 women's convents and 14 men's convents, but both she and St. John of the Cross met with much persecution from religious who were comfortable as they were and did not want to be thought of as less holy because others were living more strictly. She was often assailed with calumnies and slanders and even had to face a court of the Inquisition. Mother Teresa withdrew to her interior castle, counting the world outside as nothing. She came to the realization that the only permanence in the world is what is conducive to building virtue.

Though Mother Teresa of Avila wished her troubles would come to some resolution, she embraced them as a cross that would unite her more closely with Jesus. She once said to Jesus in prayer, "If this is how you treat your friends, no wonder you have so few of them!" In fact, one of her spiritual directors prophesied correctly that her troubles would not cease in this life. Amid the controversy in the reform of the Carmelite Order, Mother Teresa of Avila became ill and never rose from her bed. Before she died, she said, "O my Lord, and my spouse, the desired hour is now come. It is now time for me to depart hence. Thy will be done. The hour is at last come, wherein I shall pass out of this exile, and my soul shall enjoy in thy company what it hath so earnestly longed for" (*Butler's Lives*).

St. Teresa of Avila is regarded as a foundress of the Discalced Carmelite Order. It is called *discalced*, meaning barefoot, in reference to its austerity of life. St. Teresa was declared a doctor of the Church by Pope Paul VI in 1970 and is the patron saint of headache sufferers. She is often pictured with an arrow piercing her heart and with a book of her writings, which guided many in their path to holiness.

St. Teresa of Jesus, pray for us!

Prayer of St. Teresa of Avila

Let nothing disturb you,
Let nothing frighten you,
All things are passing away:
God never changes.
Patience obtains all things
Whoever has God lacks nothing;
God alone suffices.

St. Ignatius of Antioch
Bishop and Martyr, d. ca. 108
Memorial, Oct. 17

St. Ignatius of Antioch was an early bishop and martyr of
the Church. He was also known as Theophorus, or 'God-
bearer.' Taught at Antioch in Asia Minor at the feet of St.
John the Apostle, and also by St. Peter and St. Paul, Bishop
Ignatius was a direct witness and bearer of what we now
call apostolic succession. A friend of the bishop and martyr
Polycarp of Smyrna, Ignatius is remembered for the seven
letters he wrote while he was being taken in captivity to his
martyrdom in the amphitheaters of Rome. These letters
were written to various churches and to his friend Polycarp
to encourage them in the faith. They also serve as important
theological markers for the beliefs of the early Church,
especially on the Eucharist, the bishops, and the Church.

The persecution of Christians at the time was sporadic.
Emperor Trajan passed through Antioch in great pomp on
his way to war with the Parthians. To appease the gods and
ensure victory against his enemies, Trajan decreed that the
Christians of Antioch be put to death. Their leader, Bishop
Ignatius, was quickly apprehended and brought before the
emperor. Ignatius preached to the emperor about Christ
crucified who dwelt in his heart and expressed his own
desire to die for love of him. But Trajan ridiculed the
bishop, condemning him to death by being devoured by
wild beasts in the public spectacles at Rome. Ignatius,
however, rejoiced at this opportunity to attain union with
Christ as the Apostles before him had done. Ignatius
fervently believed that martyrdom would bring his soul to
glory in Christ in a way that would not have been possible
otherwise.

Ten soldiers were assigned to guard Ignatius and prevent
the Christians from rescuing him. They boarded him on a

ship, taking a circuitous path to Rome and making many stops in Asia Minor. In his letters, Ignatius called the soldiers his "ten leopards" because of their inhumanity. The more kindness he showed them, the crueler they acted toward him. However, Ignatius was allowed to disembark at Smyrna in Asia Minor. There he visited and conversed with St. Polycarp, and numerous representatives from the surrounding churches came to offer him support.

The Christians naturally wanted to rescue Bishop Ignatius, but he urged them not to. He wrote in his Letter to the Romans, "For I am afraid of your love, lest it should do me an injury. For it is easy for you to accomplish what you please; but it is difficult for me to attain to God, if you spare me…. For neither shall I ever have such [another] opportunity of attaining to God; nor will you, if you shall now be silent, ever be entitled to the honour of a better work. For if you are silent concerning me, I shall become God's; but if you show your love to my flesh, I shall again have to run my race. Pray, then, do not seek to confer any greater favour upon me than that I be sacrificed to God while the altar is still prepared" (1–2).

A major theme of his letters is Church unity. Ignatius was the first to use the word 'catholic,' or 'universal,' to describe the Church of Christ. He strongly denounced heresy and schism as marring Christ's church and urged the faithful to unite behind their bishop. In his writings, we find the structure of ministry in the early Church in terms of deacons, presbyters (priests), and bishops (overseers). He wrote, "For, since you are subject to the bishop as to Jesus Christ … without the bishop you should do nothing, but should also be subject to the presbytery, as to the apostle of Jesus Christ, who is our hope, in whom, if we live, we shall

456

[at last] be found. It is fitting also that the deacons, as being [the ministers] of the mysteries of Jesus Christ, should in every respect be pleasing to all" (Letter to the Trallians, 2).

Regarding the Eucharist, Ignatius bore witness to the early belief in Christ's words, "This is my body." He wrote against those causing division, "They abstain from the Eucharist and from prayer, because they confess not the Eucharist to be the flesh of our Saviour Jesus Christ, which suffered for our sins, and which the Father, of His goodness, raised up again" (Letter to the Smyrneans, 7).

After some delay, by which time other Christians from Antioch had already arrived at Rome, Ignatius was at last hurried to Rome for the last day of the public spectacles. The soldiers presented the emperor's letter regarding Ignatius there, and he was promptly led forth to the amphitheater. When he heard the roaring of the lions, he cried out, "I am the wheat of the Lord; I must be ground by the teeth of these beasts to be made the pure bread of Christ" (*Butler's Lives*). He was immediately devoured by two lions. The Christians greatly mourned his death, but one of them, seeking consolation, received a vision of St. Ignatius in glory. The Christians later gathered his few remaining larger bones, which were held in reverence in various churches over the centuries.

St. Ignatius of Antioch, pray for us!

St. Luke
Evangelist, First Century
Feast, Oct. 18

St. Luke is believed to be the writer of the Gospel of Luke and the Acts of the Apostles. A physician by trade, he was an early Gentile convert and a faithful associate of St. Paul, accompanying him on two missionary journeys and during his captivity.

In Acts of the Apostles 16–28, Luke begins narrating the story in the first person, using the pronoun "we." In context, this implies that Luke joined Paul at Troas, a Greek city in Asia Minor, during his second missionary journey. Luke endured many hardships together with Paul and also saw many wondrous things from the Holy Spirit in the Church. Luke accompanied Paul into Macedonia and Greece, then back to Jerusalem, and finally in Rome, where Paul was held captive.

Paul mentioned Luke in several of his letters, speaking well of his character and fidelity. In Colossians 4:14, St. Paul wrote, "Luke the beloved physician sends greetings, as does Demas." In Philemon 1:24, St. Paul named Luke as one of his "co-workers." In 2 Timothy 4:11, he even identified Luke as the only one who did not abandon him at that time, during his captivity.

According to tradition, Luke was not martyred with Paul but went on to evangelize in Italy, Dalmatia, Macedon, and possibly even Egypt before facing his own martyrdom. One tradition says Luke was crucified on an olive tree. Traditions, however, differ on the specifics of Luke's later days. Tradition also regards Luke as a skilled painter. The miraculous image of Our Lady of Czechtochowa in Poland is purported to be the work of St. Luke himself, later brought to Eastern Europe.

Much of what we know of Luke's character and personality comes from his way of writing about Jesus and his followers in his Gospel and the Acts of the Apostles. Early manuscripts give the third Gospel the title *kata Lukan*, "according to Luke," and early Church Fathers attest to Luke's authorship of this Gospel. It seems it was written before AD 70 since the events of the destruction of the Temple are not mentioned as part of the history of the early Church. Luke addressed his Gospel to the "most excellent Theophilus," a name meaning 'God-lover,' and the title 'most excellent' implies that he was a man of importance. Theophilus may have been the benefactor responsible for the publication of the Gospel.

Luke begins his Gospel in this way: "Since many have undertaken to compile a narrative of the events that have been fulfilled among us, just as those who were eyewitnesses from the beginning and ministers of the word have handed them down to us, I too have decided, after investigating everything accurately anew, to write it down in an orderly sequence for you, most excellent Theophilus, so that you may realize the certainty of the teachings you have received" (Luke 1:1–4). Luke, here, does not claim to be an immediate disciple of Jesus, but rather an investigator of the stories of eyewitnesses alive in his day. The authority in the Church behind his Gospel was that of Paul, who himself was not a disciple during Jesus' lifetime, but who had been given the rank and authority of apostleship.

Luke cites names of disciples in various stories, implying their identity as eyewitnesses. Mary herself, the mother of Jesus, may have been one of these witnesses. Residing at Ephesus, Luke would have known Mary. Luke's Gospel also uniquely shows us stories from Mary's perspective, who "kept all these things in her heart" (2:51). Luke alone tells us of the visitation of the angel Gabriel to Mary, who approached her saying, "Hail, full of grace! The Lord is with you" (1:28 [RSV]). Likewise, he alone tells of the annunciation of the birth of John the Baptist (and thus the *Benedictus*), the visitation of Mary to her cousin Elizabeth (thus the *Magnificat*), the announcement of the angels to the shepherds about the birth of Jesus (thus the *Gloria*), the visitation of the shepherds to the baby Jesus, the presentation of the child Jesus in the Temple (and thus the *Nunc Dimittis*), and the finding of the child Jesus in the Temple (*Ignatius Catholic Study Bible*).

Luke's Gospel is marked by its focus on the salvation of Jesus Christ for Jews and Gentiles alike, on its human touch and concern for the humble and lowly, and on the mercy of Jesus, the healer. Luke uniquely gives us the parable of the Lost Coin, the parable of the Good Samaritan, and the parable of the Prodigal Son.

In the Acts of the Apostles, Luke quotes Jesus telling his followers, just before ascending to Heaven, that "you will receive power when the holy Spirit comes upon you, and you will be my witnesses in Jerusalem, throughout Judea and Samaria, and to the ends of the earth" (1:8). The Acts of the Apostles shows Jesus' followers doing exactly this and recapitulating the works that Jesus himself did while on earth. The disciples preach the gospel in Acts in a pattern much like that outlined in Luke's Gospel. Peter preached to the crowds on Pentecost, "Jesus the Nazorean was a man commended to you by God with mighty deeds, wonders, and signs, which God worked through him in your midst, as you yourselves know. This man, delivered up by the set plan and foreknowledge of God, you killed, using lawless men to crucify him. But God raised him up, releasing him from the throes of death, because it was impossible for him to be held by it" (Acts 2:22–24).

A faithful follower who was open to the inspiration of the Holy Spirit, Luke left behind an everlasting witness of Christ and the early Church. He is the patron saint of physicians and surgeons.

St. Luke, pray for us!

Sts. John de Brebeuf and Isaac Jogues and Companions
Priests and Martyrs, Seventeenth Century
Memorial, Oct. 19

St. John de Brebeuf and St. Isaac Jogues were Jesuit priests and missionaries to native peoples in the New World. They died as martyrs, as did their companions, among whom were other Jesuit priests and lay associates. They became the first saints of North America.

Isaac Jogues was born in Orleans, France, in 1607 and joined the Jesuits in 1624. He served as a professor of literature at Rouen before volunteering to go to Quebec as a missionary. He was sent there in 1646, and his missionary travels among the native peoples led him as far west as Sault Ste. Marie and beyond, some one thousand miles into the interior of the continent. He planned to preach to the Sioux at the headwaters of Lake Superior, but the Iroquois captured him at Three Rivers in Quebec in 1642 (*New Advent*).

For thirteen months, Fr. Isaac Jogues was a captive and a slave. He left a diary, which recalls how he was forced to watch the torture and killing of his native converts. Subjected to the worst of conditions and punishments, and having lost fingers under torture, he was about to be burned at the stake at Ossernenon (now Auriesville, west of present-day Albany, New York) when the Dutch afforded him an opportunity to escape. The Dutch brought him to New Amsterdam (present-day New York City), from which he set sail in winter for Brittany on the western coast of France. From there, Fr. Jogues went to the nearest Jesuit college and was greeted fondly by France's queen mother. Technically, according to canon law, Fr. Jogues could not celebrate Mass anymore because of the mutilation of his fingers. Pope Urban VII, however, granted him an exception, with these words: "It would be shameful that a martyr of

Christ not be allowed to drink the Blood of Christ"
(Franciscan Media).

The following year, in 1646, Fr. Jogues insisted on returning
to the land where he had almost lost his life. Upon
returning, he was tasked with negotiating a peace treaty
with the Iroquois, at which he succeeded. He even returned
to Ossernenon, to his former captors, and was welcomed on
account of the peace treaty. Fr. Jogues returned home to
Quebec and pleaded with his superiors to allow him to
return to Ossernenon as a missionary. At last, they allowed
him to go, but sentiment at Ossernenon had changed since
an illness among the people and a blight on the crops had
struck the settlement. The leading native people there
blamed Fr. Jogues for their misfortune, saying once again
that he was a sorcerer. News of this change, however, did
not deter Fr. Jogues from continuing his journey to meet
them. They seized him near Lake George, stripped him, and
slashed him with knives. Upon bringing him into the village
of Ossernenon on October 18, 1546, they led him into a
cabin, where he was tomahawked. His body was then
decapitated and his head put on display on the walls of the
village. The rest of his body was thrown into the Mohawk
River (*New Advent*).

A few decades later, the village of Ossernenon would
produce the first Native American saint, St. Kateri
Tekakwitha. Eight Jesuit martyrs of the New World were
canonized together with St. Isaac Jogues in 1930 by Pope
Pius XI (Franciscan Media). Fr. Jean de Brebeuf was the
superior and had spent 24 years among the native peoples.
Rene Goupil was a lay associate of the Jesuits who was
tortured along with Fr. Jogues in 1642 and was martyred in
that same year. Jean de Lalande was another lay associate

who was captured with Fr. Jogues in 1646 and was martyred the day after Fr. Jogues. Fr. Anthony Daniel was killed by the Iroquois while working with the Hurons. His chapel was burned together with his body. Fr. Gabriel Lalemant had taken a fourth vow to sacrifice his life for the native peoples, and he died alongside Fr. Brebeuf. Fr. Charles Garnier was ambushed while performing baptisms. Fr. Noel Chabenel was a reluctant missionary who wanted to return to France but offered his life as a martyr when the time came (Franciscan Media).

St. John de Brebeuf, St. Isaac Jogues, and Companions are the patron saints of North America.

St. John de Brebeuf, St. Isaac Jogues, and Companions, pray for us!

Sts. Simon and Jude
Apostles, First Century
Feast, Oct. 28

Saints Simon and Jude were among Jesus' Apostles. They walked with him, witnessed his life, death, and resurrection, and spread the gospel after his Ascension. Both are also believed to be martyrs.

The Roman calendar celebrates Saints Simon and Jude together on October 28, though they are celebrated on separate dates in the East. Simon and Jude were listed next to each other in the lists of Apostles in the Gospels, and there was a tradition (though rather uncertain) that later on, they preached together in Persia or Syria before being martyred there.

Simon is listed by name in all four Gospels. Jude, on the other hand, is so named in Luke and John, but seems to be called Thaddeus in Matthew and Mark. Whereas Jude was a common Jewish name related to Judah, one of the 12 sons of Israel, Thaddeus is a related Greek name. It was common to have a compound Jewish and Greek name, so Jude and Thaddeus were probably the same person. The name Jude is identical to Judas but is spelled differently in English translations to highlight the distinction from Judas Iscariot, Jesus' betrayer.

St. Jude was the one in John's Gospel who asked Jesus at the Last Supper, "Master, [then] what happened that you will reveal yourself to us and not to the world?" (Jn. 14:22). The Lord responded, "Whoever loves me will keep my word, and my Father will love him, and we will come to him and make our dwelling with him. Whoever does not love me does not keep my words; yet the word you hear is not mine but that of the Father who sent me" (Jn. 14:23-34).

Jude was often thought to be the author of the Epistle of St. Jude in the New Testament, but this is not certain, and there are other men named Jude in the early Christian community who could just as well have been the author. The letter, which is written in very skilled Greek, warns a specific Christian community about the dangers of false teachings and uses sophisticated means of exegesis from the Old Testament to make its points. Those who reject St. Jude Thaddeus as the author of the epistle note that the apostle was probably an unlettered Galilean tradesman, unlikely to have written in that manner.

Jude is listed in Luke and John as the son of James. Elsewhere, a Jude, brother of James, and a Simon are named as being among the brothers (in our sense, cousins) of Jesus. It is debated whether or not the Apostles Jude and Simon were the same as Jesus' brothers by those names.

Simon is called the "zealot" in Matthew, Mark, Luke, and Acts to distinguish him from Simon Peter. While some commentators tell us that he is called a zealot because of his zeal for Jesus, it is more commonly thought that Simon belonged to the party of the Zealots before his call to follow Jesus. The Zealots were a party of Jews who sought a political redemption of Israel through force. Inspired by the success of Judas Maccabeus, who won independence for Israel from the Greeks through military campaigns in a time of great religious oppression, some resorted to guerilla tactics to disrupt Roman control and any other powers that cooperated with it. The Zealots were motivated by the goals of correcting the injustices of the oppressors, restoring Israel to its rightful place, and putting a son of David on the throne. Though we do not know Simon's specific involvement with the Zealots, the party was also responsible for the assassinations of hostile officials and soldiers and for destroying munitions and supplies.

469

The Zealots sought a Messiah, but a political one. Though Jesus strongly rejected their reliance on force and violence, it makes sense that he would appeal to them in their desire for a Messiah, converting some of them to a new and peaceful understanding. Jesus, in fact, was often concerned that if the crowds prematurely recognized him as the Messiah, they would mistake him for the kind of Messiah that the Zealots sought. Thus, we read in John 6:15: "Since Jesus knew that they were going to come and carry him off to make him king, he withdrew again to the mountain alone." A generation after Jesus' Ascension, the Zealots proposed Simon bar Giora as the Messiah, even convincing the Temple officials to join the cause. The ultimate result was the destruction of the Temple by the Romans in AD 70, the slaughter of countless Jews, and the deportation of all surviving Jews out of Jerusalem.

Jesus prayed for his followers just before his suffering and death, "I revealed your name to those whom you gave me out of the world. They belonged to you, and you gave them to me, and they have kept your word.... When I was with them I protected them in your name that you gave me, and I guarded them, and none of them was lost except the son of destruction, in order that the scripture might be fulfilled" (Jn. 17:6, 12). Simon the Zealot left his former cause completely behind, finding the true Prince of Peace instead. He remained with Jesus and is believed to have been martyred for him without any recourse to violent resistance.

According to some traditions, St. Simon the Zealot was sawed in two and St. Jude Thaddeus was martyred by a club. Thus, St. Jude is depicted in sacred art with a club, representing his martyrdom, whereas St. Simon is depicted with a saw. St. Jude is also depicted bearing an image of the face of Jesus. According to one story, St. Jude healed Agbar, King of Edessa in modern-day Turkey, from leprosy by giving him a cloth on which to wipe his face. The cloth left an imprint of the face of Jesus, and the king was converted to Christianity.

St. Simon the Zealot is the patron saint of tanners, and St. Jude Thaddeus is the patron saint of hopeless causes. St. Jude apparently became the patron of hopeless causes because prayerful people in desperate situations had exhausted recourse to all the saints they knew until they finally went to the one who bore the same name as Judas, the one who betrayed the Lord. They found powerful intercession from St. Jude Thaddeus, who became a very popular saint for that reason (StJudeShrine.org). Today, St. Jude's Children's Hospital, which specializes in childhood cancer treatment, is named after the patron of hopeless causes.

Saints Simon and Jude, pray for us!

St. Charles Borromeo
Bishop, 1538–1584
Memorial, Nov. 4

St. Charles Borromeo was the Archbishop of Milan and a crucial church reformer in the sixteenth century.

He was born a nobleman. His father was a count and his mother a Medici. An uncle, on his mother's side, was a cardinal and later a pope. Charles was given the best of education. He was always very pious, and he wanted to take the tonsure—a commitment to the ecclesiastic life—at the age of 12, which he was allowed to do. He was given an abbey, and then another abbey to secure wealth, but he would only allow enough money to be kept for his education, with the rest given to the church and the poor. When Charles' uncle was elected pope, he did not celebrate with his fellow townspeople in Milan, but instead went to Confession and received Holy Communion together with his brother. Since Charles had received a doctorate in civil and canon law, his uncle, Pope Pius IV, gave him important roles in the Roman Curia. Charles did not care for the honors given to him and tried to refuse them when possible. Instead, he focused on the duties incumbent on him. Charles was made a cardinal-deacon, papal secretary of state, and papal penitentiary. Later, he was named administrator of the see of Milan, the largest diocese in the Church at the time.

After the untimely death of Charles' only brother, Count Federigo, Charles was pressured by his family, through the pope himself, to renounce the ecclesiastical life and to marry so as to secure the inheritance of his family's wealth for himself and future generations. Charles, however, very much wanted to continue in the Church and to become a priest, so he had himself secretly ordained as a priest by another cardinal at the Basilica of St. Mary Major in Rome,

473

in order to make his state in ecclesiastical life permanent. Having taken this route, Charles was soon ordained as a bishop and then made Archbishop of Milan by the pope.

Cardinal Borromeo was highly in tune with the need for reform in the Catholic Church following the Protestant Reformation. The Council of Trent had been convoked to respond to the Protestant Reformation and to reform the Catholic Church, but there was little interest in it among the bishops, many of whom did not want to change the status quo in the Church. The council was in danger of coming to an end without completing its purpose, but Cardinal Borromeo exerted influence behind the scenes to keep it going and on task.

Often in those times, the Archbishops of Milan did not reside in their own diocese. Likewise, Cardinal Borromeo was required to remain outside his diocese, both because of responsibilities with the pope in Rome and because of the Council at Trent. Cardinal Borromeo saw the need to guide the reform personally at the local level, however, so he finally received permission from the next pope to return permanently to Milan to live in his own diocese.

Back in Milan, he led by example. When the plague struck Milan, priests refused to help and even the government fled the city. Archbishop Borromeo himself went to care for the plague victims, eventually coaxing the priests to join him.

One of the reforms for which the Council of Trent called was education and catechesis to ward off misunderstandings that might fuel heresies. It called for a seminary system to educate priests and a catechism for the formation of the faithful. Cardinal Borromeo established a seminary at Milan and promoted the new Confraternity for

Catholic Doctrine by implementing catechism classes in all the parishes of his diocese. He also trimmed away excessive or non-edifying artwork in churches, as called for by Trent, so as to avoid scandal to those influenced by Protestant critiques of Catholic art. He was tough on corruption, which was rampant in the church, and established effective administration through his appointed leaders. Cardinal Borromeo understood that these and other measures were necessary to prevent Protestant inroads into Italy, since the climate in the church was ripe for their criticisms.

The cardinal was the target of two assassination attempts from those opposing his reforms. Once, while he was boldly confronting his opponents and refusing to give in to their demands, the cross he was holding was shot from his hands. Another time, he suffered an indirect hit from a gunshot (*New Advent*).

Cardinal Borromeo shunned any luxuries available to him. He slept most nights in a chair, and only for a few hours. At most, he would sleep on a bed of hay. He also fasted strictly, often going without basic nourishment. He was worn out and sickly later in life and died in 1584, at the age of 46. He was immediately celebrated by his people as a saint, but was officially canonized in 1610. St. Charles Borromeo is the patron saint of bishops, catechists, cardinals, seminarians, and spiritual leaders (Catholic Online).

St. Charles Borromeo, pray for us!

St. Leo the Great
Pope and Doctor of the Church, d. 461
Memorial, Nov. 10

Pope St. Leo I was popularly given the title "the Great" because of his decisive and holy leadership of the Church in times when it was challenged both by heresies and by the collapse of the Roman Empire.

Leo was from Tuscany and was well-educated, focusing especially on theology but also excelling in other areas of learning. He was made a deacon of Rome, serving Pope Celestine I. The next pope, Sixtus III, sent Leo on a diplomatic mission. When Pope Sixtus died, Leo, returning to Rome from Gaul, was elected to take his place. Leo was consecrated as bishop of Rome in 440.

Various heresies, including Pelagianism and Manicheism, were making inroads throughout the Church and into the hierarchy, and Pope Leo took action against them. He identified and excommunicated heretical clergy and bishops and also centralized mission churches under his authority to guard against heresy. Eutyches became a leading voice among the monophysite heretics, denying the distinct human and divine natures of Christ. Eutyches was excommunicated by Flavian, Archbishop of Constantinople, but appealed to Rome. Leo wrote to Flavian, reaffirming the excommunication and strongly denouncing Eutyches. A synod of heretical bishops assembled in 449 to affirm Eutyches' heretical doctrine, but Pope Leo denounced them as the "Robber Synod" and called together the ecumenical Council of Chalcedon, in Asia Minor, in 451. He sent his legate to read the letter he had written to Flavian, known as Leo's Tome, and the council celebrated and approved it. Standing on the authority of previous authentic councils and with the blessing of Rome, the Council of Chalcedon produced the most complete orthodox formulation of Christ's Incarnation.

The Council of Chalcedon pronounced:

> Following, then, the holy Fathers, we all unanimously teach that our Lord Jesus Christ is to us One and the same Son, the Self-same Perfect in Godhead, the Self-same Perfect in Manhood; truly God and truly Man; the Self-same of a rational soul and body; co-essential with the Father according to the Godhead, the Self-same co-essential with us according to the Manhood; like us in all things, sin apart; before the ages begotten of the Father as to the Godhead, but in the last days, the Self-same, for us and for our salvation (born) of Mary the Virgin Theotokos as to the Manhood; One and the Same Christ, Son, Lord, Only-begotten; acknowledged in Two Natures unconfusedly, unchangeably, indivisibly, inseparably; the difference of the Natures being in no way removed because of the Union, but rather the properties of each Nature being preserved, and (both) concurring into One Person and One Hypostasis; not as though He were parted or divided into Two Persons, but One and the Self-same Son and Only-begotten God, Word, Lord, Jesus Christ; even as from the beginning the prophets have taught concerning Him, and as the Lord Jesus Christ Himself hath taught us, and as the Symbol of the Fathers hath handed down to us.

The Holy See's diplomatic service traces its roots back to Pope Leo the Great's legate to the Council of Chalcedon, making it the most ancient diplomatic service in operation.

Pope Leo the Great is also remembered in history for peacefully shielding the city of Rome from the onslaught of the greatly feared Atilla the Hun, who had unscrupulously left a trail of death and destruction wherever he went. Leo met with Atilla in 452 in upper Italy before his planned raid on Rome. No one knows for sure what words Leo spoke to Atilla, or if the barbaric warrior was given a vision from Heaven, but the result of his meeting with the pope was that he turned his armies away from their march on the Eternal City (*New Advent*). Later when the Vandals approached to pillage Rome in 455, Leo likewise met them on the way. He was able to dissuade them from killing and destroying; they only plundered valuables to take as booty.

Pope Leo the Great is also remembered for his eloquent sermons, 95 of which have survived to the present day. Leo died in 461 and was buried with honor in the old St. Peter's in Rome. Today, his body lies under the altar of St. Leo the Great in the main church of St. Peter's Basilica. In 1754, he was declared a doctor of the Church by Pope Benedict XIV.

St. Leo the Great, pray for us!

St. Martin of Tours
Bishop, 316 or 336–397
Memorial, Nov. 11

St. Martin, the saintly bishop of Tours, is the patron saint of soldiers and was an important early evangelizer in western France. He was born either in 316 or 336 in modern-day Hungary, at a time not long after the legalization of Christianity in the Roman Empire. Martin's father was a tribune in the Roman army, and Martin was conscripted into service as an adolescent (*New Advent*). From an early age, he was drawn to Christianity. Because of Emperor Constantine, Christianity was popular among the soldiers. Once, Martin refused his wages rather than participate in a military campaign that violated his conscience. Thus, he became the patron saint of conscientious objectors. On one chilly day, Martin came across a poor, half-naked beggar, so he took his cloak, cut it in two, and gave the beggar the better part. Martin was still a catechumen when this happened, but he was baptized shortly afterward. Jesus came to him in a vision and told him that it was he himself whom Martin had clothed.

When Martin was able to be discharged from the army, he came under the direction of the famous early theologian and bishop Hillary of Poitiers in Gaul, who guided him in the spiritual life. Hillary, however, was exiled by the Arian heretics, so Martin returned to his own homeland. Upon hearing of Hillary's later restoration, he returned to Gaul with the bishop. Bishop Hillary helped Martin to become a hermit, and numerous other men followed him in that life. Martin also engaged in evangelistic missions to the outskirts of western Gaul, preaching the gospel to people in the countryside who still worshiped the pagan gods. Many converted to Christianity.

Martin was made bishop of Tours but refused to live in the city. Instead, he lived in a small cell outside the city, taking care of the affairs of the church from there. He established parishes throughout his diocese, which he visited annually, and the numbers of Christians grew through his preaching and example.

St. Martin of Tours is the patron saint of the poor, soldiers, conscientious objectors, tailors, and winemakers.

St. Martin of Tours, pray for us!

St. Josaphat
Bishop and Martyr, 1580–1623
Memorial, Nov. 12

St. Josaphat Kuntsevych was a bishop and a martyr for Church unity between East and West. He was born in 1580 in present-day Ukraine, then Poland-Lithuania, and was christened as John. His father wanted him to become a merchant, but as a young man, John realized a vocation to become a monk. An Eastern Christian, John became a Basilian monk and priest, taking the name Josaphat. Known for his preaching and strict asceticism, he was later appointed as an abbot. His favorite prayer was to touch his head to the ground while crying out, "Jesus, Son of God, have mercy on me, a poor sinner" (*New Advent*).

During this time in the Eastern Church, the clergy was in a state of laxity and spiritual decay. In 1596, certain Ruthenian eparchies (dioceses) came into union with the Bishop of Rome at the Union of Brest. Josaphat, whose adult career came a few years afterward, wholeheartedly embraced this movement toward Christian unity under the successor of Peter.

Most of the other Orthodox in his area, however, did not, because of differences in culture, liturgy, and certain points of theology—most notably, the *Filioque* of the Nicene Creed—that the Holy Spirit "proceeds from the Father *and the Son*." When Josaphat became the abbot of another monastery, many of the monks opposed him. Likewise, many people opposed him when he was appointed bishop of Brest-Litovsk, even though it was one of the eparchies that had already chosen to unite with Rome. Josaphat won over many, however, both to himself and to unity with Rome, through his saintly example and the careful reforms he instituted. As bishop, he published a catechism to instruct the faithful, reformed the clergy, and held synods to discuss church affairs.

His opponents were vocal, charging that he had "gone Latin" and was taking the people with him. The Catholic bishops of Poland did not support him, either, because he insisted on the integrity of the Eastern rite liturgy rather than assimilation into the Roman rite. He decided to return to Litovsk despite rumors of trouble. His opponents sought his life, and he knew it. At this time, there were martyrs on both sides of the issue. Josaphat's enemies rallied a mob and hoped that Josaphat's supporters would strike the first blow to justify their plot against the bishop. Josaphat, however, called for peace and preached from the gospel, "Indeed, an hour is coming when those who kill you will think that by doing so they are offering worship to God" (John 16:2 quoted by Catholic Online).

So, Josaphat's opponents sent a priest named Elias to hurl constant insults in the streets against the bishop and his supporters. After some time of enduring much abusive language and many vicious lies, Josaphat's servants asked for permission to arrest Elias. Josaphat gave permission if Elias persisted, and his opponents used this to incite the mob, who began to beat Josephat's men. Josephat went out to them to speak peace, but they hit him with a stick, pierced him with a battle weapon, shot him through the head, and then dumped his dead body in the river. Only some of the Jews of the city dared to intervene to save his followers and to accuse his killers, risking their own safety (Catholic Online). St. Josaphat was canonized a saint by the Catholic Church in 1867—the first Eastern Catholic to be raised to the honors of the altar by Rome. Many Eastern Catholic churches are named after him.

St. Josaphat, pray for us!

St. Frances Xavier Cabrini
Virgin, 1850–1917
USA Memorial, Nov. 13

St. Frances Xavier Cabrini, a religious foundress, educator, and patron of immigrants, was the first American citizen to be canonized. She was born in Italy in 1850. Christened Maria Francesca, Cabrini wanted to enter religious life but was turned away at the age of 18 due to her health. She ultimately discerned that she should start her own religious order, dedicated to missions abroad. Cabrini took religious vows together with seven other women, founding the Missionary Sisters of the Sacred Heart in 1880. Taking the name Frances Xavier, her plan was to be a missionary to China, like St. Francis Xavier. When she spoke to Pope Leo XIII, however, he told her to go "not to the east, but to the west," to New York, to serve the immigrants there.

Mother Cabrini and her sisters arrived in New York in 1889. She organized classes for the children of immigrants to learn catechism and receive schooling. Despite facing many obstacles, she ultimately founded some 67 institutions, including schools, hospitals, and orphanages serviced by her sisters and their lay collaborators (cabrini.edu). During her lifetime, the Missionary Sisters of the Sacred Heart spread to other major cities in the United States, and beyond to Buenos Aires, Rio di Janeiro, and Paris. She made some 24 transatlantic voyages to care for her order and institutions. Mother Cabrini became an American citizen in 1909. She died in 1917 in Chicago, while still in active ministry, due to complications from dysentery. St. Frances Xavier Cabrini was canonized in 1946 by Pope Pius XII. She is the patron saint of immigrants and hospital administrators (Catholic Online).

St. Frances Cabrini, pray for us!

St. Elizabeth of Hungary
Religious, 1207–1231
Memorial, Nov. 17

Wife, mother, noblewoman, ruler, penitent, and charitable laborer, St. Elizabeth of Hungary is an example of a lay woman who achieved sanctity in the Middle Ages. Though at the end of her short life she became a secular Franciscan and lived a consecrated single life, she lived most of her saintly life very much in the secular world.

Elizabeth was born to King Andrew II of Hungary and his wife, Queen Gertrude. Her brother Bela IV succeeded their father as king of Hungary. In Elizabeth's infancy, King Andrew promised Elizabeth in marriage to another very young noble. The boy was named Ludwig IV, and his father Hermann was the landgrave of Thuringia and Hesse, in modern-day Germany. "Landgrave" was a title in the Holy Roman Empire for a count with jurisdiction over a territory. Hermann requested that Elizabeth be sent to be raised in his court, and she was brought there in her childhood. There she was raised well, by Hermann's wife Sophia, who was a pious lady. Elizabeth had an inclination for the things of God from an early age, even though she was surrounded by luxuries. She spent much time in prayer and found ways of doing penance and works of mercy. Elizabeth's father gave her a yearly allowance and established a court of ladies for her. She directed the money and the ladies to help the less fortunate.

Hermann, the landgrave, soon died, so his wife served as a regent until their young son Ludwig became of age. As a child, Elizabeth was educated together with Hermann's daughter Agnes. They were both to wear jeweled coronets, but Elizabeth always took hers off when they went to church because she could not bear to wear it in front of him who wore a crown of thorns. She would stop at every altar and pray, and when no one was around, she would prostrate herself. She had a devotion to the saints and to her guardian angel. At table, Elizabeth would find ways of avoiding the finer foods through conversations, by serving others, and using other tactics. She also dressed simply whenever she could.

Agnes came to despise Elizabeth and began to speak around the court against Elizabeth marrying her brother, saying she should join a convent and leave the matters of courtly life to others. Opinion around the court turned against Elizabeth, but she accepted her sufferings and focused only on pleasing God. She prayed, "O sovereign spouse of my soul, never suffer me to love any thing but in Thee, or for Thee. May every thing which tends not to Thee, be bitter and painful, and Thy will alone sweet" (*Butler's Lives*). When Ludwig arrived from his education abroad, they went to him and asked if he agreed with many of the courtiers that Elizabeth was unsuitable for him. Ludwig disagreed and said he admired her very much for her virtue (*Butler's Lives*). The two were married in 1221 and were given a full royal wedding, and the people adored them.

Elizabeth, now titled as margravine (the wife of the landgrave), was generous in distributing alms from the treasury for the poor of the land. When famine struck, she dug deeply into the treasury to distribute provisions to those who had none. Elizabeth would feed the poor every day at the castle, but many could not climb to its gates because of their infirmity, so she built a hospital for them at the bottom of the hill. She would often feed and nurse them herself, tending lovingly even to those with repulsive illnesses. Elizabeth was criticized by the courtiers for her extreme generosity, but Ludwig defended her, saying that surely God would bring blessings to them on her account.

Elizabeth bore three children for her husband: Hermann II, Sophia, and Gertrude. Hermann became a nobleman but died in his late teens, Sophia married a duke, and Gertrude became a nun and an abbess. Ludwig set out on crusade to meet with Emperor Frederick Barbarossa but fell ill and died along the way in 1227. He was given the sacrament of the sick, and though young, passed this world in a blessed state. He was remembered by historians as a pious ruler, and legends grew among the people of miracles performed after his death.

Elizabeth was greatly sorrowed at the news of her husband's passing, but clung even more tightly to God. She now ruled in place of her husband, with the title of landgravine. She continued her focus on the needs of the poor, but Ludwig's brother Heinrich stirred up sentiments against her, accusing her of squandering the treasury. With the help of forceful demagogues, he was able to incite a mob to make him landgrave in place of Elizabeth, thereby seizing power.

By traditional accounts, Heinrich expelled Elizabeth from the castle and forbid the townspeople from giving her lodging in their homes (*Butler's Lives*). It should be noted that some research from the late nineteenth and early twentieth centuries, however, concluded that Elizabeth renounced her right and left the castle voluntarily and that the stories surrounding the passage of power from Ludwig to Heinrich are inaccurate (*New Advent*). But according to the traditional story, she had to go to the common inn for lodging, and her young children were brought to her afterward, happy just to be reunited with her (*Butler's Lives*). Elizabeth, her children, and her maids all had to stay together in a single room in the common inn, so Elizabeth went to the Franciscan friars at midnight, when the friars gathered to sing the *Te Deum*. Henry's men, however, found her and sent her back to the common inn. Again, Elizabeth rejoiced in her sufferings: "Ah, my Lord and my God, may Thou be all mine, and I all Thine. What is this, my God and my love? Thou all mine and I all Thine. Let me love Thee, my God, above all things, and let me not love myself but for Thee, and all other things in Thee. Let me love Thee, with all my soul, with all my memory" (*Butler's Lives*). She received much consolation in prayer.

Elizabeth's aunt, the abbess of Kitzingen, sent for her to come to her monastery in the diocese of Wurtzburg (*Butler's Lives*). She advised Elizabeth to speak to the bishop of Bamberg, another relative and a good man. The bishop and his associates were very concerned about the injustice that Elizabeth had suffered. He thought perhaps it would be best to arrange for another good marriage for her, but she decided instead to live the rest of her life in celibacy for God. Meanwhile, her husband's bones were finally brought back to Germany in great ceremony after having been recovered from their first, far-off grave.

Public sentiment swelled in favor of the good landgrave Ludwig IV and his wife Elizabeth. The bishop rallied the barons to start talks to restore Elizabeth to her position. The barons grew so impassioned to restore justice in the land that Elizabeth had to temper them to speak to Heinrich civilly. They did so and were able to change his stance toward her. Heinrich took her back into the castle as a member of the royal family. Persuaded by the barons, he even offered her the government, but she declined.

Elizabeth instead devoted the rest of her short life to growing in holiness, having placed herself under the direction of a holy priest named Conrad of Marburg. He was severe as a spiritual director, even requiring her to dismiss one of her maids because their friendship had grown too close. Conrad guided Elizabeth in following St. Francis' new order as a secular member rather than as a nun. In place of vowing poverty, she would vow to renounce the pomps of the world so she would be able to continue generously serving the poor from her great wealth.

Elizabeth eventually left the palace and chose to live in a little cottage in the countryside. She dressed simply and wore a Franciscan habit underneath her ordinary clothing. She also ate very meagerly and worked hard among the poor. Three years after becoming a secular Franciscan, she fell ill and died at the age of 24. Having been given knowledge four days before that she would soon go to God, she wrote up her will, with Christ and his poor as her heirs.

Many great healing miracles were attributed to her intercession, such that her tomb became a popular pilgrimage site. St. Elizabeth of Hungary is the patron saint of bakers, beggars, brides, charities, and those suffering on account of the death of their children (Catholic Online).

St. Elizabeth of Hungary, pray for us!

St. Cecilia
Virgin and Martyr, d. ca. 230
Memorial, Nov. 22

A young virgin and martyr of the early Church, St. Cecilia is celebrated as the patron saint of musicians, especially church musicians. This seems to derive from the references to her singing to the Lord in the legendary *Acts of St. Cecilia*. There we also find her as a stunning example of a successful person-to-person evangelizer.

According to her *Acts*, St. Cecilia professed that she had never worshiped "demons." Accounts differ, but the *Acts*, which tells us that the young Cecilia was "prudent, sensible and wise," also tells us she was raised by parents who were idolators but always had the sense to worship only the true God. As a young girl, she practiced a life of prayer, penance, and almsgiving. Her parents, however, gave her in marriage to a wealthy young pagan named Valerian. St. Cecilia had vowed her virginity to God, but was nonetheless obliged to marry Valerian. During the wedding festivities, she went into her chamber and, lying prostrate, prayed that God would save her virginity. While the musicians were singing, she secretly sang only to God in her heart.

The *Acts* tells how St. Cecilia not only got out of this difficult situation but also won over her pagan husband to heroic virtue for Christ:

> When the wedding guests departed, Valerian and Cecilia were alone in the bridal-chamber. As he was preparing to retire, the all-wise maiden said, "Vow to me that you will not divulge what I shall tell you, and then I shall reveal to you a great secret." He then swore that he would tell her secret to no one. Continuing, she uttered, "Know that I have a fearful and wonderful angel of God Who diligently guards my body, so that no man might defile me. Now if he

sees that you desire to touch me out of carnal desire, he shall become angry and shall slay you instantly. Thus, you shall lose the flower of your youth. However, if he sees that you love me in a clean and pure fashion, as your sister, he shall love you as me, and shall reveal himself to you!"

The youth marveled at her words, and said, "If you would have me believe you, show me the heavenly protector. If, in truth, he is an angel, I shall do whatever you command from now and henceforth." She replied, "If you will not first cleanse yourself from the defilement of idols, and then be baptized in the name of the Holy Trinity—Father, Son and of the Holy Spirit—and believe in the One and Tri-Hypostatic God, then you will not be granted to behold his fiery angels." Valerian then asked, "And who is able to cleanse me?" The maiden answered, "Go out of the city, nearby the third milestone of the Via Appia, in that terrible place of suffering where the indigent abide. When certain of the poor seek alms from you, then ask them on my behalf, since they know me as having given them alms frequently, to show you to Archbishop Urban. You may disclose to him the secret, and he shall perform whatever is needed. Then, you will behold the holy angel."

Valerian did as his wife urged him. He went to Archbishop Urban (Pope Urban I, who reigned 222–230), told him the story, and was heartily received and baptized by him after some questioning. We are told by the *Acts* that Valerian's eyes were opened by the graces of baptism. Valerian went home to St. Cecilia, whom he saw conversing with the angel about whom she had told him. The angel gave them each a heavenly crown of roses and lilies and said, "Preserve, without defilement of soul and body, these elect and wonderful crowns which are sent to you by the Master Christ from Paradise. As an unfeigned sign that these are heavenly crowns and not earthly ones, their scent shall never diminish, nor shall their leaves wither. Moreover, no one, save those who guard prudence and wisdom, and believe in Christ, such as yourselves, may behold these crowns."

Then Valerian, too, became an evangelizer. The angel told Valerian that he would grant him a favor as a reward for his act of faith. Valerian asked only for the conversion of his brother, Tiburtius. The angel was pleased and told him that Christ desired this also. Soon after, Tiburtius entered the chamber and smelled a heavenly fragrance. Valerian took this as his sign to share with his brother about Christ and about the wonderous things he had experienced. Tiburtius listened, but it was only when St. Celicia herself confidently explained that there is but one true God and that idols are mere fabrications that Tiburtius was convicted in his heart and sought baptism from Archbishop Urban. He experienced a visit from the angel of St. Cecilia, as well, after his baptism.

Later on, Valerian, Tiburtius, and Cecilia, deploring how the bodies of Christian martyrs were left on the streets exposed, went out to recover them for proper burial and veneration. Valerian and Tiburtius were caught, however, and were brought to the hostile Roman eparch Dalmatius and thrown in prison. St. Cecilia visited them there and encouraged them in the faith. Upon questioning, the brothers boldly professed their belief in Christ and their rejection of idols. They were beheaded for refusing to burn incense to idols. All present witnessed angels taking the brothers' souls up to heaven, and many conversions came as a result.

Meanwhile, the authorities went to Valerian's house to confiscate his belongings, and there they found and arrested St. Cecilia. When she was brought to Dalmatius, she too refused to burn incense to idols, declaring, "I have never worshiped demons!" She was tortured, but refused to give in. The executioners admired and pitied her and tried to convince her to save her life, yet she said to them, "I, my brothers, rejoice for the love of my Christ amid these dread chastisements. I am only sorry for you because you submit yourselves to evil and heartless rulers, and provoke your Creator and Savior, the all-good and most compassionate One, Who can bestow on you life eternal." She also said to them, "O thoughtless ones! This is not to be reckoned as a loss of life, but rather a wise exchange, because I am giving dishonorable clay and will receive precious gold. In return for this temporal and short death, I shall receive life unending; and for small torments, instead, I shall receive eternal glory."

St. Cecilia's wisdom, grace, and courage is said to have inspired many at that very time, resulting in hundreds of conversions, and the church kept vigil throughout the night of her passion. She was condemned to be shut in and boiled or steamed to death in her baths. The fires were heated to the maximum, but the saint was found unharmed, singing to the Lord. Then St. Cecilia was struck thrice with a dagger. She did not die, but no further blows were allowed for a Roman citizen, so she was left to die. Later, when the Christians went to collect her relics, they found her still alive. She said to them, "I asked a favor of the Lord that I not yet die until I make my house a church, dedicated to the Master Christ, and that I preach the truth." St. Cecilia survived another three days and preached to those who would listen, and many were converted. Her house in Rome was, indeed, secretly made a church by Archbishop Urban, and her relics were kept there.

Though there is a tradition that St. Cecilia invented the pipe organ, this is unlikely. She is, however, venerated as the patron of church music because of her heartfelt singing to the Lord. Her popularity spread throughout the ages, and she is even mentioned in the canon of the Mass.

St. Cecilia, pray for us!

St. Clement I
Pope and Martyr, d. 99
Memorial, Nov. 23

St. Clement was an early pope, or bishop of Rome. He is said to have received the apostolic faith from St. Peter himself.

St. Clement of Rome, as distinguished from the later St. Clement of Alexandra, is remembered in the canon of the Mass as the fourth pope after Peter, Linus, and Cletus. He is believed to have been bishop of Rome from the years 88 to 99. Little is known factually about his life. He is thought to have been a Jewish convert, since the writing he left behind shows an extensive familiarity with the Old Testament. Rome had many Jewish Christians at the time. It is also thought that Clement may have been a freedman from among the thousands of slaves in Emperor Nero's household (*New Advent*).

While numerous letters have been incorrectly attributed to Clement, his First Letter to the Corinthians is believed to be authentic. It is an important and lengthy letter to the Corinthian church, admonishing them against following the leaders of a sedition in that church, in which numerous presbyter-bishops were deposed. The letter references several of the New Testament epistles, but not any of the Gospels. Clement also mentioned St. Paul's letter to the Corinthians, as a reminder to them.

Written on behalf of the church of Rome, the letter seems to be an early testimony to the primacy of the Roman See over other churches. It seems that at the time, as in the New Testament itself, bishops and presbyters were not yet distinguished from each other, but were distinguished from deacons. It also seems that the local churches were ruled by a college of presbyter-bishops rather than only one bishop, as would be the case later on. The earliest of those later remembered as popes, therefore, may have been chief among the college of presbyter-bishops at Rome.

In his Letter to the Corinthians, Clement tells us about the meaning of apostolic faith:

> The apostles have preached the gospel to us from the Lord Jesus Christ; Jesus Christ [has done so] from God. Christ therefore was sent forth by God, and the apostles by Christ. Both these appointments, then, were made in an orderly way, according to the will of God. Having therefore received their orders, and being fully assured by the resurrection of our Lord Jesus Christ, and established in the word of God, with full assurance of the Holy Ghost, they went forth proclaiming that the kingdom of God was at hand. And thus preaching through countries and cities, they appointed the first fruits [of their labours], having first proved them by the Spirit, to be bishops and deacons of those who should afterwards believe (Ch. 42).

The bones of St. Clement are believed to be housed in the Basilica of St. Clement in Rome, alongside those of the early bishop and martyr St. Ignatius of Antioch. There is a legendary account of St. Clement's martyrdom. According to an unlikely but pious story, Clement was exiled by Emperor Trajan to Crimea, where he was placed in a labor camp. The captives were deprived even of easy access to water, having to walk six miles to the spring. St. Clement saw a lamb on a hill, so he took a pickaxe and struck the ground. A spring of water came up, and many in the whole region were converted to Christianity. His captors, however, had him tied to an anchor and drowned in the Black Sea. His bones were said to be collected later, because the sea was made to recede once a year to reveal a miraculous shrine, which entombed his relics.

The story was written centuries later, but the fact that Clement was honored with an altar in the very early days of the Church suggests the he was, indeed, believed to have died as a martyr. At the time, only martyrs received the honor of having an altar built over their remains.

St. Clement I, pray for us!

St. Andrew
Apostle, First Century
Feast, Nov. 30

St. Andrew, a Galilean fisherman from Bethsaida and brother of Simon Peter, was one of Christ's twelve Apostles. He is mentioned several times throughout the Gospels, interacting with his Master.

Simon and Andrew feature early in John's Gospel. Right after the Gospel's prologue and introduction of John the Baptist, Simon and his brother Andrew are presented as being disciples of John the Baptist who hear John's testimony about Jesus. We read,

> The next day John was there again with two of his disciples, and as he watched Jesus walk by, he said, "Behold, the Lamb of God." The two disciples heard what he said and followed Jesus. Jesus turned and saw them following him and said to them, "What are you looking for?" They said to him, "Rabbi" (which translated means Teacher), "where are you staying?" He said to them, "Come, and you will see." So they went and saw where he was staying, and they stayed with him that day. It was about four in the afternoon. Andrew, the brother of Simon Peter, was one of the two who heard John and followed Jesus. He first found his own brother Simon and told him, "We have found the Messiah" (which is translated Anointed). Then he brought him to Jesus. Jesus looked at him and said, "You are Simon the son of John; you will be called Cephas" (which is translated Peter) (John 1:35-42).

In Matthew 4 and Mark 1, we likewise find Simon and Andrew as Jesus' first disciples, but their call happens while fishing on the Sea of Galilee. We read in Matthew's Gospel, "As he was walking by the Sea of Galilee, he saw two brothers, Simon who is called Peter, and his brother Andrew, casting a net into the sea; they were fishermen. He said to them, 'Come after me, and I will make you fishers of men.' At once they left their nets and followed him" (Matthew 4:18–20). While there may have been some literary license, it is possible to reconcile this narrative with John's story, interpreting Matthew and Mark's account as a second meeting and deepening of the call for Simon and Andrew. As fishermen from Bethsaida, they may have broken from fishing for the winter season and followed John the Baptist at the River Jordan, where they first met Jesus and followed him before making a permanent commitment to him back at the Sea of Galilee. Meeting Jesus previously would also help to explain how quickly they dropped everything and followed Jesus. Luke's Gospel has a story mentioning only Simon by name, in which Jesus causes a miraculous catch of fish and Simon leaves everything to follow him, responding to the call to "catching men" (Luke 5:10). Luke directly implies that Simon already knew Jesus since he had already cured Simon's mother-in-law in Luke 4.

In John's Gospel, Andrew was the one who stepped forward to offer Jesus the five loaves and two fishes from a boy, not knowing that Jesus would multiply them for the masses (John 6). After the entry into Jerusalem and the obvious approach of a climactic tension in Jesus' ministry, Andrew was together with Peter, James, and John in asking Jesus about the sign for the beginning of the end. Jesus said to them, "See that no one deceives you. Many will come in my name saying, 'I am he,' and they will deceive many. When you hear of wars and reports of wars do not be alarmed; such things must happen, but it will not yet be the end.

Nation will rise against nation and kingdom against kingdom. There will be earthquakes from place to place and there will be famines. These are the beginnings of the labor pains" (Mark 13:5–8).

Andrew is listed whenever the Apostles are listed. When named with his brother Simon Peter, his name always comes second. Andrew is last mentioned in Scripture in the Upper Room, awaiting the coming of the Holy Spirit (Acts 1:13).

According to tradition, Andrew evangelized in Scythia. Some say he went to Sogdiana, Colchis, Greece, and Acaia (*Butler's Lives*). Wherever he went, he took on Jesus' call to be a "fisher of men." St. Andrew is believed to have been martyred in Acaia, dying on a cross made in a shape of an *X*. The symbol is thus referred to as St. Andrew's Cross. He is the patron saint of fishermen, singers, Scotland, Romania, Russia, Ukraine, and Patras.

St. Andrew, pray for us!

St. Francis Xavier
Priest, 1506–1552
Memorial, Dec. 3

St. Francis Xavier, the Apostle of the East Indies, was a founding member of the Jesuits, the Society of Jesus, and is said to have baptized some 700,000 people in his mission work abroad.

Francis was born in a castle in Navarre to a noble family and aspired to worldly ambition. He went to Paris to study philosophy, where he developed a friendship with Peter Favre. St. Ignatius of Loyola, who was also studying in Paris and was in the early stages of founding the Society of Jesus, tried to befriend Peter and Francis. Peter Favre was interested in what Ignatius had to say about the spiritual life, but Francis ridiculed him for his disheveled appearance. Ignatius worked hard to get through to Francis and finally did so with these words of Jesus: "What will it profit a man to gain the whole world, and lose his own soul?" (Mk. 8:36, quoted in *Butler's Lives*). Ignatius gained Francis' trust and respect, converting him to a spiritual path and to joining him in starting the Society of Jesus. A few years later, in 1537, Ignatius of Loyola, Peter Fevre, Francis Xavier, and four others would take their vow of Montmartre—an important step in the formation of the Jesuits (*New Advent*).

The new order, soon to be approved by the pope, involved extensive formation and then missions to serve the needs of the Church. After Xavier had been ordained a priest together with Ignatius, and had done some ministry in Venice and then in Rome, the king of Portugal sought for Xavier to be sent to evangelize to the East Indies, which were under Portuguese control. The king even influenced the pope to make Fr. Francis Xavier papal nuncio to the East Indies and sent him off with two companions. The appointment gave Fr. Xavier added authority to take action in the Church and to work in diplomacy with rulers.

Fr. Francis Xavier set sail from Lisbon in April of 1541. On board, his kind but authoritative voice put an end to swearing and quarrelling among the sailors. He did not arrive in Goa, India, until May of 1542. Fr. Xavier visited the sick in Goa and evangelized them. He would also walk through the streets and ring a bell to gather the children to teach them about God. In the fall of 1542, he traveled south to do ministry at the pearl fisheries, and then to island of Ceylon, which is modern-day Sri Lanka. Fr. Xavier encountered many difficulties, both from the local pagan rulers and from the Portuguese soldiers. He faced them bravely, once speaking so authoritatively in God's name to the leader of a pillaging band that the latter dispersed his men and left Fr. Xavier and his people alone.

Fr. Xavier made many converts, and miracles and healings accompanied his preaching. He was said to have the gift of tongues, sometimes conversing in languages and dialects that he had never learned (*Butler's Lives*). He also tended to the structure of the church, even establishing a seminary in Goa for native men to study for the priesthood.

Fr. Xavier went on to do work in southeast Asia—to the Portuguese colony of Malacca, near modern-day Singapore and Malaysia, and even to the Maluku Islands in modern-day Indonesia. Returning to Malacca, Fr. Xavier made the acquaintance of a noble Japanese man named Angeroo, who had escaped Japan after killing a man, but who was remorseful for what he had done. Fr. Xavier converted the man to Christianity to receive Christ's forgiveness and also learned more about Japan and their culture from him. Fr.

Xavier resolved to set out for Japan, first spending time there to learn the language and develop a kind of Japanese catechism before evangelizing and establishing a church there. Fr. Xavier and his companions, however, were expelled from the city where they had evangelized and baptized many. They then went to the Japanese capital but had little success there, so Fr. Xavier sought to arrange an audience with the emperor himself to tell him about Christ. Unfortunately, such an audience required a great fee, which he could not afford.

While in Japan, Fr. Xavier came across sailors and traders from China and next resolved to go there to bring the gospel. He managed to have himself appointed ambassador to China by the Viceroy of India and then set sail for the Chinese mainland. While on board, Fr. Xavier became very ill and required a surgery, which did not go well (*Butler's Lives*). The ship was able to land on the island of Sancian, just off the coast of China. A small shelter was built there for Fr. Xavier, and that is where he died in 1552, at the age of 46. In just a decade, Fr. Xavier had managed to evangelize a large portion of the world.

The body of St. Francis Xavier was buried in Goa, but his right arm, which had baptized so many, was enshrined in Rome at the Gesu, the mother church of the Jesuits. He is the patron saint of missionaries and Catholic missions, and of Goa, India, China, and numerous other places.

St. Francis Xavier, pray for us!

St. Nicholas (of Myra)
Bishop, Fourth Century
Optional Memorial, Dec. 6

St. Nicholas was bishop of Myra. He suffered in prison for the faith and became known for his generosity. He is patron saint of children and is culturally associated with Christmas and gift-giving to children.

A tradition places the birth of St. Nicholas in 270 in the region of Lycia in Asia Minor, but little to nothing is known for certain of his early days—or of the details of much of his life, for that matter. According to one story, Nicholas was pious from a young age. His parents, however, died when he was young and left him with a large inheritance, which he gave away to the poor, the sick, and their children (*Butler's Lives*). After making a pilgrimage to Egypt in his youth, he became bishop of Myra in Lycia, just off the Mediterranean coast (*New Advent*).

Persecution of the Christians broke out under the emperor Diocletian in 303, and many Christians throughout the empire were killed or imprisoned. Bishop Nicholas was arrested and thrown in prison. Bishop Nicholas was released at some point years later because of the rise of Constantine. Emperor Constantine began his conversion to Christianity in 312, when he conquered under the sign of the cross at the Battle of Milvian Bridge. In 313, he issued the Edict of Milan, granting religious toleration to the Christians.

After Bishop Nicholas was released, he returned to Myra. There is a story that he participated in the great Council of Nicaea in 325, in Asia Minor, which defined the Son as one in being with the Father, equal in dignity and majesty. According to the story, Bishop Nicholas, moved by a perhaps over-impassioned zeal for Christ's Incarnation, slapped the heretic Arius on the face after his blasphemous speech at the Council on the Son being unequal to the Father.

Bishop Nicholas had a special love for children and would teach them lessons about God and guide them to virtue. Legends arose about Nicholas' generosity, especially to young people. According to one such story, Bishop Nicholas stayed at an inn where he received a dream from God that the innkeeper had robbed and murdered three boys, who had stayed there on their way to Athens to study for the priesthood. The innkeeper had dismembered their bodies and pickled their remains in three large jars. In the dream, Bishop Nicholas confronted the innkeeper and prayed. Through his prayers, the boys were resurrected in real life (St. Nicholas Center).

According to another legend, a father could not pay the dowry for his three daughters. No one would marry them, so the young maidens were likely destined for a life of slavery. Therefore, Bishop Nicholas slipped pouches of gold coins for each of them through an open window at night. He tossed the pouches into their shoes next to the fireplace. In the morning, the girls were thrilled to discover the coins, which changed the course of their lives forever. This is how the custom began of children placing their shoes before the fireplace for St. Nicholas to fill. Originally, they did this on the feast of St. Nicholas, which was December 6. Over the centuries, the custom took on various turns, and now children around the world eagerly wait for Santa Claus to fill their stockings on Christmas Eve.

Accounts offer varying years for the death of St. Nicholas, which most certainly took place in the mid-fourth century, possibly 343. He was buried in his own cathedral in Myra.

St. Nicholas' popularity began in the East, where the Emperor Justinian built a church to his honor in 430 and where he was named in the liturgy of St. John Chrysostom. He also became popular in the West. While the region of Lycia was under Muslim rule, Italian sailors broke in and stole St. Nicholas' body, bringing it to Bari in the Kingdom of Naples in 1087 (*Butler's Lives*). It remains in Bari to this day. Many cures and miracles have been attributed to St. Nicholas. He is celebrated in the Roman calendar with an optional memorial on December 6.

St. Nicholas, pray for us!

St. Ambrose
Bishop and Doctor of the Church, d. 397
Memorial, Dec. 7

St. Ambrose, Church Father and one of the four original Doctors of the Church, was bishop of Milan and instrumental in the conversion of St. Augustine.

St. Ambrose was the son of Ambrosius, Roman prefect of Gallia, which included France, Spain, and Britain. Ambrose was well-educated in Greek and Roman language and literature and also in law. His sister Marcellina, who was ten years older and helped raise him in the Catholic faith, became a nun and inspired him to celibacy for the Kingdom.

Bishop Dionysius of Milan, an orthodox Catholic, was exiled in chains in 355 by the Arians, who denied the full divinity of Christ. He was replaced with a fiercely Arian bishop from Cappadocia, Auxentius, who enforced that heresy upon the church in Milan. The common faithful, however, despised the Arians and longed for the orthodox faith. When Auxentius died in 374, they called for Ambrose, an orthodox Catholic and skilled rhetorician, to be made bishop. Ambrose objected, but they would not let him refuse. Ambrose was still a catechumen and had not yet been baptized, according to the customs of the time, but he accepted baptism and then was ordained and made a bishop. At the news, Ambrose's brother Liberius resigned his prefecture to help his brother so Ambrose would not have to tend to worldly affairs (*New Advent*).

Though he was not as well-versed in theology as in the classics, Bishop Ambrose's fame spread because of his impassioned and beautiful rhetoric in defense of Catholic orthodoxy. With his familiarity with Greek, as well as in his correspondence with St. Basil the Great, he helped maintain close ties between East and West in the Church. Bishop Ambrose was staunch in his support of the cause of orthodoxy against the real threat of the Arian heresy, eliminating Arianism in Milan. But simply being orthodox was not enough to please Bishop Ambrose. Rather than turning a blind eye to the sins of a powerful ally, Bishop Ambrose publicly denounced the orthodox emperor Theodosius after the latter allowed his men to commit a massacre. Bishop Ambrose barred the emperor at the doors of the church, forbidding him to enter until he repented. Theodosius was moved by the words of Ambrose, repented of his crime, and did public penance. Later on, when Theodosius died, Ambrose delivered the emperor's funeral homily and praised him for submitting himself to penance (*New Advent*).

The future St. Augustine was not yet a Catholic when he heard of St. Ambrose, but he was interested to hear Ambrose's rhetorical skills for himself. Already growing wary of the former heresies into which he had been deluded, Augustine engaged in dialogue with Ambrose, who helped him over his remaining hurdles to Catholicism. Augustine respected Ambrose, at first because his preaching carried an erudition than many other Catholic preachers lacked. In fact, St. Ambrose baptized St. Augustine, receiving the future Doctor of Grace into the Church. St. Ambrose was also a spiritual director to St. Augustine's mother, St. Monica, who had urged her son to go to the good bishop to have his questions answered while they were in Italy.

The writings of St. Ambrose are treasured to the present day and have been cited authoritatively for centuries. As St. Ambrose was a scholarly but busy administrator, his writings have practical aims. He wrote sermons, commentaries on Scripture, dogmatic texts, moral treatises, and even hymns, helping to develop sacred chant. The Ambrosian rite of the liturgy, celebrated in Milan, and Ambrosian chant bear his name.

St. Ambrose, pray for us!

An Exhortation from St. Ambrose

Do not desert a friend in time of need, nor forsake him nor fail him, for friendship is the support of life.

If friends in prosperity help friends, why do they not also in times of adversity offer their support? Let us aid by giving counsel, let us offer our best endeavors, let us sympathize with them with all our heart.

There is your brother, naked, crying, and you stand there confused over the choice of an attractive floor covering.

It is a better thing to save souls for the Lord than to save treasures. He who sent forth his apostles without gold had not need of gold to form his Church. The Church possesses gold, not to hoard, but to scatter abroad and come to the aid of the unfortunate.

If you have two shirts in your closet, one belongs to you and the other to the man with no shirt. (quoted on Aletia)

St. Stephen
The First Martyr, d. ca. 34
Feast, Dec. 26

St. Stephen was one of the first seven deacons appointed in the Church and is honored as the first Christian martyr. He "fell asleep" at his martyrdom by stoning, crying out, "Lord, do not hold this sin against them" (Acts 7:60). The Acts of the Apostles tells us he was "a man filled with faith and the holy Spirit" (Acts 6:5). It seems he was a convert and a Greek-speaking Jew. He was assigned in his ministry to the poor and the widows among Greek-speaking Christians.

In Acts of the Apostles chapter 6, the apostles decide to appoint seven worthy men to tend to the needy. The needs of poor Gentile Christians were being neglected, and the Apostles knew that they could not do all the work themselves. The Apostles were the chief witnesses of Christ's life, death, and resurrection and thus had to focus on preaching. The term 'deacon,' which means 'one who serves,' does not appear in this chapter, but we see it used in other parts of the New Testament to describe an assisting ministry. In Acts 6, we find that these seven men received the laying on of hands, which is traditionally understood to be ordination.

All seven of these ordained men are mentioned by name. They were all Gentile Christians. Stephen is listed first and is singularly praised for his exceptional character. We are then told that "Stephen, filled with grace and power, was working great wonders and signs among the people" (Acts 6:8). This, however, provoked some of the Jews who were opposed to Jesus as the Christ. They tried to argue with him, but could not win, so they resorted to agitating a crowd against him. The crowd brought Stephen to the Sanhedrin— the same body that had insisted that Pilate have Jesus put to death not so long before.

We read that "they instigated some men to say, 'We have heard him speaking blasphemous words against Moses and God'.... They presented false witnesses who testified, 'This man never stops saying things against [this] holy place and the law'" (Acts 6:11, 13). Stephen's speech to the Sanhedrin is the longest speech recorded in Acts. We are told, "All those who sat in the Sanhedrin looked intently at him and saw that his face was like the face of an angel" (Acts 6:15). Stephen addressed the members as his brothers and fathers and went through the whole of salvation history, speaking of how the people turned away from God and did not listen to the prophets, or even to Moses, and also how God's presence is not limited only to the Temple in Jerusalem. Stephen summed up his speech by convicting the present generation of doing the same as their ancestors and of putting Jesus the Christ to death.

He concluded, "You stiff-necked people, uncircumcised in heart and ears, you always oppose the holy Spirit; you are just like your ancestors. Which of the prophets did your ancestors not persecute? They put to death those who foretold the coming of the righteous one, whose betrayers and murderers you have now become. You received the law as transmitted by angels, but you did not observe it" (Acts 7:51–53). This was enough for them, and they immediately charged at Stephen to stone him for blasphemy.

We read of Stephen's martyrdom:

> When they heard this, they were infuriated, and they ground their teeth at him. But he, filled with the holy Spirit, looked up intently to heaven and saw the glory of God and Jesus standing at the right hand of God,

and he said, "Behold, I see the heavens opened and the Son of Man standing at the right hand of God." But they cried out in a loud voice, covered their ears, and rushed upon him together. They threw him out of the city, and began to stone him…. As they were stoning Stephen, he called out, "Lord Jesus, receive my spirit." Then he fell to his knees and cried out in a loud voice, "Lord, do not hold this sin against them"; and when he said this, he fell asleep. (Acts 7:54-60)

Saul was an approving witness to Stephen's martyrdom, since those who were stoning Stephen laid their garments at Saul's feet. But as Tertulian later said, "The blood of the martyrs is the seed of the Church." In the following chapters in Acts, we read of Saul's dramatic conversion to Christ and, moreover, his historic mission to the Gentiles, like those to whom Stephen was so dedicated in bringing the love of Christ.

St. Stephen, pray for us!

St. John the Evangelist
Apostle and Evangelist, First Century
Feast, Dec. 27

Known as the "beloved disciple," St. John the Evangelist was one of the inner circle of Jesus' Apostles and is believed to be the author of the Gospel of John, the three Letters of St. John, and possibly also the book of Revelation in the New Testament. St. John was a son of Zebedee. His mother was Salome, and St. James the Greater was his brother.

John was a Galilean fisherman, together with his father and brother. He was among the first disciples to be called by Jesus, and he left everything to follow him. In Matthew's Gospel, we read, "[Jesus] walked along from there and saw two other brothers, James, the son of Zebedee, and his brother John. They were in a boat, with their father Zebedee, mending their nets. He called them, and immediately they left their boat and their father and followed him" (Mt. 4:21-22).

Jesus nicknamed the sons of Zebedee "Boanerges," or "sons of thunder" (Mk. 3:17). This is likely because of their fiery and zealous temperament. It was the sons of Zebedee who asked Jesus if they should call down fire from heaven on unrepentant Samaritan towns (Mk. 9:28) and who asked him, at their mother's urging, for a privileged place on his right and on his left (Mt. 20:20–22). Writing in old age and more humbly, John never mentioned himself by name in the Gospel traditionally attributed to him, even though he was named often in the other Gospels. He did, however, refer to himself there as the "beloved disciple," or the "disciple whom Jesus loved." An analysis of the text rules out other possibilities for this disciple except John himself. In John's Gospel, the beloved disciple is seen resting his head on the bosom of Jesus at the Last Supper (Jn. 13:23), standing at the foot of the cross (Jn. 19:26), and then running to the empty tomb ahead of Peter, whom he let enter before him (Jn. 20:2). At the end, we find a prophecy about the beloved disciple, in which Jesus says, "What if I want him to remain until I come? What concern is it of yours? You follow me" (Jn. 21:22).

Not only was John a disciple and one of the 12 Apostles, but he was in an even more select group, together with Peter and James. John and James, who was likely his older brother, were fishing partners with Simon, later called Peter. They were all present together at the miraculous catch of fish, when Jesus told Simon to put out into the deep (Lk. 5). Peter, James, and John alone were admitted by Jesus to accompany him at the Transfiguration, into the chamber of Jarius' daughter who had died, and at his agony in the Garden of Gethsemene. When Jesus was at his most distressed, he turned to Peter, James, and John. We read in Matthew's Gospel of the agony in the garden: "He took along Peter and the two sons of Zebedee, and began to feel sorrow and distress. Then he said to them, 'My soul is sorrowful even to death. Remain here and keep watch with me'" (Mt. 26:37–38). After taking their fill of food and wine at the Last Supper, none of them remained awake with Jesus, but John was the only of the Apostles to accompany Jesus to the end, standing with Mary and the women at the foot of the cross. One of the women there was his own earthly mother, Salome (Mt. 27:56). But it was also there that Jesus gave John his own mother, Mary. We read, "When Jesus saw his mother and the disciple there whom he loved, he said to his mother, 'Woman, behold, your son.' Then he said to the disciple, 'Behold, your mother.' And from that hour the disciple took her into his home" (Jn. 19:26–27). This is seen in Catholic theology as Jesus' entrustment of his mother not only to the beloved disciple John, but also to every beloved disciple. Mary is believed to have spent her final days in Ephesus, where John later settled.

John's Gospel is the latest of the canonical gospels to be written, typically dated in the AD 90s. The symbol attributed to it is the eagle, since it soars above the other gospels in its spiritual symbolism. The Gospel begins with a prologue, introducing themes of the contrast of light and darkness, and comparing the new creation in Jesus to the creation of the world:

> In the beginning was the Word,
> and the Word was with God,
> and the Word was God.
> He was in the beginning with God.
> All things came to be through him,
> and without him nothing came to be.
> What came to be
> through him was life,
> and this life was the light of the human race;
> the light shines in the darkness,
> and the darkness has not overcome it. (Jn. 1:1–5)

A number of the stories of John's Gospel are organized around seven "I am" statements of Jesus, in which he manifests his divine identity:

1. I am the bread of life. (Jn. 6:35)
2. I am the light of the world. (Jn. 8:12)
3. I am the door of the sheep. (Jn. 10:7)
4. I am the good shepherd. (Jn. 10:11)
5. I am the resurrection and the life. (Jn. 11:25)
6. I am the way, the truth, and the life. (Jn. 14:6)
7. I am the true vine. (Jn. 15:1)

John's Gospel emphasizes the love of Christ, a theme that continues into his epistles. In 1 John 4, we read, "We have come to know and to believe in the love God has for us. God is love, and whoever remains in love remains in God and God in him" (1 Jn. 4:16). John wrote in his Gospel and in his epistles as a witness to the love of God and the life he offers. We read in the prologue of his first epistle:

> What was from the beginning,
> what we have heard,
> what we have seen with our eyes,
> what we looked upon
> and touched with our hands
> concerns the Word of life—
> for the life was made visible;
> we have seen it and testify to it
> and proclaim to you the eternal life
> that was with the Father and was made visible to
> us—
> what we have seen and heard
> we proclaim now to you,
> so that you too may have fellowship with us;
> for our fellowship is with the Father
> and with his Son, Jesus Christ.
> We are writing this so that our joy may be complete.
> (1 Jn. 1:1–4)

John's Gospel and his three epistles are similar in language and themes. Many scholars believe that the epistles, however, may have been penned by his own disciples, according to the tradition and teaching that he left. The book of Revelation, which directly claims to have been written by a "John," is different in language and themes, though the earliest of traditions also attributes it to St. John the Apostle. Many scholars, however, believe it was written by another John. The book speaks of visions and prophecies, which reveal the gospel in its heavenly context and the world in God's ultimate domain. The John of Revelation was exiled to the island of Patmos. Thus, if the author is indeed St. John the Evangelist and Apostle, he probably spent his last days on the island. Some traditions vary on how John entered eternity, and the Gospel of John insists that Jesus' prophecy—"What if I want him to remain until I come?"—does not mean that John would not die (Jn. 21:22–23).

St. John the Evangelist, pray for us!

The Holy Innocents
Martyrs
Feast, Dec. 28

The feast of the Holy Innocents is celebrated during the octave of Christmas to highlight their connection to the Christ child. Unlike St. Stephen, the first Christian martyr, they did not die by choice, but they did die in place of Christ, as the Christ child would one day die in their place.

The story only appears in Matthew's Gospel. Guided by the star to the newborn king of the Jews, the Magi first stopped in Jerusalem, thinking that surely the new king was to be born in the palace of King Herod the Great. But when they told the king of the portent in the heavens, he was troubled and gathered the chief priests and scribes to inquire where the Messiah was to be born (Mt. 2:3–4). Citing the prophets, they told him the child was to be born in Bethlehem. Herod told the Magi to find the child in Bethlehem, but then to return to him so that "I too may go and do him homage" (Mt. 2:8). The Magi found the child in Bethlehem, at the place the star came to rest, and did homage to the Christ child, but "having been warned in a dream not to return to Herod, they departed for their country by another way" (Mt. 2:12).

Meanwhile, an angel appeared to Joseph in a dream and said, "Rise, take the child and his mother, flee to Egypt, and stay there until I tell you. Herod is going to search for the child to destroy him" (Mt. 2: 13). Thus, Joseph took Mary and the infant Jesus and fled to Egypt, where they remained until the death of Herod the Great a few years later. Having to leave everything and flee to protect Jesus in an unknown land is traditionally remembered as the second of the seven sorrows of Our Lady.

Herod, however, became enraged when he realized that the Magi did not return, and ordered his men to go to

Bethlehem and slaughter all male children two years old and younger. Many paintings try to depict the anguish of the mothers of Bethlehem as their babies were pierced through, many perhaps dying themselves while trying to protect their beloved children. Matthew recalls a prophecy of Jeremiah:

> A voice was heard in Ramah,
> sobbing and loud lamentation;
> Rachel weeping for her children,
> and she would not be consoled,
> since they were no more. (quoted in Mt. 2:18)

The direct meaning of this prophecy from Jeremiah 31 was regarding the exile of the people of Judah to Babylon. They were first led to the city of Ramah, just north of Jerusalem, before being deported. Many were killed there. Their ancestral mother Rachel weeps for them because of their sad fate. Matthew presents the typology as pointing further, to the pain of the mothers in Bethlehem at the slaughter of their infants.

There is no historical record of the slaughter of innocents outside Matthew's Gospel. It is an established fact, however, that Herod the Great, who did rule at the time, was a cruel man who perpetrated massacres. The first-century historian Josephus tells us how Herod even executed three of his own sons and his once-beloved wife. He also tells us how zealous Herod was for protecting his own kingdom against any other claims to it, including destroying written genealogies that countered his own claims.

After the death of Herod the Great, the angel again appeared to Joseph in a dream and said, "Rise, take the child and his mother and go to the land of Israel, for those who sought the child's life are dead" (Mt. 2:20). They returned, but not to Bethlehem, because of news of the cruelty of Herod Archelaus in Judea. Instead, they settled in Nazareth, where Luke's Gospel tells us that Mary and Joseph had lived before Jesus' birth.

Holy Innocents, pray for us!

Addendum
St. Marianne Cope
Virgin, 1838–1918
Optional Memorial, Jan. 23

St. Marianne Cope is an American saint canonized in 2012 by Pope Benedict XVI. Christened as Barbara, she was a German-American immigrant who settled in Utica, New York, with her family. Barbara was a factory worker until she entered the Sisters of the Third Order of St. Francis in Syracuse, New York, in 1862. She took the name Marianne and served at first as a teacher. In 1877, Mother Marianne was elected provincial, and she was reelected in 1881. She was also one of the founders of the first general hospital in Syracuse. In 1883, the government of Hawaii sent a request to some 50 religious communities in the United States to come to Hawaii to service the Kakaako Receiving Station for those believed to have leprosy. Leprosy, or Hansen's disease, was greatly feared, and none of the other communities responded favorably. Only the sisters under the leadership of Mother Marianne volunteered unanimously to go. Only 6 of the 35 who volunteered were taken, and Mother Marianne herself was among them (Franciscan Media).

Not only did the sisters do the job requested of them in Hawaii, but they also opened a school for orphaned girls and took on a mission to lepers started by St. Damien de Veuster. Ultimately, St. Damien himself contracted leprosy and died. Mother Marianne and her sisters, however, never contracted the disease, likely owing to their modern practices in hygiene, which they had learned through their work in their hospital back at Syracuse.

Mother Marianne and her sisters restored a sense of dignity and joy to the lepers and orphans they served. Mother Marianne died in Hawaii in 1918 at the age of 80. St.

Marianne Cope is the patron saint of lepers, outcasts, those suffering from HIV/AIDS, and Hawaii.

St. Marianne Cope, pray for us!

Poem for Sister Marianne Cope by Robert Louis Stevenson

To see the infinite pity of this place,
The mangled limb, the devastated face,
The innocent sufferers smiling at the rod,
A fool were tempted to deny his God.

He sees, and shrinks; but if he look again,
Lo, beauty springing from the breast of pain! –
He marks the sisters on the painful shores,
And even a fool is silent and adores. (NCR)

About the Author

Michael J. Ruszala, the author of numerous religious books, holds an M.A. in Theology & Christian Ministry and a B.A. in Philosophy and Theology *summa cum laude* from Franciscan University of Steubenville in Ohio. He currently serves as a pastoral associate for faith formation and evangelization and as a parish music director. Michael has also been teaching for a number of years as an adjunct lecturer in religious studies at Niagara University. He lives outside Buffalo, New York, with his wife Katie, who also works in church ministry and with youth.

www.ingramcontent.com/pod-product-compliance
Lightning Source LLC
Chambersburg PA
CBHW030532100426
42813CB00001B/232